Hermann Sautter (ed.)
Indebtedness, Economic Reforms, and Poverty

Göttinger Studien
zur Entwicklungsökonomik
de Desarrollo Económico
in Development Economics
2

Göttinger Studien zur Entwicklungsökonomik,
de Desarrollo Económico

Indebtedness, Economic Reforms, and Poverty

Hermann Sautter (editor)

Vervuert · Iberoamericana 1995

Die Deutsche Bibliothek - CIP-Einheitsaufnahme

Indebtedness, economic reforms and poverty / Hermann
Sautter (ed.). - Frankfurt am Main : Vervuert ; Madrid :
Iberoamericana, 1995
  (Göttinger Studien zur Entwicklungsökonomik, de desarrollo
  económico, in development economics ; 2)
  ISBN 3-89354-172-1 (Vervuert)
  ISBN 84-88906-10-2 (Iberoamericana)
NE: Sautter, Hermann [Hrsg.]; Göttinger Studien zur
  Entwicklungsökonomik

© Vervuert Verlag, Frankfurt am Main 1995
© Iberoamericana, Madrid, 1995
Reservados todos los derechos
Printed in Germany

Contents

Foreword 7

Rolf Schinke
Poverty and Indebtedness in Latin America:
The Influence of Changing Prices
of Tradables and Nontradables 9

Eduardo Lizano
Economic Policy in Latin America:
Moving toward Consensus? 45

Moritz Kraemer
Stabilization and Poverty in Latin America during the 1980s 75

Moritz Kraemer
Programa Nacional de Solidaridad -
Poverty and Power Politics in Mexico 123

Hermann Sautter
International Poverty Reduction.
A Discussion of the Possibilities of Development Cooperation 169

Hermann Sautter
Problems of an International Social Order 193

List of authors 213

Foreword

Following the critical discussion of recent economic reforms in Latin America, published in vol. 1 of the Ibero-America Institute's Göttinger study series, this volume focuses on the incidence of poverty after the reforms and the scope for poverty reduction policies, a high priority issue on the international agenda in the 1990s.

The book contains six articles written by staff members and guests of the institute. *Rolf Schinke* and *Moritz Kraemer* analyze the influence of debt-creating capital flows and stabilization policies on poverty. *Moritz Kraemer* further examines the possibilities and limits of Mexico's PRONASOL program, an example of the new social policy packages implemented in Latin America. *Eduardo Lizano's* essay argues for the need to initiate a poverty-reducing growth process within the context of the 'New Economic Policy' framework in the region. Finally, *Hermann Sautter* discusses the possibility of an international coordination of poverty reduction policies and the feasibility of an 'international social order'.

The editor is indebted to Mrs. von Schierstaedt for her diligence and patience in the final preparation of the manuscript.

Göttingen, February 1995.

Hermann Sautter
Director

Poverty and Indebtedness in Latin America: The Influence of Changing Prices of Tradables and Nontradables [1]

Rolf Schinke

1. Introduction

There is a growing body of research on the evolution of poverty in severely indebted countries. These studies aim to explain why poverty increased in the years following the implementation of adjustment programs. Although it may be tempting to explain this phenomenon by resorting to the weakness of growth as a result of the debt overhang (Krugman 1989), difficulties arise when the causal chain is extended to the period of increasing indebtedness. There exists some empirical evidence on the relation between growth and poverty (Fields 1989). However, the link between indebtedness, or more generally, capital imports and growth is far from clear (Scheide 1993).

This analysis follows a different path. It demonstrates that capital inflows change the pattern of production and consumption in such a way that, via increases in the prices of nontradables, production of these goods is enlarged while the relative decrease of the prices of tradables discourages production of the latter. The relative change in profitability in both sectors has consequences for employment and sectoral wage rates. The result of the employment analysis can then be used to show the consequences for the development of the headcount index. The analysis is extended to include the effects of an expenditure switching policy.

Section two gives a description of the development of poverty during the pre- and post-debt crisis periods. It is shown that the headcount index seems to follow a u-shaped pattern during both periods taken together, decreasing during the period of rising indebtedness and increasing after the outbreak of the crisis. The third section is

---

[1] Revised version of a paper presented at the DSA Conference 1993 in Brighton. The author expresses his thanks to Ulrich Hiemenz for his valuable comments on an earlier draft and to Anne Brooks-Senftleben for her comments on the final draft. Further, I wish to thank Anke Scholz for her graphical representations, and Margret von Schierstaedt for typing the manuscript.

devoted to the theoretical analysis. In part three, some empirical findings are given that underline the results from the theoretical analysis. It is demonstrated that relative prices of nontradables increased with capital inflows, and further, that the labour markets revealed changes in the relative wage rates as indicated by the theoretical analysis. Conclusions are drawn in section five.

2. The Situation

During the 1970s and 1980s the majority of developing countries experienced a remarkable increase in their external indebtedness (table 1)[1]. High inflows of foreign capital are bound to influence relative factor scarcities and consequently factor prices: the expectation is that while capital is more abundant, unskilled labour gets scarcer and therefore more expensive.[2] As the poors' wealth consists mainly of unskilled labour one should expect a decline of poverty. Table 1 demonstrates this was only partly the case. The data in this table are the percentage changes of the debt-GNP-ratios for 38 LDCs between 1975 and 1985 as well as the percentage changes of their headcount indexes (separately for rural and urban areas) between the mid-seventies ("1975") and the most recently available in the eighties ("1985").[3] Well-known facts are revealed with respect to external indebtedness: On average there is a tripling of the debt-GNP ratio in Latin American and Asian countries and a quadrupling for African countries in 1975 - 1985.[4] During this time many countries also experienced a severe change of poverty measured by their headcount index as the most widely available indicator of poverty. While Latin American countries suffered a sharp increase in their headcount indexes, there was a noticeable decline of poverty rates elsewhere.

---

[1] Table 1 is a condensed version of appendix table 1.

[2] For the sake of exposition it is assumed that the rise in external indebtedness is equal to a net inflow of foreign capital and that it is exclusively utilized in the formation of capital. Of course, this is a very strong assumption as empirical research shows that foreign transfers normally lead to an increase in consumption as well - although to a lesser extent. See Corsepius, Nunnenkamp, and Schweickert (1989). This assumption will be relaxed later on.

[3] In this study poverty is measured by the headcount index. Although this index has some shortcomings with respect to the underlying axioms it is the most widely available measure. Further, this index is a valuable input in the calculation of the α - group of poverty indices. See Foster, Greer, and Thorbecke (1984, 761-766).

[4] Data in table 1 and annex table 1 refer only to those countries for which headcount indices are available. Generally, data for African countries included in these tables cannot be regarded as being representative for the majority of African countries.

Table 1

Relative Changes in Indebtedness and Poverty Indexes: 1975-1985

	Indebtedness [1]	Poverty [2] Urban	Poverty [2] Rural
Latin America			
1 Argentina	369.1	66.7	5.3
2 Bolivia	249.5	..	1.2
3 Brazil	158.2	11.8	-2.9
4 Chile	108.7	..	..
5 Colombia	99.1	0.0	-6.3
6 Costa Rica	235.6	33.3	7.1
7 Domin. Republic	303.0	..	..
8 Ecuador	359.7	0.0	0.0
9 El Salvador	101.3	..	..
10 Guatemala	309.2	27.7	-4.8
11 Haiti	269.9	18.2	2.6
12 Honduras	126.5	428.6	45.5
13 Jamaica	319.4	..	..
14 Mexico	221.7	15.0	-12.2
15 Nicaragua	485.6	..	..
16 Panama	141.6	0.0	4.0
17 Paraguay	281.3	..	..
18 Peru	172.2	36.8	-10.0
19 Trinidad and Tobago	232.5	..	2.6
20 Uruguay	303.3	46.2	7.4
21 Venezuela		50.0	-2.3
Asia and Oceania			
22 Bangladesh	233.3	-30.9	-38.6
23 China	..	..	-80.0
24 India	24.8	-17.4	-16.9
25 Indonesia	24.0	-48.7	-60.0
26 Korea, Rep.	68.3	-72.2	-66.7
27 Malaysia	263.5	-55.6	-47.9
28 Nepal	1008.0	-13.6	19.4
29 Pakistan	-18.2	-37.5	-24.4
30 Philippines	360.7	10.5	0.0
31 Sri Lanka	134.0	-25.0	33.3
32 Syria	566.7	..	-10.0
33 Thailand	426.4	-53.8	3.0
Africa			
34 Egypt	150.2	..	-22.7
35 Ghana	94.0	..	25.6
36 Madagascar	794.4	-58.0	-26.0
37 Morocco	603.4	-26.3	-28.9
38 Tunisia	107.5	-52.9	-27.9

Sources: World Debt Tables, various issues; ILO, World Labour Report 1992.

[1] Percentage Change in Total External Debt (EDT) as a percentage of GNP.

[2] Headcount Index, percentage change.

.. Data not available.

Latin American countries experienced a growing disparity in poverty between urban and rural areas, while in non-Latin American countries poverty in rural and urban areas developed in the same direction (with the exception of Nepal and Syria). As a rule, there was a severe increase in urban poverty in nearly all Latin American countries. On top of the ranking is Honduras with a 400 per cent increase in urban poverty. Changes in the 30 to 50 per cent range are frequent (Argentina, Costa Rica, Guatemala, Peru, Uruguay, and Venezuela). Taking into account the relatively high degree of urbanization in Latin America the increase in urban poverty rates usually meant an increase in overall poverty. With respect to rural poverty, the rates of change were lower. Some countries even succeeded in reducing rural poverty (Brazil, Colombia, Guatemala, Mexico, Peru and Venezuela). It is striking that the Latin American oil exporters (Mexico, Peru, and Venezuela) and Colombia (a further exporter of raw materials) are prominent members of those who lowered poverty in rural areas.

Summarizing table 1 leads to the following conclusions:

a) There is ample evidence of a positive correlation between the development of the debt-GNP ratio and urban poverty in Latin America while

b) the relationship between changes in the debt-GNP ratio and rural poverty is far less pronounced.

c) In other countries the change in poverty seems to be negatively correlated with the debt-GNP ratio.

A correlation coefficient of 0.8 between poverty and indebtedness is evidence for proposition a) above while these coefficients were practically zero for b) and c). The expected relationship between these two variables, however, is negative due to the utilization of external savings to finance additional domestic investment. A capital stock which is higher than that resulting from domestic savings should lead to higher incomes. According to the scarce existing empirical evidence on the relationship between poverty and growth the latter seems to be a necessary - although not a sufficient - condition for the reduction of poverty. [1]

---

[1] In his survey Fields (1989, 175) states that "... in almost all cases poverty declines as the economies grow."

The data presented in table 1 may be misleading inasmuch as they do not unveil developments during the period. In Latin American countries growth of indebtedness was finished as early as 1982 while low income countries' debts began to grow thereafter. If there is a relation between poverty and indebtedness it is possibly not a linear one. Figure 1 provides some evidence in this respect. This figure shows the development of the headcount index for those three countries for which data are available for the period 1960 to 1988 (Brazil, Colombia, and Costa Rica). These three countries show a u-shaped development of their headcount index with the minimum somewhere at the beginning of the eighties. During the phase of rising external debt poverty rates declined while they increased again after the debt crisis broke out.[1)]

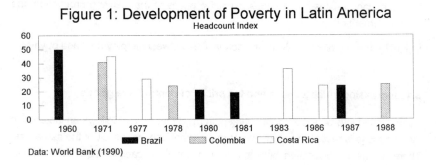

Figure 1: Development of Poverty in Latin America
Headcount Index

Data: World Bank (1990)

Figure 1 demonstrates that a comparison of the poverty and debt situations of the mid-seventies and mid-eighties may lead to wrong conclusions. The trend in the development of poverty until the beginning of the eighties seems to be different from that prevailing thereafter which was mainly influenced by terms of trade and the real interest rate shocks, misguided policy responses as well as the finally resulting adjustment efforts.

[1)] Note, that from these three countries Costa Rica had a local maximum of poverty around the year 1983.

3. Theoretical Analysis of the Relationship between Indebtedness and Poverty

Section 3 of this study suggests a theoretical explanation for the u-shaped path of poverty in the course of the last two decades. The theoretical analysis is based on the following hypotheses: capital inflows have some kind of Dutch disease effects as they change relative prices of tradable and nontradable goods, and thus influence the development of poverty rates via their effect on the labour market.

More explicitly, the hypothesis consists of three building blocks:

- The first of them concerns the relationship between indebtedness (or more generally: capital inflows) and the change in relative prices of tradable and nontradable goods.
- The second relates the changes in relative prices to the resulting production and employment effects.
- Finally, the last block analyzes the connection between employment and poverty.

3.1. Increasing Indebtedness and the prices of nontradable goods

Before going into details it should be kept in mind that in what follows an increase in indebtedness is meant to be equivalent to a current account deficit of the same size. There will be no distinction between different forms of capital inflows. It is simply assumed that indebtedness is the only way of importing capital. [1]

Figure 2 demonstrates what happens to a country's prices of tradables and nontradables in the case of massive inflows of foreign capital. Nontradables (NT) are measured on the vertical axis, and tradables (T) are depicted on the horizontal axis. The country's transformation curve is CD. Originally, the quantities produced and consumed in the country are given by F. The relative price of tradables, i.e. the price of tradables in terms of nontradables is represented by the slope PQ. [2] Assuming that the country in question imports foreign capital equal to FG, defined to be equivalent to net imports of goods and non-factor services, the quantity of tradable goods

---
[1] This is not very far from reality if one considers the situation in Latin America during the late seventies and early eighties.
[2] It is assumed that both categories of goods are composite commodities. Within each group there are no changes in relative prices.

increases by the same amount while the quantity of nontradables remains unchanged.[1] As a result of this capital import nontradables are relatively scarcer and therefore become more expensive than before. The new price line is given by RS (or UV). The new point of optimal production is I while the new consumption bundle is represented by J. Producing nontradable goods has become more profitable and therefore their production has been expanded while that of tradables has been reduced. The first result of this analysis is that inflows of foreign capital raise the prices of nontraded goods relative to those of tradables.

Figure 2: Capital Inflows and the Relative Price of Tradables

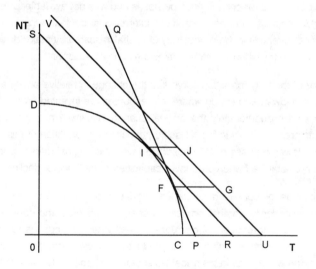

Source: Michaely (1981, 314)

---

[1] Note that, by definition, imports must be tradables.

This result may be criticized by pointing to the fact that a transfer of resources may shift the transformation curve in a northeastern direction. Expanding production of nontradables the pre-transfer relative prices might be reestablished. Therefore, as far as the long-run effects of the transfer are concerned, capital inflows may be neutral in their effect on relative prices. However, this reasoning is not convincing for two reasons:

a) The outward shift of the transformation curve does not only depend on the amount of the transfer but also on its utilization. Usually, when external indebtedness increases so does the debt service. From 1980 to 1982 the national savings rate declined between two (Mexico) and 13 (Chile) percentage points in six out of seven severely indebted Latin American countries (IDB, 1985, p. 43). With a given transfer of resources, and under ceteris paribus assumptions this leads to a massive decline in the ratio of investments to GNP. An extensive part of the transfer has been used for consumption purposes and was not available for expanding productive capacity. Furthermore, in an international context account has to be taken for differences in the productivity of capital indicated by major differences in GNP growth rates when investment rates are nearly the same.

b) The shift of the transformation curve and the change in relative prices as a result of capital inflows depends on where the resources are invested. When both sectors expand proportionately the original change in relative prices will prevail. If growth is predominantly in the NT sector, expanding production of this sector will lead to a lower increase of NT prices. However, the original ratio of prices could only be reestablished when productive capacities in the T sector decline.

When a situation of continued capital inflows lasts for some time the country in question will experience another process of changing prices in the course of which the relative price of tradables will decrease as well when it succeeds to expand its production.[1] In countries where labour productivity is low international competition ensures that the wage rates in the tradables sector must be low. Usually, in this situation, wage rates in the nontradables sector are low, as well, even though between less developed and advanced countries productivity differs to a lesser extent in this

---

[1] From the vast body of literature on this phenomenon, Balassa (1964) has to be mentioned. Later, Kravis, Heston, and Summers (1982) were concerned with this problem. The latter as well as Balassa gave the Ricardian explanation of a one factor world described in the text above. An analysis using a two-factor-model is given in Bhagwati (1984). Both types of models and explanations have been criticized by Lancieri (1990), who bases his reasoning on market failures.

sector. In the course of economic development it is expected that labour productivity predominantly increases in the tradables sector, raising wage rates throughout the country while in the nontradables sector productivity increases at a much slower rate. As a result of this process the prices of nontradable goods will increase relative to that of tradables.

Both developments imply that in a regression

(1) $$(e/PPP)_i = f(\Delta D_i, PCY_i)$$

the coefficients of both exogenous variables are expected to have a negative sign. In equation (1) e is the nominal exchange rate, PPP the purchasing power parity, ΔD the inflow of foreign capital (net increase in external debts), and PCY the income per capita of country i.

3.2. Relative prices and employment

In order to draw conclusions about the employment situation resulting from the change in relative prices it is necessary to introduce a few additional assumptions:

- Labour is the poors' only source of income.
- Rigidities that may cause unemployment exist either in the T or in the NT sector.

Under these conditions entrepreneurs will expand their demand for labour until the value of its marginal product equals the wage rate. Assuming no rigidities in either the T or NT sector then, according to the Stolper-Samuelson Theorem relative wage rates in the NT sector will increase as a result of higher prices of NT goods if their production is more labour-intensive than in the T sector. If the majority of the poor is employed in the NT sector an increase in capital inflows may lead to a reduction of poverty via higher wage rates in that sector.

However, this simple model of the labour market in LDCs may be criticized for several reasons. At any wage rate total labour supply is given and constant. Therefore, it does not account for a change of the number of persons willing to initiate work, and the change of hours of work supplied by those already in work. First, a rise in the wage rate increases the reservation wage and thus the number of those willing to work, and second, depending on the relative strength of the income and substitution effects, a higher wage rate may increase or decrease the number of hours worked of the already employed. In what follows this argument will be left aside because it may be reasonably assumed that the reservation wage of the poor is extremely low and therefore, an increase of the wage rate may not change the number of the working poor. Instead, discussion will be concentrated on a different point of critique of the model: rigidities may exist in either the tradables or nontradables sector.

Figures 3 and 4 are a representation of this situation. In figure 3 wages in the tradables sector are inflexible while in figure 4 there are rigid wages in the nontradables sector. In both figures, the horizontal axis measures the total labour force available in the economy: on the left of Q_{NT} the quantities of labour demanded and supplied in the nontradables sector and on the right of Q_T the respective quantities of labour in the tradables sector. The wage rates in both sectors (w_T and w_{NT}) are measured on each vertical axis. Within this model total labor supply is inelastic. There is equilibrium in the unprotected sector where the wage rate equals labour supply, given the job opportunities in the protected sector. There, a higher wage rate is paid whose expected value - given the probability of being unemployed - equals the wage rate in the unprotected sector.[1]

Specifically, in figure 3 it is assumed that labour in the tradables sector is protected. L^0_T is the labour demand schedule in the tradables sector where the minimum wage is fixed at $\dot{w}_T$. Employment in this sector is $Q_T C$. Line HT^0 is the Harris-Todaro-curve that represents the equivalent of the certain wage rate in the unprotected sector to that of the higher but less certain wage rate $\dot{w}_T$ in the protected sector. According to figure 3 the wage rate in the unprotected (nontradables) sector is given by the point of intersection (A) of the Harris-Todaro curve (HT^0) with the labour demand schedule (L^0_{NT}) of that sector. In this model a part of the labour force (CF) is voluntarily unemployed. Increasing prices of nontradables imply an upward movement of the labour demand schedule L_{NT}^0 to the left to L_{NT}^1 with the new point of intersection at A'. As this process does not alter the wage rate in the protected sector of tradable goods - where the minimum wage rate $\dot{w}_T$ still applies - the increase of NT prices results in higher wages

---

[1] This representation of the problem is familiar and has been used in several studies. For further details see Addison and Demery (1993), Demery and Addison (1993) and Edwards (1988) as well as the literature cited therein.

Figure 3: Wage Inflexibility in the Tradables Sector

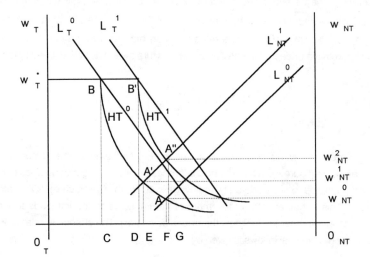

and employment in the nontradables sector and a reduction of unemployment in the tradables sector.

Thus, rising indebtedness leads to an increase of the wage rate in the nontradables sector. Under the assumptions of this model the relationship $w^*_T > w^1_{NT} > w^0_{NT}$ applies. This implies that the inflow of foreign capital results in the following ratio of wage rates:

$$(2) \qquad \left(\frac{w^*_T}{w^0_{NT}}\right) : \left(\frac{w^*_T}{w^1_{NT}}\right) > 1$$

When indebtedness has been excessive so that adjustment programs will become necessary an "expenditure switching" policy will lead to an increase in the prices of tradables vis-à-vis those of nontradables. When this increase in the prices of tradables leads to only a moderate increase in labour demand in the tradables sector, the HT curve and the labour demand curve will move to HT^1 and L^1_T, respectively. Still the wage rate in the tradables sector will be unchanged at w^*_T and the wage rate in the nontradables sector will rise to w^2_{NT} as a result of the shift of the HT curve to the right. Once again, the ratio of the wage rates between both sectors before and after the change in relative prices (this time due to expenditure switching) will exceed unity:

$$\text{(3)} \qquad \left(\frac{w^*_T}{w^1_{NT}}\right) : \left(\frac{w^*_T}{w^2_{NT}}\right) > 1$$

In the same manner rigidities in the labour market can exist in the sector of non-tradable goods (figure 4). When during the process of increasing indebtedness labour demand expands only moderately the wage rate in the (protected) NT sector is constant. This, together with a movement of the HT curve to the left leads to higher wage rates in the other sector (now the tradables sector). The change in relative wage rates caused by capital inflows is given by

$$\text{(4)} \qquad \left(\frac{w^0_T}{w^*_{NT}}\right) : \left(\frac{w^1_T}{w^*_{NT}}\right) < 1$$

When excessive debt levels require adjustment measures by pursuing policies that lead to expenditure switching and to a rise in the prices of tradables then again the change in the ratio of wages is given by

$$\text{(5)} \qquad \left(\frac{w^1_T}{w^*_{NT}}\right) : \left(\frac{w^2_T}{w^*_{NT}}\right) < 1$$

when in the post-adjustment situation the wage rate in the tradables sector is lower than the protected wage rate in the nontradables sector. An important result of this analysis is the change in the level of unemployment and the changes in the wage ratios.

Figure 4: Wage Inflexibility in the Nontradables Sector

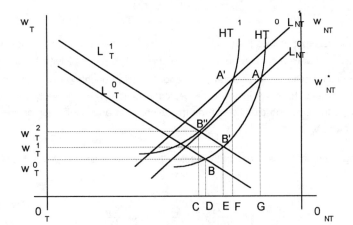

3.3. Changes in Unemployment and Poverty

The next step consists in elaborating how these changes in unemployment will affect poverty when the latter is measured by the headcount index. To proceed in a straight-forward manner it is proposed to use the class of α-measures developed by Foster, Greer, and Thorbecke (1984). This group of poverty measures is given by the following index (PV_α):

(6)
$$PV_\alpha = \frac{1}{n}\sum_{i=1}^{q}\left(\frac{Y_p - Y_i}{Y_p}\right)^\alpha$$

where n is the population, q the number of those living below the poverty line (Y_p), Y_i (i=1,...,q) the income of the poor and α a parameter of poverty aversion. Setting α equal to zero makes equation (6) equivalent to the headcount index (HCI). Using the PV index with α equal to zero and Kanbur's result (Kanbur 1987), the effect of an expenditure switching policy (π) on this index is given by:

(7)
$$\frac{dPV_\alpha}{d\pi} = \frac{dx_T}{d\pi}\left(PV_{\alpha,T} - PV_{\alpha,NT}\right)$$

For the analysis that follows it should be noted that a crucial assumption underlying equation (7) is that workers leaving a sector dx_i (i=T, NT) are completely absorbed by the other sector where the sectoral distribution remains unchanged. Whether this migration will lead to in an increase or decrease of the overall poverty measure, depends on the size and direction of the migration flows and on the sector-specific HCI (PV_T and PV_{NT}).

When wages are inflexible in one of the sectors the overall change in poverty is given by

(8)
$$\frac{dPV_\alpha}{d\pi} = PV_T\frac{dx_T}{d\pi} + PV_U\frac{dx_U}{d\pi} + PV_{NT}\frac{dx_{NT}}{d\pi}$$

where PV_U is the poverty index (HCI) of the jobless. The change in the number of unemployed is given by dx_U. As before, the flows of migrants add up to zero. In figures 3 and 4 the respective migrations dx_i (i = T, NT, U) are indicated. With rigidities in one of the sectors (either the tradable or the nontradable sector) changes in overall poverty depend on sectoral HCIs and on changes in sectoral employment. When these changes are given, assumptions on the ranking of the sector-specific HCIs are necessary to infer the direction of change in the overall HCI.

Table 2 lists the poverty effects of the terms in (8) for the alternative policy cases of rising indebtedness and expenditure switching. In part one of the table it is assumed that rigidities are in the nontradables sector while in part two rigidities are assumed to exist in the sector of tradable goods. In either part there are two sets of assumptions with regard to the ranking of the sector-specific HCIs. Case a) holds when the HCI of the tradables sector is always higher than that of the nontradables sector. This is indicated by (T>N) [1]. The opposite is true for case b) where the poverty ranking of the nontradable sector is always higher than that in the tradables sector (N>T). [2]

---

[1] To improve legibility of the table the sectoral HCIs are indicated by their respective suffixes (T,N,U). Thus, T>N means $PV_T > PV_N$.

[2] For convenience in the first two lines of table 2 the sectoral changes in employment resulting from figures 3 and 4 are repeated.

Table 2
Wage Inflexibility and Poverty

Part 1: Wage inflexibility in the nontradables sector

Rising Indebtedness: $dX_T < 0$ $dX_U < 0$ $dX_{NT} > 0$
Expenditure Switching: $dX_T > 0$ $dX_U < 0$ $dX_{NT} = 0$

Poverty Ranking	Rising Indebtedness					Expenditure Switching			Combined Effects	
	$\frac{dX_T}{d\pi}$	$PV_T - PV_{NT}$	$\frac{dX_U}{d\pi}$	$PV_U - PV_{NT}$	Effect of Rising Indebtedness	$\frac{dX_T}{d\pi}$	$PV_T - PV_U$	Expend. Switching Effect		
	(1)	(2)	(3)	(4)	(5)	(6)	(7)	(8)	(9)	(10)
a) T > N										
T > N > U	−	+	−	−	?	+	+	+	?	+
T > U > N	−	+	−	+	−	+	+	+	−	+
U > T > N	−	+	−	+	−	+	−	−	−	−
b) N > T										
N > T > U	−	−	−	−	+	+	+	+	+	+
N > U > T	−	−	−	−	+	+	−	−	+	−
U > N > T	−	−	−	+	+?	+	−	−	?	−

Table 2 (continued)
Wage Inflexibility and Poverty

Part 2: Wage inflexibility in the tradables sector

Rising Indebtedness: $dX_T = 0$ $dX_U < 0$ $dX_{NT} > 0$
Expenditure Switching: $dX_T > 0$ $dX_U < 0$ $dX_{NT} < 0$

Poverty Ranking	Expenditure Switching					Rising Indebtedness			Combined Effects	
	$\frac{dX_T}{d\pi}$	$PV_T - PV_{NT}$	$\frac{dX_U}{d\pi}$	$PV_U - PV_{NT}$	Expend. Switching Effect	$\frac{dX_{NT}}{d\pi}$	$PV_{NT} - PV_U$	Effect of Rising Indebtedness		
	(1)	(2)	(3)	(4)	(5)	(6)	(7)	(8)	(9)	(10)
a) T > N										
T > N > U	+	+	−	−	+	+	+	+	+	+
T > U > N	+	+	−	+	?	+	−	−	?	−
U > T > N	+	+	−	+	?	+	−	−	?	−
b) N > T										
N > T > U	+	−	−	−	?	+	+	+	?	+
N > U > T	+	−	−	−	?	+	+	+	?	+
U > N > T	+	−	−	+	−	+	−	−	−	−

During the process of increasing indebtedness and with rigidities in the nontradables sector the changes in employment are $dx_T < 0$, $dx_U < 0$ and $dx_{NT} > 0$. When a successful policy of expenditure switching is pursued the respective changes are $dx_T > 0$, $dx_U < 0$, and $dx_{NT} = 0$.[1] Table 2 shows the signs of the terms in equation (8) according to the assumptions indicated above. The column headed by "total effect" lists the overall poverty effects of rising indebtedness (left part of the column) and expenditure switching (right part). The opposite is true for columns 9 and 10 of part two of the table: the effect of the expenditure switching policy is repeated in column 9 while that of rising indebtedness is listed in col. 10. In this analysis a u-shaped HCI curve consistent with the Latin American experience during the last twenty years can be explained only by the sectoral poverty ranking T>U>N when rigidities exist in the NT sector.

Difficulties arise when one relies exclusively on the model with rigidities in the tradables sector to explain the u-shaped HCI curvature because either the single terms in the debt and in the expenditure switching case show the same sign or the expenditure switching effect is inconclusive as the single terms of equation (8) are of opposite sign. At best the poverty rankings T>U>N or U>T>N may be used to explain the u-shaped curvature of the HCI in some Latin American countries.

So far, the assumption underlying the interpretation of table 2 has been that rigid sectors remain so during both phases, i.e. during that of growing debts and that of expenditure switching. However, this does not seem to conform to reality. The competitive pressure initiated by the opening-up of economies as a result of the execution of adjustment programs is mostly felt in the tradables sector. Therefore, if at all, it is the NT sector that is relatively protected after the implementation of an expenditure switching policy. Relying exclusively on one model of rigidities doesn't seem to be very convincing. Assuming the existence of wage rate inflexibility in the production of tradables during the building-up of foreign debts while wage inflexibility exists in the NT sector in the course of the adjustment process, and assuming that in both phases the same ranking of sectoral poverty holds, only the ranking T>U>N results in the observed changes in poverty during both phases.

---

[1] This latter result explains why table 2 contains only two terms under the heading "expenditure switching" in part one and "Increasing Indebtedness" in part 2.

Against this reasoning one may argue that it does not seem to be convincing that the sector that received most protection before the opening of the economy, namely the tradables sector, should be the one with the highest ranking in poverty. However, it should be kept in mind that the real wage ruling in the tradables sector has been eroded as a consequence of the constancy of the money wage rate and the inflationary process that is the result of the protracted increase in the price of nontradables as a consequence of the increase in indebtedness.[1] When this process lasts for some time, this ranking of poverty is not implausible. According to these findings one may formulate the hypothesis that the relative wage rate (w_T/w_{NT}) will decline during the building-up of external debts and rise during the period of economic adjustment.

4. Empirical Analysis

This analysis consists of two parts. In the first part the empirical relationship of equation (1)[2] is tested. Only when it can be shown that rising external debts have a significant influence on the relative price of tradables further analysis is worthwhile.

4.1. Indebtedness and the Price Ratio of Tradables and Nontradables

The results of the regression analysis of equation (1) are given in table 3. Two sets of data have been used. Parts I to III of that table show the results of a cross section analysis carried out with World Bank data for 1990. Part IV contains the results of a time series analysis with Chilean data from 1970 to 1988.[3]

The regressions have been calculated for the whole sample of countries, and separately for low and middle income countries. Additionally, in part III calculations using an interaction term are reproduced. As the separate calculations for low and middle-income countries show larger differences in the values of the coefficients, it is suspected that there was a significant shift in the elasticity of the exchange rate-PPP ratio with respect to the capital variable during the course of economic development.

---

[1] Compare section 3.1.

[2] Section 3.1.

[3] The analysis used different data series for the capital or debt variable. Details are explained in the notes to that table. In most cases that variable has been calculated as percentage of the GDP. The income variable is either per capita income from the International Comparison Project (ICP) or the conventional GDP per capita (PCY).

Table 3

Regression Results [1] (I)
Purchasing Power Parity and Indebtedness

$$\frac{e}{PPP} = b_0 + b_1 \, PCY + b_2 \frac{CADXTR}{Y}$$

	LDCs		LICs		MICs	
	n=69	n=71	n=30	n=31	n=39	n=41
Intercept	3.68	3.95	3.89	4.29	3.19	3.28
	(18.78)	(19.86)	(5.97)	(6.92)	(16.79)	(14.61)
PCY	-0.00055	-0.00064	-0.00023	-0.00055	-0.00037	-0.00039
	(-5.28)	(-5.77)	(-0.13)	(-0.30)	(-4.51)	(-3.98)
CADXTR/Y	-3.93	-6.60	-6.79	-11.70	-2.27	0.35
	(-1.89)	(-3.69)	(-1.63)	(-4.01)	(-1.32)	(-0.20)
R^2_{adj}	0.28	0.34	0.09	0.33	0.33	0.30
F	13.99	18.99	1.33	8.44	10.23	9.49
SSR	58.50	76.97	42.46	46.48	12.16	18.69

Source: Own calculations with data from World Development Report (1992).

[1] t-values in parentheses

Symbols:

PCY	GDP per capita
ΔD	Net increase in foreign debts
AID	Foreign aid
FDI	Foreign Direct Investment
ΔR	Change in international reserves
CAD	Current Account Deficit-GDP-Ratio (90)
CADXTR/Y	Current Account Deficit excluding official transfers in percent of GDP
PPP	Purchasing Power Parity
LDCs	Less Developed Countries
LICs	Low Income Countries
MICs	Middle Income Countries
e	Exchange rate
Y	GDP
dk	Capital inflow

Table 3 (continued)

Regression Results [1] (II)
Purchasing Power Parity and Indebtedness

$$\frac{e}{PPP} = a_0 + a_1 \, PCY + a_2 \, (dK)/Y$$

1. dK = ΔD + AID + FDI − ΔR

	(1) LDCs (n=67)	(2) LICs (n=30)	(3) MICs (n=36)
Intercept	3.794 (17.24)	4.977 (6.45)	3.101 (17.35)
PCY	-0.00063 (-4.95)	-0.000202 (-1.09)	-0.000378 (-4.48)
dK/Y	-3.366 (-1.98)	-8.641 (-2.68)	-2.699 (-1.70)
R^2adj	0.26	0.16	0.34
F	12.86	3.66	10.06
SSR	65.17	41.30	11.11

2. dK = CAD

	(1) LDCs (n=70)	(2) LICs (n=30)	(3) MICs (n=39)
Intercept	3.892 (16.78)	4.861 (6.94)	3.316 (16.97)
PCY	-0.000602 (-5.40)	-0.00124 (-0.77)	-0.000407 (-5.01)
dK/Y	-3.442 (-2.26)	-8.753 (-3.09)	-3.264 (-2.21)
R^2adj	0.28	0.21	0.38
F	14.62	4.86	12.57
SSR	64.69	38.61	11.23

[1] t-values in parenthesis

Table 3 (continued)

Regression Results [1] (III)
Purchasing Power Parity and Indebtedness

$$\frac{e}{PPP} = c_0 + c_1\, PCY + c_2\, dK/Y + c_3\, (PCY \cdot dK/Y)$$

	dK/Y = CADXTR/Y without Lesotho and Jordan	dK/Y = CAD/Y all countries
Intercept	3.52 (14.88)	3.36 (12.73)
PCY	-0.00053 (-4.29)	-0.00045 (-3.39)
CADXTR/Y	5.08 (1.82)	
CAD/Y [2]		4.95 (3.51)
PCY·CADXTR/Y	-0.0039 (-1.89)	
PCY·CAD/Y		-0.0036 (-2.23)
R^2_{adj}	0.29	0.34
F	10.12	13.40
SSR	86.40	101.29

Source: Own calculations with data from World Development Report (various issues).

[1] t-values in parentheses

Table 3 (continued)
Regression Results (IV)
Purchasing Power Parity and Indebtedness: Chile 1970/71 - 88 [1)]

coefficients of the test equation [2)]	(1)	(2)
a_1	3,47 (10,08)	3,47 (8,63)
a_2	2,47 (9,64)	1,93 (20,59)
a_3	5,50 (8,66)	5,50 (7,42)
b_1	-0,0018 (-5,62)	-0,0018 (-4,82)
b_2	-0,00046 (-2,24)	.. ..
b_3	-0,0016 (-4,28)	-0,0016 (-3,66)
c_1	0,00092 (2,28)	-0,00092 (1,95)
c_2	0,00000 (0,49)	-0,00015 (-3,47)
c_3	-0,00033 (-3,24)	-0,00033 -2,78)
R^2 (adj.)	0,92	0,89
F	27,65	22,65
LM-Test (Prob.)	0,58	0,50
Ramsey RESET (Prob.)	0,90	0,64
Dickey-Fuller t	-5,44*	-4,84

Source: Own calculations with data from World Bank (1992b).

[1)] t-values in parantheses

[2)] see text

* significant at 10% level

.. data not available

According to the hypotheses explained in part 3.1. of this paper both coefficients of the variables on the right hand side of the test equation (1) show the expected negative sign. Furthermore, they are usually significantly different from zero when the whole sample is considered [1]. Although the coefficients of determination are rather low, the F - values of the regressions indicate an acceptable degree of significance for the estimates. However, it should be noted that small changes of the sample size can lead to sizable changes in the values of the coefficients. This result may be interpreted as a weak indicator that multicollinearity may be a problem.

Partitioning the sample into low- and middle-income countries (LICs and MICs) considerable differences in the value and significance of the coefficients result. In the case of the LICs the income variable is insignificant while the coefficient of the capital variable is much higher and more significant than in the whole sample. Income differences are not reflected in the exchange rate-PPP ratio. The opposite holds in the sample that consists of MICs only. Here, the income variable is usually highly significant. However, despite these results, the Chow test reveals that both samples can be pooled as the hypothesis of stable coefficients for the whole sample cannot be rejected. This justifies the regression with an interaction term, the results of which are reproduced in part III of table 3. The coefficients indicate that the elasticity of the exchange rate PPP-ratio with respect to capital transfers decreases with the level of development indicating that the weights of the variables change in the course of economic development.

The results obtained in the cross-section analysis dampen the expectations with respect to the quality of the estimates in a time series analysis with Chilean data. As Chile belongs to the group of middle-income countries problems with the significance of the income coefficient and with multicollinearity could be expected. A first round of estimates (the results of which are not reproduced here) demonstrated that these fears were partially justified. The coefficient of the income variable had the correct (negative) sign and was significant while the coefficient of the capital variable was positive or insignificant when only these two variables had been included. In these cases usually the adjusted R^2 was relatively low and the value of the Durbin-Watson statistic indicated that first-order autocorrelation could not be excluded. Inclusion of a trend variable resulted in a strong increase of the R^2 statistic. These results point to

---

[1] The sample size varies according to different methods used in the detection of outliers.

the possibility of a misspecification of the equation. The result of a Ramsey test further strengthened this suspicion.

The estimation strategy pursued was to hold the number of independent variables as small as possible. Therefore, in a second step stability of the estimates was checked. The result of the Chow test indicated structural breaks in 1976 and 1983. There are plausible reasons for breaks in these years which mark the stabilization efforts of the mid-seventies and the first completed year under the rules of the debt crisis. For this reason dummy variables were used to test the stability of all coefficients. The test equation was defined as follows:

(9) $(e/PPP)_i = a_1 D_1 + a_2 D_2 + a_3 D_3 + b_1 D_4 + b_2 D_5 + b_3 D_6 + c_1 D_7 + c_2 D_8 + c_3 D_9 + u$

where

$$D_1 = \begin{cases} 1 \text{ for the years 1970-75} \\ 0 \text{ else} \end{cases}$$

$$D_2 = \begin{cases} 1 \text{ for the years 1976-82} \\ 0 \text{ else} \end{cases}$$

$$D_3 = \begin{cases} 1 \text{ for the years 1983-88} \\ 0 \text{ else} \end{cases}$$

$$D_4 = \begin{cases} \text{PCY for the years 1970-75} \\ 0 \text{ else} \end{cases}$$

$$D_5 = \begin{cases} \text{PCY for the years 1976-82} \\ 0 \text{ else} \end{cases}$$

$$D_6 = \begin{cases} \text{PCY for the years 1983-88} \\ 0 \text{ else} \end{cases}$$

$$D_7 = \begin{cases} \text{CAD for the years 1970-75} \\ 0 \text{ else} \end{cases}$$

$$D_8 = \begin{cases} \text{CAD for the years 1976-82} \\ 0 \text{ else} \end{cases}$$

$$D_9 = \begin{cases} \text{CAD for the years 1983-88} \\ 0 \text{ else} \end{cases}$$

and CAD as current account deficit and PCY as GDP per capita, both measured at prices of 1985.

Part IV of table 3 shows the results of this analysis. Compared with those of the cross section analysis the results show a relatively high coefficient of determination. The augmented Dickey-Fuller test reveals that the variables used for the results in col. 1 are cointegrated. According to the Ramsey test a misspecification can be excluded at reasonable levels of probability. However, the result of the LM test points to the possibility that the residuals may be correlated.

In part IV of table 3 the signs of the independent variables are as follows:

Variable	**Result of columns**	1970 - 75	1976 - 82	1983 - 88
PCY	(1)	-	-	-
	(2)	-		-
CAD	(1)	+	not significant	-
	(2)	+	-	-

This result is astonishing. Although the income variable has the expected sign in all periods, the sign of the capital variable is persistently positive in the first period and negative later on. One might be tempted to interpret this outcome as influence of multicollinearity between the independent variables as the correlation between both is 0.86.

However, a high coefficient of correlation between independent variables does not tell much about multicollinearity in the current estimation. Multicollinearity leads to unacceptable results when the estimated coefficients deviate to a large extent as a result of omitting or introducing one observation. In this respect the result was not clear. Omitting the first observation (1970) resulted in insignificant coefficients of the current account deficit in the first and second subperiod. Restricting the analysis to the period 1970 to 1987 led to a result that was nearly identical with that of col. 1 in table 3 part IV. It was therefore concluded that multicollinearity was not a serious problem.

The fact that the negative sign expected for the coefficient of the capital variable (CAD) resulted only during the eighties implies that in the 1970s Chile's external debt did not cause an increase in the relative price of nontradables. One may explain this a) by the fact that the abnormally high increase in Chile's foreign debt began in 1980 and b) by the extraordinary events in the seventies (Allende's government, the military revolt, and the stabilization process in the mid-seventies).

4.2. Analysis of the Changes in the Wage Rates

According to the theoretical analysis the following changes in the relative wage rates $w = (w_T/w_{NT})^t /(w_T/w_{NT})^{t+n} \gtrless 1$ between periods t and t + n are to be expected:

	Rigidities in the Sector of Tradables	Rigidities in the Sector of Tradables
Capital Inflow	$w > 1$	$w < 1$
Expenditure Switching	$w > 1$	$w < 1$

The assumptions on sectoral inflexibility correspond to different types of LDCs. To give an example, wage rigidity in the tradables sector may be expected in those countries where industrialization already achieved an advanced level, and where production of tradables is situated in urban areas. Another example for countries with inflexibilities in the tradables sector are those which overwhelmingly export agrarian products, and where labour is effectively protected by minimum wage legislation. On the other hand, protected labour in the nontradables sector may exist in countries where production is concentrated in urban areas while tradables may be produced either in rural or urban areas.

If one differentiates production in rural and urban areas and in tradable and nontradable sectors the Latin American countries can be arranged according to their relative sectoral and regional shares of production. Table 4 demonstrates the result of this kind of partitioning. In rural areas production of tradables dominates that of nontradables in countries like Bolivia, El Salvador and Paraguay as well as the oil-exporting countries Trinidad and Tobago, Peru, Venezuela and Ecuador while production of nontradables dominates that of tradables in Mexico. In no country there is a dominant production of tradable goods in urban areas (first part of table 4) although production of tradables is two-to four times higher in urban than in rural areas in Brazil, Argentina, Mexico, and Uruguay. Finally, there is a strong urban domination in the production of nontradables (second part of table 4). This leads one to suggest that in principle, one can distinguish two groups of countries. In the first of them production of tradables and nontradables is concentrated in urban areas (Argentina, Brazil, Mexico, Uruguay, Panama, Chile, Costa Rica, and Colombia). The second group consists of countries where tradables are mostly produced in the countryside while nontradables production is situated in urban areas (Trinidad and Tobago, Bolivia, Peru, Venezuela, and Ecuador).

If competition is an effective instrument to diminish the protection of labour and to lower rigidities in the wage rates, when the economies become more open, wage inflexibility is expected to be more prevalent in the production of nontradables than in that of tradables. As a consequence, the model depicted in figure 4 (rigidities in the production of nontradables) is likely to better reflect reality during the adjustment process than that of figure 3 (wage inflexibility in the tradables sector) which corresponds more to the Latin American situation in the seventies. If this judgement is correct one must expect that the relative wage rate $w = (w_T/w_{NT})^t / (w_T/w_{NT})^{t+n}$ exceeds

Table 4
Sectoral and Regional Orientation of Production in Latin America
- Sectoral Orientation - [1)]
when the region is given

Orientation on	Strength of Orientation	Production in Urban Areas	Production in Rural Areas
Tradables	strong		Bolivia 262 Trinidad and Tobago 299 Venezuela 177 Paraguay 158 El Salvador 156 Peru 150 Colombia 138 Ecuador 128 Chile 113 Costa Rica 100
	weak		
Nontradables	weak	Venezuela 91 Uruguay 89 Brazil 75 Colombia 59 Argentina 57	Uruguay 69 Argentina 52 Brazil 62 Panama 55
	strong	Mexico 49 Paraguay 47 Chile 47 Ecuador 45 Panama 43 Costa Rica 42 Bolivia 39 El Salvador 38 Trinidad 22	Mexico 43

Source: Own calculations with data from UN, Handbook of National Accounts Statistics, various issues.

[1)] The numbers indicate how strong production of tradables relative to nontradables is concentrated in urban or rural areas.

Table 4 (continued)
Sectoral and Regional Orientation of Production in Latin America
- Regional Orientation -[1)]

when the sector is given

Production of	Strength of Orientation	Urban Orientation		Rural Orientation	
Tradables	strong	Brazil Argentina Mexico Uruguay	4,1 2,3 2,2 2,0	Trinidad and Tobago Bolivia El Salvador Paraguay	0,2 0,4 0,5 0,5
	weak	Paraguay Chile Costa Rica Colombia	1,6 1,2 1,1 1,0	Peru Venezuela Ecuador	0,7 0,7 0,8
Nontradables	strong	Brazil Venezuela Bolivia Chile Costa Rica Colombia Trinidad and Tobago Uruguay	3,4 3,3 2,9 2,8 2,5 2,4 2,4 2,3		
	weak	El Salvador Ecuador Argentina Panama Peru Mexico Paraguay	2,2 2,2 2,1 2,1 2,1 2,0 1,8		

Source: Own calculations with data from UN, Handbook of National Accounts Statistics, various issues.

[1)] The numbers indicate how strong regional production is concentrated in the tradables or nontradables sector.

Table 5
Changes of Relative Wage Rates in Latin America

Ratio of Wage Rates in the Production of Tradables to Nontradables: w_T / w_{NT}

	Urban Production of Tradables / Urban Production of Nontradables			Rural Production of Tradables / Urban Production of Nontradables			Urban Production of Tradables / Rural Production of Tradables		
	Sectors*)	1976-81 (1)	1982-90 (2)	Sectors*)	1976-81 (3)	1982-90 (4)	Sectors*)	1976-81 (5)	1982-90
Brazil	(1):(3)	..	0.91	(2):(3)	..	0.76 1)			
	(1):(4)	..	1.04	(2):(4)	..	0.27 1)			
Bolivia	(1):(3)	1.3	..	(2a):(3)**)	1.29	..			
	(1):(4)	1.36	..	(2a):(4)**)	1.33	..			
				(2b):(3)**)	0.80	..			
				(2b):(4)**)	0.83	..			
Costa Rica	(1):(3)	1.03	1.10	(2):(3)	1.13	0.86 3)	(1):(5)	1.16	..
	(1):(4)	0.93	1.05	(2):(4)	1.01	0.87			
Chile	(1):(3)	..	1.28	(2):(3)	1.10	..	(1):(2)	0.87	..
	(1):(4)	..	1.17	(2):(4)	1.02	..			
Ecuador							(1):(2)	1.05	..
Honduras	(1):(3)	1.86	0.88 4)	(2):(3)	2.88	0.37 4)	(1):(5)	1.79	..
	(1):(4)	2.06	0.99 4)	(2):(4)	3.23	0.41 4)			
Mexico	(1):(3)	0.90	0.94 4)						
Peru	(1):(4)	1.21	1.07 6)	(2):(3)	0.83 5)	..	(1):(5)	1.12	..
				(2):(4)	1.17 5)	..			
Uruguay	(1):(3)	1.07	0.96 2)						
	(1):(4)	1.02	1.03 2)						
Paraguay	(1):(3)	..	1.08 2)	(2):(3)	2.08 2)	..			
	(1):(4)	..	0.76 2)	(2):(4)	1.54 2)	..			

Sources: ILO, Yearbook of Labour Statistics, various issues.

1) 1984-1988 *) Sectors: (1) Manufacturing Tradable Sectors: (1), (2) and (5)
2) 1983-1990   (2) Mining and Quarrying Nontradable Sectors: (3) and (4)
3) 1987-1990   **) (2a) Mining, (2b) Oil
4) 1982-1989   (3) Construction
5) 1986-1989   (4) Transport
6) 1984-1990   (5) Agriculture

Note: A ratio exceeding unity indicates that wage rates in the production of nontradables increased by more than those in the production of tradables.

.. Data not available.

unity during the process of rising external debt and is lower than unity during the process of adjustment. Then, with respect to the first group of countries - where production of tradables and nontradables is concentrated in the cities - the first column of table 5 must show values that exceed unity while in the second column they must be less than 1. For the second group of countries (production of tradables in the countryside and that of nontradables in urban areas) the entries in column three must exceed unity and those in column four should be less than one.

Table 5 demonstrates that to a large extent these expectations conform to reality. In their tendency the entries in columns (1) and (3) are significantly higher and those in columns (2) and (4) smaller than one. Therefore, these empirical results are an indirect indication of the influence that capital flows may exert on poverty.

5. Concluding Remarks

Investigating the influence that debt-creating capital flows may have on poverty one is tempted to analyze the causal chain going from capital inflows via domestic investment and growth to the alleviation of poverty. Although there are clear empirical findings that poverty is reduced during the process of economic growth (Fields 1989, 167 - 185), empirical evidence on the relation between capital inflows and growth is somewhat inconclusive. For this reason this study relied on a different path of analysis to explain the relationship between capital flows and poverty: the change in the price ratio of tradable and nontradable goods. Capital inflows increase the prices of nontradables vis-à-vis those of tradables. The phenomenon that changes in relative prices of nontradables exert an effect on poverty has already gained some interest in the discussion of the social dimensions of adjustment programs (Addison and Demery 1993; Demery and Addison 1993, and Kanbur 1987). New is that this relationship is an important ingredient in the explanation of lower poverty rates during the process of rising indebtedness. The above analysis suggests that external capital flows may exert a strong influence on the development of poverty when the latter is measured by the headcount index. A policy aimed at reducing poverty has to take these relationships into account. Foreign capital can be used for the purpose of poverty alleviation although it may have negative effects on the production of tradables inasmuch as it provides negative incentives on the development of this sector.

However, it must be recognized that poverty alleviation via capital inflows is not without risks. Table 3 gives some evidence in this respect. There are combinations of sectoral poverty indices and changes in sectoral employment that allow for an increase in poverty even in times of capital inflows, regardless whether the wages are inflexible in the T or NT sectors (although looking at the number of cases this seems to happen more probably when rigidities govern the NT sector.) In the same manner, but with an opposite effect, expenditure switching does not always lead to an increase in poverty. Besides, there are cases where both policies may lead to a reduction in poverty in either scenario of inflexibility.

Evidently, the tradables - nontradables scenario with price rigidities, first in the tradables sector when external debts are rising, and later on in the nontradables sector when adjustment policies are introduced seems to fit quite well into the picture revealed by most Latin American countries during the late 1970s and 1980s. When, by and large, higher capital flows to LDCs lead to lower overall poverty rates measured by the headcount index, then a policy of poverty alleviation should take this into account as well. More specifically, economic policy on a micro- and macroeconomic level has to prepare the conditions that investors and creditors alike realize an investment-friendly environment. Some studies made this relationship rather explicit (Corsepius, Nunnenkamp, Schweickert 1989; Hiemenz, Nunnenkamp et al. 1991). Therefore, developing countries in Latin America and elsewhere should increase their efforts to become more attractive as host countries for foreign capital. Whether these capital inflows raise the growth rate of the recipient countries is not clear at all. However, according to the results of this study via changes in relative prices of nontradables they exert a relatively direct influence on the reduction of poverty.

In the political debate on development aid it has been claimed that funds need to be allocated in a way that maximizes poverty reduction, otherwise alleviation of poverty will not result. In this context, it is frequently pointed out that trickle-down effects from economic growth are insufficient. With respect to poverty-oriented allocation of development aid this claim may be criticized. It has been mentioned above, that only in periods of economic growth decreases of poverty have been realized (Fields 1989, 1734). From these findings one has to conclude that poverty orientation does not make much sense when aid is allocated in a way that hinders economic growth. That this may happen can be explained with reference to the model above. Decreasing poverty during the period of capital transfers, and increasing poverty as a result of expenditure switching was compatible with the sectoral poverty ranking T > U > N when during the period of expenditure switching prices in the nontradables sector were inflexible. Probably, a poverty-oriented aid policy would aim to alleviate the higher poverty of those employed in the tradables sector which when combined with a transfer of capital will lead to a result that is detrimental to that of the intended adjustment policy as the transfer increases the price of nontradables. As adjustment is a necessary input for future development, poverty oriented allocation of funds may reduce future growth and thus making further poverty alleviation more difficult.

References

Addison, T., and L. Demery. 1993. "Labour Markets, Poverty, and Adjustment." *Journal of International Development* 5:135-143.

Balassa, B. 1964. "The Purchasing Power Parity Doctrine: A Reappraisal." *Journal of Political Economy* 72:584-596.

Bhagwati, J. 1984. "Why Are Services Cheaper in Poor Countries?" *Economic Journal* 94:279-286.

Corsepius, U., P. Nunnenkamp, and R. Schweickert. 1989. "Debt versus Equity Finance in Developing Countries." *Kieler Studien.* No.229. Tübingen.

Demery, L., and T. Addison. 1993. "The Impact of Macroeconomic Adjustment on Poverty in the Presence of Wage Rigidities." *Journal of Development Economics* 30:331-348.

Edwards, S. 1988. "Terms of Trade, Tariffs, and Labour Market Adjustment in Developing Countries." *World Bank Economic Review* 2:165-187.

Fields, G. S. 1989. "Changes in Poverty and Inequality in Developing Countries." *World Bank Research Observer* 4:167-185.

Foster, J., J. Greer, and E. Thorbecke. 1984. "A Class of Decomposable Poverty Measures." *Econometrica* 52:761-766.

Hiemenz, U., and P. Nunnenkamp et al. 1991. "The International Competitiveness of Developing Countries for Risk Capital." *Kieler Studien.* No.242. Tübingen.

IDB. 1985. *Economic and Social Progress in Latin America. External Debt: Crisis and Adjustment. 1985 Report.* Inter-American Development Bank. Washington.

ILO. 1992. *World Labour Report 1992.* Geneva.

———. Various issues. *Yearbook of Labour Statistics.*

Kravis, I., A. Heston, and R. Summers. 1982. "The Share of Services in Economic Growth." In G. Adams and B. Hickman, eds. *Global Econometrics: Essays in Honor of Lawrence Klein.* Cambridge, MA.

Krugman, P.R. 1989. "Market-Based Debt Reduction Schemes." In J.A. Frenkel, M.P. Dooley, and P. Wickham, eds. *Analytical Issues in Debt.* International Monetary Fund. Washington, D.C.

Lancieri, E. 1990. "Purchasing Power Parities and Phase IV of the International Comparison Project: Do They Lead to "Real" Estimates of GDP and its Components?" *World Development* 18(1):29-48.

Michaely, M. 1981.
"Foreign Aid, Economic Structure, and Dependence." *Journal of Development Economics* 9:313-330.

Ravi Kanbur, S. M. 1987. "Structural Adjustment, Macroeconomic Adjustment, and Poverty: A Methodology for Analysis." *World Development* 15:1515-1526.

Scheide, J. 1993. "Does Economic Growth Depend on External Capital? Some Evidence from 116 Countries." *Applied Economics* 25:369-377.

United Nations. *Handbook of National Accounts Statistics.* Various issues.

World Bank. 1992a. World Development Report 1992. Washington, D.C.

———. 1992b. *World Tables 1992.* Washington, D.C.

———. 1990. *World Development Report 1990.* Washington, D.C.

———. Various Issues. *World Debt Tables.*

Appendix Table 1

Poverty and Indebtedness: A Statistical Survey

Country	External Debt (EDT/GNP)		Poverty Indicator (%) (Population in Poverty)			
			Urban		Rural	
	1975	1985	1975	1981-1990	1975	1981-1990
Latin America						
Argentina	17.95	84.20	9	15	19	20
Bolivia	50.53	176.60	..	..	85	86
Brazil	19.48	50.30	34	38	68	66
Chile	68.66	143.30	12	..	25	..
Colombia	21.40	42.60	40	40	48	45
Costa Rica	36.00	120.80	18	24	28	30
Domin. Republic	20.84	84.00	45	..	43	..
Ecuador	16.84	77.40	40	40	65	65
El Salvador	23.34	47.00	20	..	32	..
Guatemala	6.79	27.80	47	60	84	80
Haiti	9.65	35.70	55	65	78	80
Honduras	34.70	78.60	14	74	55	80
Jamaica	56.00	234.90	..	..	80	..
Mexico	17.16	55.20	20	23	49	43
Nicaragua	40.01	234.30	21	..	19	..
Panama	43.46	105.00	36	36	50	52
Paraguay	15.21	58.00	19	..	50	..
Peru	31.34	85.30	38	52	80	72
Trinid. and Tobago	6.32	21.00	..	..	39	40
Uruguay	22.24	89.70	13	19	27	29
Venezuela	5.41	..	20	30	43	42
Asia und Oceania						
Bangladesh	12.75	42.5	81	56	83	51
China	..	5.7	..	6	65	13
India	15.46	19.3	46	38	59	49
Indonesia	33.07	41.0	39	20	40	16
Korea, Republic	31.20	52.5	18	5	12	4
Malaysia	19.56	71.1	18	8	48	25
Nepal	2.13	23.6	22	19	36	43
Pakistan	49.38	40.4	32	20	41	31
Philippines	19.34	89.1	38	42	58	58
Sri Lanka [1]	20.38	47.69	20	15	27	54
Syria	9.96	66.4	..	..	60	36
Thailand	9.08	47.8	13	6	33	34
Africa						
Egypt [1]	44.51	111.37	..	34	44	34
Ghana	25.93	50.3	..	59	43	54
Madagascar	10.13	90.6	50	21	50	37
Morocco	19.42	136.6	38	28	45	32
Tunesia	29.64 [2]	61.6	34	16	43	31

Sources: External debt: Data from World Debt Tables (various issues).
Poverty: Data from ILO, World Labour Report 1992.
[1] Public debt/GNP.
[2] 1976.
.. Data not available.

Economic Policy in Latin America:
Moving toward Consensus?

Eduardo Lizano [1]

> "The basic principles of our economic policy are once more in the melting pot."
> (Meade 1948, 1)

> "... progress in our discipline has come to a standstill ...its former vitality is no longer there..."
> (Hirschman 1980, 1055)

I. Introduction

Literature on economic development in Latin America has been proliferating of late. One of the outstanding features of these contributions is that they place considerable emphasis on the issue of economic policy. Most of the work has looked at the wealth of experience accumulated in the countries of the region, attempting to identify the most significant features and shared components of economic policy approaches. Terms like "convergence," "consensus", "agenda", "plan of action" and "program" are becoming common currency.

This paper will examine three publications. The first is an article on the Washington "consensus" prepared by John Williamson and published in a compiled volume entitled *Latin American Adjustment: How much has happened?* (Williamson 1990a) [2] According to Williamson, the consensus is an attempt to be objective. He collects and classifies all the trends commonly seen in Washington, avoiding his own personal preferences and opinions. The author then proceeds to expand the range of his

---

[1] Academia de Centroamérica, Apartado 4633, 1000 San José, Costa Rica.

[2] Published by the Institute for International Economics (April, 1990). Williamson's main contributions can be found in Chapter 2 ("What Washington means by Policy Reform," 5-20) and Chapter 9 ("The Progress of Policy Reform in Latin America," 351-420). Chapter 9 separately was also published as number 28 of the institute's *Policy Analysis in International Economics* series (Williamson 1990b).

position by introducing items he would recommend. The second document is the ECLAC paper *Equity and the Transformation of Production: An Integrated Approach* (ECLAC 1992). Finally, we will analyze the agenda proposed by Enrique Iglesias in his book *Reflexiones sobre el desarrollo económico: Hacia un nuevo consenso latinoamericano* (Iglesias 1992).

This paper does not pretend to offer a systematic analysis of the rich content of these three publications. Rather, the idea is to look at each author's proposals for hastening economic development in Latin America, and compare them. Other important elements of these contributions to literature on Latin American economies are not addressed here. The second section gives an analytical summary of the message in each of the three documents. The third is a comparative exploration of common viewpoints. The fourth outlines theoretical positions that could provide a basis for a common economic policy. The fifth and final section discusses directions in which to orient future efforts at building a new consensus. The paper closes with some final comments.

A few questions are worth asking here: Why have these positions emerged? What is the source of these new contributions? A number of explanations could be given. The most important are:

i) The need to respond to the so-called lost decade. In the 1980s, Latin America not only failed to make satisfactory progress; it actually regressed in a number of important ways, such as real income per capita, employment, the level of poverty, macroeconomic stability, the foreign debt burden, and the distribution of income.

ii) The need to capitalize on the valuable experiences already beginning to build up in many countries of Latin America through the present "silent transformation" (Sagasti 1991, 2). These transformation experiences are taking place in the political arena as reflected in the process of democratization, as well as in economics, including programs for stabilization, economic opening, privatization, and renegotiation of the foreign debt.

iii) The need to assimilate lessons learned from the resounding failures of the centrally planned economic model, and the other model, so fashionable in Latin America, based on guilds, paternalism and populism (GPP). Both approaches have brought only economic stagnation, poverty, and political repression for vast segments of the population.

iv) The need to make better use of advances in the academic discipline of economics. Today, as Williamson states (1992a, 4), we know much more than 20 or 25 years ago about appropriate and inappropriate economic policies. Iglesias (1992, 156) agrees that Latin America now knows better than ever the fundamental codes of economic growth.

There are two main messages in the three contributions reviewed here. First, the need to roll up the sleeves and set to work immediately. Second, the real possibility that the boat can be steered into safe harbor. Although external events are important for explaining trends in the Latin American economy, it is now clear that the burden of responsibility lies at home. It makes little sense to continue blaming external factors for the blatant inadequacies of economic and social development in the region. The ideas studied in the following pages are geared in this direction and for this purpose. We will explore, identify, specify, and systematize the components of an appropriate economic policy that, as we stand at the threshold of a new century, holds the promise of achieving better standards of living for the population of Latin America.

II. The Proposals

In this section, we will analyze the three position papers introduced above from two different angles: their objectives, and the economic policy tools by which they propose to meet those objectives.

1. The Washington Consensus

A correlation matrix between Williamson's objectives (columns) and high-priority areas of economic policy (rows) is presented in table 1. The first four objectives are included in his original paper (Williamson 1990a). The fifth objective is added later (Williamson 1991): concerned with achieving greater equity, he proposes and details a number of inter-related measures to improve income distribution.[1] Table 1 traces

---

[1] He suggests more expenditures on primary education, preventive health care and housing; higher taxes on real estate; tax on income derived from foreign investment; and credit for micro-enterprises.

Table 1
The Washington Consensus

Objectives / Priority Areas	Growth	Inflation	Balance of payments	Environment	Income distribution
- Fiscal deficit	Crowding out	Inflationary pressure	Real demand	-----	Inflationary tax
- public expenditures	Infrastructure	-----	-----	Resource allocation	Education, health, housing
- Fiscal reform	Incentives for production and accumulation	-----	-----	Tax for environmental impact	Net impact of public finances
- Financial liberalization	Profitability of investments	-----	External capital flows	-----	-----
- Exchange rate	Competitiveness of local producers	Prices of imported goods	Level of imports and exports	-----	Prices of imported goods
- Trade policy	Competition and investment opportunities	Supply of imported goods	Level of imports and exports	-----	-----
- Direct foreign investment	Additional investment resources	-----	External capital flows	-----	-----
- Privatization	Productivity of public assets	Public sector financing	-----	-----	Democratization of ownership
- Deregulation	Market operations	Elimination of distortions and rents	-----	-----	Elimination of distortions and rents
- Property rights	Promotion of investments	-----	-----	-----	-----

Source: compiled from Williamson (1990a).

the relationship between objectives and instruments; it is in no sense comprehensive as, in general, every measure has indirect impacts and affects all the objectives simultaneously.

2. ECLAC's integrated approach

The 1992 ECLAC paper on equity and the transformation of production, marks the culmination of a slow, intensive process of study and reflection. [1] Table 2 summarizes ECLAC's position. The three main objectives are: to foster economic growth, to ensure an equitable distribution of national income, and to achieve environmentally sustainable development. The requirements for meeting these objectives are: technological progress, productive employment, and investment in human resources. Policy measures focus on five essential areas: First, economic opening should be promoted if the countries are to participate in the international economy more effectively. Second, a larger proportion of development projects needs to be funded with locally-derived resources. Third, the labor market needs reform through deep-seated changes in labor relations, geared toward avoiding confrontation and

Table 2
Equity and the Transformation of Production

High priority areas for economic policy	... to bring about	... and thus meet objectives for ...
- Penetrating the international economy	- Technical progress	- Economic growth
- Savings and investment		
- Labor market	- Productive employment	- Equity
- Social measures		
- Participation and consensus-building	- Investment in human resources	- Environmental sustainability

Source: based on ECLAC (1992).

raising productivity. Fourth, social policy measures should be two-pronged, including both investments in human resources, and increases in transfers, so as to break the inter-generational chain of poverty. Fifth, participation and consensus-building among workers and the general population should be encouraged. This is the only way to organize society democratically which is in turn a precondition for economic growth and equity.

3. Enrique Iglesias' Agenda

Iglesias has set two main objectives. The first is modernization of the economy, meaning growth. The second is equity to ensure an economic modernization process that is socially and politically sustainable. In order to attain these two objectives, Iglesias proposes ten high-priority points, which he calls "fronts," around which to mold an authentic Latin American consensus (Iglesias 1992, 156-170):

a) Facilitate the modernization of production. This means that macroeconomic balances need to be maintained, the price system must function properly, markets must operate predictably, and the opening of the economy should be promoted.

b) Make sure the model is socially sustainable by incorporating sectors now sidelined from the production process. This requires a full frontal attack on poverty.

c) State reform. Certain government activities need to be curtailed, while others should be reinforced. It is not a question of doing "more" or doing "less," but of doing "better" by building a more efficient public sector. If the government can be modernized, it will provide the support the private sector needs if it is to perform to its full potential.

d) Strengthen the private sector. The private sector needs to be reinforced, as private enterprise is called upon to play a leading role.

e) Promote technological modernization. The ability to compete depends on swift progress in this area.

---

[1] This exercise had begun at least seven years earlier, when in 1985 ECLAC published *Bases y opciones estratégicas para reorientar el desarrollo.*

f) Train human resources. This factor is fundamental for the region's economic development, not only to satisfy social concerns, but also for strictly economic reasons. The new market calls for a massive, modern process of training human resources at every educational level.

g) Pursue economic integration in the region. The integration process will facilitate changes in the production structure, and improve the competitive position of countries participating in the international economy.

h) Participate in the international economy. Under present circumstances, Latin American economies need to be much more open. New approaches will have to be sought for meeting this goal.

i) Pursue environmental sustainability. Any economic development model for Latin America must be environmentally sustainable. This means that the needs of future generations must be taken into account whenever measures are taken to expand production or raise standards of living.

j) Ensure a favorable political setting. Economic development requires a favorable political environment. This can be created only by consolidating and deepening democracy. This, in turn, means moving away from confrontation and toward convergence and consensus-building, and anchoring governments to basic political agreements. There is a need for a new, very broad social pact.

In Iglesias' view, if these two objectives and ten "fronts" are accepted, it would then become possible, as stated earlier, to build a true Latin American consensus and design economic and social policies appropriate for the 1990s, and attuned to this region.

III. Moving Toward Consensus?

This analysis of the three positions points to a certain consensus, or at least a convergence of opinions. The commonality revolves around the points listed below.

1. Assessment of the Situation

The assessment of the situation in Latin America features three items. First, socio-economic conditions in these countries leave a great deal to be desired, with the events of the 1980s having worsened a situation that was already precarious. Second, although substantial efforts will be needed, today's problems can be overcome. Third, some countries of the region have already made considerable strides in advancing major economic, social and political reforms.

2. Causes

The present situation can be attributed to three main causes:

– The crisis of the inward oriented growth model based on import substitution. Excessive protectionism, which occurred in opposition to the oft-repeated recommendations of Prebisch for avoiding excessively high customs duties and promoting exports, lies at the heart of this crisis.

– Heavy-handed, poorly oriented government intervention that brought manifold rents to diverse interest groups – business, labor and professionals. These programs brought a proliferation of subsidies, exemptions, controls, prohibitions, permits, rules and regulations, all of them producing significant, profound distortions in goods and factor markets. Moreover, they opened avenues for powerful interest groups to manipulate the government to their own ends. The government, instead of safeguarding and promoting the common good, was occupied with the creation and distribution rents.

– The backlash of certain traditional economic policies based on deficit spending, monetary expansion, easy credit, price controls, an overvalued currency, and foreign indebtedness. Much of the crisis experienced in the 1980s resulted directly from such policies.

Latin America wasted the valuable opportunities made available through the international economy and the incorporation of new scientific and technological knowledge. The results were not slow in coming. The economies grew either not at all or precariously little, and the distribution of income worsened. In the wake of this stagnation followed serious problems of poverty, unemployment and social marginalization.

There is no sense in trying to hang on to a few safe patches or repair the sinking ship. Instead, a decisive new tack is needed. This means, first, to open the economy and move toward a greater and better participation in the international market. Second, macroeconomic prudence is required to maintain the overall balance. Third, the implementation of domestic liberalization measures to allow markets to function properly. Fourth, a more equitable distribution of incomes to help create sociopolitical conditions favorable for economic development.

It is very important not to overlook the way external events have influenced development in the countries of Latin America. However, even while it is necessary to recognize the obvious role of such events, one must never forget that the main responsibility lies in domestic economic policies. Local efforts and discipline, the basis for sound economic policy, are in the hands of Latin Americans themselves. If they do not take the reins, no one will do it for them.

3. Policy Objectives

The main objectives of economic policy can be summarized as follows:

- Economic growth, either by transforming production or by modernizing the production structure.

- Equity, through a better distribution of national income and wealth.

- Environmental sustainability, so that today's development will not endanger tomorrow's possibilities for development.

4. Policy Tasks

The main tasks for economic policy stand out quite clearly. They revolve around:

- The need to restore and maintain macroeconomic balances. Stability is viewed as a necessary precondition for a reduction of the economic uncertainty economic agents face in decision making. Fiscal, monetary, exchange-rate, and wage policies need to be developed cautiously.

- The need to develop effective procedures for national economies to move as quickly as possible toward penetrating the international economy. The economies of Latin America are so small that their domestic markets cannot provide a broad enough base for development over the medium term. They need to become active players in international markets if they are to fully exploit their own comparative advantages, and attain a better allocation of their resources.

- The proper functioning of goods and factor markets is an integral part of the development process. Efficient markets are indispensable; by revealing relative shortages via undistorted price signals, they steer the decisions of economic agents, and orchestrate their actions under conditions in which available information is necessarily incomplete.[1] This is why we need to deregulate and liberalize the economy, eliminating distortions and rents.

- The inevitability of state reform. Only an efficient government can ever create and maintain the conditions needed for markets to function properly and, at the same time, counteract the common undesirable effects of markets that do not operate satisfactorily.

- The inescapable need to allocate a significant share of public expenditures for the training of human resources. Only through training can new knowledge be incorporated into the production process, raising productivity and improving the ability to compete. The pressing need for a major drive to improve training should serve as a focal point of any economic policy, not only as a means to boost production, but also to bring about a more equitable distribution of national income.

- Incorporation of science and technology into the development process. This point is of paramount importance. Macroeconomic stability, the rule of law, and the socio-political setting are all essential to the process of economic growth. However, only technological change will allow human and environmental

---

[1] Compare Hayek (1945).

resources to perform up to their true potential in creating more added value, controlling unit costs of production and, finally, improving the ability to compete successfully. This is why technological change must never be seen as an exogenous variable, but as endogenous to growth.

- Finally, the critical need to reform public finances. This goes far beyond merely improving fiscal balances by avoiding high, chronic fiscal deficits. In the first place, the crowding out of the private sector by the public sector needs to be avoided. Second, major changes are needed in the allocation of public expenditures: cutting back spending on the military and indiscriminate subsidies, and boosting outlays for education, health, sanitation and housing. Finally, the tax system needs to be overhauled. The reform of public finances is a factor of overriding importance for achieving growth and equity.

Disagreements over these points are few and fading. Certain differences persist concerning priorities and emphasis. However, clear possibilities are emerging for a common agenda and perhaps even the outlines of a certain policy consensus.

IV. The Foundations of Consensus [1]

The emerging consensus outlined in the last section is built on certain economic underpinnings. This section will explore those foundations and then attempt to crystallize the most important points.

1. Market size

The dimension of the market is a critical factor, strongly shaping possibilities for factor allocation, specialization, economies of scale, capital accumulation, technological change, and earnings from trade. Larger markets bring stronger and faster economic growth. It is only in this setting that efforts to participate in the international economy make sense. Similarly, programs for regional economic integration can be meaningful only if they help member countries consolidate their international market position, and

---

[1] Some of the ideas in this section and the next were set out by the author in the seminar "Central America after the Crisis," organized by Canning House and the University of London Institute of Latin American Studies (London, 30 November and 1 December, 1992).

do not become a means for protecting domestic markets. The process of opening national economies must move ahead vigorously. As it offers economic agents greater opportunities for investment and consumption, it will also intensify competition and force national producers to improve the allocation of factors of production.

2. Properly Functioning Markets

Markets need to operate properly. Because the market is the only way to reveal relative scarcities through prices, its proper functioning is essential for sound economic decision-making of all agents (consumers, producers, savers and investors). Markets play an irreplaceable role in the basic processes of the economy: they promote the effective allocation of factor resources, smoothing production processes, and assuring a reasonable distribution of national income. In the final analysis, producers must attune their decisions to the preferences of consumers, not vice-versa. The ultimate objective of the economy is to satisfy the needs of consumers as determined by themselves, and not by some benevolent dictator, over-enthusiastic planner, or monopolist.

3. Expectations

When economic agents make decisions, they carefully weigh their expectations, especially in two areas – stability and credibility. The first has to do with changes in the macroeconomic setting. In the second area, credibility, decision-makers need to believe that economic policy will remain consistent and have continuity. Economic agents faced with decisions attach overriding importance to these two points. This is why macroeconomic policy must be handled wisely, if the basic balances in the economy are to be maintained.

4. Market Limitations

Even though proper markets are essential, very often they do not function properly. Many different causes of market failure have been identified.[1] Markets are not a

---

[1] A good analysis of this topic can be found in Bator (1958).

product of spontaneous generation. Economic freedom, as Robbins (1953) has insisted, requires a detailed legal and institutional framework. Only this can guarantee property rights, the validity of contracts, and freedom of labor, enterprise and consumption. These fundamental economic rights, indivisible and interdependent, offer citizens the secure foundation they need for their business decisions. In the absence of such a setting, markets cannot function as they should. Market results may also be skewed by the presence of monopolistic and oligopolistic structures, even when market-clearing prices keep supply and demand in balance. Indeed, as Adam Smith declared, nothing good for consumers ever comes from a conclave of producers; businesses always try to prevent the market from providing a true reflection of consumer sovereignty. The market can never be raised to the category of dogma, but instead must remain a means to discipline the tumultuous forces of self-interest, as Robbins stated in 1953 [1].

This is why state intervention is needed in three specific directions. First, it must create an overall setting and maintain a legal and institutional framework by which markets can operate properly. Second, it must adopt measures to block monopolistic structures and break them apart if they should appear. Third, it must make provisions to buffer social groups that are hurt when markets do not operate well. The World Bank philosophy is worth remembering at all times: "To justify [government] intervention, it is not enough to know that the market is failing; it is also necessary to be confident that the government can do better". [2]

5. The cohesiveness of production and distribution

Over the medium term, the dichotomy between production and distribution is a fallacy. No one can set the priority on one of these two tasks, leaving the other for later. In essence, they are not two processes at all, but a single one. The very act of specifying the volume and structure of overall supply (domestic production)

---

[1] The specific quotation by Robbins (1953) says, "...not so much that the system of markets was always tending to some refined equilibrium adjustment, but rather that it provided a rough pointer and a rough discipline whereby the tumultuous forces of self-interest were guided and held in check" (16). He does not refute the position of Meade when he says that "state foresight and intervention is required to guide the economy from war to peace, to prevent inflationary and deflationary pressures, to ensure a tolerably equitable distribution of income and property, and to prevent or to control the anti-social rigging of the market by private interest, but that these objectives can be achieved in an efficient and a free society only if an extensive use is made of the mechanisms of competition, free enterprise and the free market determination of prices and output" (1948, V-VI).

[2] World Bank (1991, 131).

automatically defines the demand for the different production factors and fixes their price based on availability. This, in turn, dictates the actual distribution of national production [1]. Two considerations should be kept in mind:

a) In the final analysis, real wage levels depend on profit trends in the private sector. Labor unions should never overlook the cause-and-effect relationship between profits and investments, investments and demand for labor, and demand for labor and wage levels. When they press their demands, they would do well to focus on investment levels by private businesses and the public sector, rather than just on nominal wage levels.

Profits, in turn, are closely bound to changes in real wages. This is because of the cause-and-effect relationship between, on the one hand, the social environment (peace and stability) and the economic setting that encourage new investment, and on the other, the standards of living of labor groups. In large measure, the standard of living for labor depends on real wages. This is why businesses need to be constantly alert to real wage trends. Thus, the processes of production and distribution must be seen as inseparable.

b) For most of the population, "trickle down" works. This position can be found in A. Marshall (1887) [2] and in the W.A. Lewis model (1954). In both cases, the demand for labor is the driving force behind expanding employment and the subsequent rise of real wages. Companies cannot retain the full surplus they generate, but must transfer it to the workers. Overall worker compensation increases, first, due to the expansion of "q" (employment), and later, with the rise of "p" (wages). As capital accumulation advances and production expands, "the reserve army" tends to diminish, and after some time labor groups see an improvement in their standards of living. However, this topic must be explored in more depth, a task which will be taken up in the following paragraph.

---

[1] Nonetheless, some authors such as Fajnzylber (1990, 163) see the process as sequential, rather than unitary.

[2] "In the ordinary course of things, the first benefit of an improvement in the demand for their wares goes to the employers, but they are likely to want to increase their output while prices are high, and make high profits while they can. So they soon begin to bid against one another for extra labour; and this tends to raise wages and hand over some of the benefits to the employed. This transfer may be retarded, though seldom entirely stopped, by a combination among employers, or it may be hastened on by the combined action of the employed." (Marshall, 216-217).

6. Poverty

Even though the two basic conditions for improving living standards may be met [1], all too often large groups of society continue to live in undesirably precarious conditions. Many factors can be mentioned as the cause of such difficulties for certain social groups. Some are economic (technological development, cyclical fluctuations, structural adjustment). Others are social (power structure, relations of dependency). Still others are difficult to categorize (natural disasters, misfortune, illness, old age).

This is not a new problem (IDB, 1993). It has nagged at most Latin American countries for decades, but neither the agro-export model nor the import-substitution model and even less the GPP model has successfully addressed the problems of poverty and flagrant inequality [2]. It demands a solution, or at least some relief. Merely ethical motives are bolstered by important social and economic reasons. No situation characterized by increasingly unfulfilled expectations can offer a social milieu favorable to the process of private investment, so necessary for economic development. Moreover, the ongoing process of technological change demands workers who are better and better trained, which is difficult to achieve if a very high proportion of the population is living in poverty [3].

7. The importance of economic policy

The supply of factors of production is a critical issue for understanding economic growth. Access to more factors can shift the production possibilities curve to the right. However, it is becoming increasingly evident that the supply of factors is only part of the picture. It is the way those factors are used that keeps the economy closer

---

[1] First, markets function as they should so the "trickle down" effect can take place, and second, the government has effective tools to offset the detrimental effects of market failure.

[2] Economists have been concerned about the issue of poverty for a long time. Hume (1752) states, "A too great disproportion among the citizens weakens any state...where the riches are in few hands, these must enjoy all the power, and will readily conspire to lay the whole burden on the poor." A. Smith stated in 1776, "No society can surely be flourishing and happy of which the far greater part of the members are poor and miserable..." (Vol. I, 80). A century later, Cairnes wrote "...the rich will be growing richer; and the poor, at least relatively poorer. It seems to me...that these are not conditions which furnish a solid base for a progressive state" (340). Marshall (1893) added, "I have devoted myself for the last twenty-five years to the problem of poverty; and very little of my work has been devoted to any inquiry which does not bear upon that." (Memorials, 70).

[3] J.R. McCulloch (1843) had already stated it very clearly: "An ignorant and under-educated people, though possessed of all materials and powers necessary for the production of wealth, are uniformly sunk in poverty and barbarism." As cited by Robbins (1968, 75-76).

to or further from the production possibilities curve. If factors are used inefficiently, the economy can never come near the curve. Great potential exists in such a situation for increasing production simply by changing the allocation of factor endowments. Factor allocation is closely linked to economic policy. This is why today it is widely accepted that economic policy truly matters. The World Bank devoted its 1991 annual report to this very subject, and Fischer (1991) has stressed it emphatically. Programs for economic liberalization have taken on considerable importance, along with programs to eliminate distortions and rents. As a result, factors of production can be allocated better, making it possible to produce more with the same endowment of factors, or even with less.

8. The process of change

It is a mistake to attempt to deal separately with "economic issues," "social issues" and "political issues." From a broader view economic, social and political factors are all part of the same general process of social change. They are closely related and interdependent, which means that economic development, social progress and democratization all contribute to a single process. One cannot occur without the others.[1]

Over the long term, the process of change serves to raise standards of living and enhances citizen participation. However, as the process of change unfolds, the interplay of factors does not necessarily benefit all social sectors equally. Certain groups find themselves losing social status, political power and relative income levels when society moves from an inward-oriented development model to an outward-oriented model, and from an economic-social-political organization based on the GPP model to one characterized by the operation of free markets, social mobility and democracy. This is why the process of change depends ultimately on the power struggle between those who defend the status quo and those who foster change. If defenders of the status quo are powerful, change becomes very difficult. This explains why certain

---

[1] Pourgerami (375) recently reached the following conclusion: "...the positive and significant development-democracy-growth associations demonstrate that countries achieving high levels of development are more likely to establish and sustain democracy, and nations with democratic political institutions are more likely to accelerate economic growth. Failure to understand the multidimensionality of societal progress will result in 'uneven' development, a phenomenon most common in the developing world, in which a few modernizing units operate to benefit the dominant politico-economic elite, while other units remain impoverished and repressed."

communities continue for decades to post no economic, social or political progress whatsoever. In the final analysis, no society is condemned to progress [1].

Having now analyzed the foundations that undergird convergence and consensus, we can close by summarizing the three basic guidelines. i) Go back to basics and remember the principles of Economics 101, understanding that the simplest is generally the most important. ii) Abandon false dichotomies, especially the one that pits the market against the state. iii) Recognize the overriding importance not only of what ought to be done (economic theory), but also of how to do it (economic policy). This, in turn, leads to a broader view of economic development, embracing the whole process of social change.

V. Toward a Broader Consensus?

Although major progress has been made toward identifying consensus points several issues remain unresolved pending a more detailed analysis. The most important will be discussed in this section.

1. State Reform

All three positions presented above agree on the pressing need for profound state reform in Latin America [2]. Countries can develop only if the state openly supports the private sector and provides what the market cannot. All too often, however, the barriers blocking this objective are underestimated. True, the state is no longer seen as the executive committee of the ruling political party or of some business or industry group, nor as a simple guardian of the public interest. Even so, much remains to be done.

The government in Latin America today represents an institution based on a concentration of power whose decisions are binding for all the members of the community. It is no wonder that governments have so often been taken over literally by assault through pressure groups. Those who would harness government's power

---

[1] Recent contributions on the theory of economic growth (Lucas, 1988; Barro and Sala-i-Martín, 1992) make this very clear. The conditions for convergence between wealthy countries and poor countries do not commonly occur in the real world, and poor countries can very easily remain poor.

[2] Compare sections II and III.

in this fashion are not much concerned with placing it at the service of the community. Instead, they have their own special interests, and some of them are part of the state itself, including the government bureaucracy, labor unions of public-sector entities, and the armed forces. Others operate from outside the government, such as certain business, labor or professional groups. Most of them have been established for the express purpose of promoting and defending their own interests. They have developed many different ways to do this, ranging from lobbying to funding political groups, to outright corruption. They compete with each other, individually or through alliances or coalitions, to transform the government into a creator and distributor of rents. The public interest or the common good slip to second or even third place.

What can be done in such a setting to promote state reform, or to scale down and modernize government structures? How can interest groups be persuaded to support measures that, while profitable for society as a whole, may prove detrimental to themselves? What can be done to create extra maneuvering room so the process of change can begin?

A resolution of these issues demands unstinting effort and dedication.[1] No matter what steps are taken, progress in this direction will be time-consuming. Without it, there can be neither economic development nor equity. In such a complex setting, with its major political stumbling blocks, it would be an error to stake too many hopes on the prospect of state reform.

2. Transition from Inward- to Outward Oriented Development

There is broad agreement that the inward-oriented development approach, based on import substitution, no longer has anything to offer. No one questions the need for and usefulness of a model based on outward-oriented development through bold participation in the international economy. However, the countries have yet to grasp how very difficult it will be to make the transition from one model to the other. This is due primarily to the legacy of the GPP model based on guilds, paternalism and populism.

---

[1] Grindle (1991) and Nelson (1990) recently developed a promising approach.

This GPP model, which has been embraced in nearly all the countries of Latin America over the past few decades, has done considerable damage. It rejected both the planning approach and the market approach in favor of an economic, social and political organization based on the proliferation of special-interest groups (industry, labor, bureaucracy, professional, political, etc.) that have manipulated the government to obtain every imaginable kind of privilege (rents) for their own benefit. It is no exaggeration to say that the government does little more than make decisions to favor certain groups.

The basic components of the system are the formation of pressure groups, practices of political and electoral patronage and corruption, and spurious, temporary alliances and coalitions. Government intervention, overextended and poorly channeled, has sparked many profound distortions that prevent agents from receiving the signals they need for making economically sound decisions. Economic agents, instead of busying themselves with boosting productivity and cutting unit costs of production as competition looms and technological change flourishes, find they obtain greater benefits if they concentrate on obtaining additional rents from the government or tenaciously defending those they have already won.

The results of the widespread practice of the GPP model are well known. They include macroeconomic instability, economic stagnation, woeful income distribution, and social and political marginalization of a substantial share of the population. Under these circumstances, each group behaves in ways that are rational for them but ultimately lead to consequences detrimental to society as a whole. The economic, social and political power structure that grew out of the GPP model now stands as a nearly impenetrable barrier to changing the model. The different power groups are unflinching in their zeal to protect the rents they obtain through the status quo. Greater economic freedom poses a clear threat to the economic, social and political advantages enjoyed by the interest groups. Like calves clinging to the udder, they hang on to their privileges for dear life. As a result, the process of social change is severely hampered. Very often, the forces fighting to protect the status quo are more powerful than those advocating change. Structural adjustment policies in Latin America have proven much more difficult to implement than anyone had anticipated. Economic reform in general has advanced much more slowly and produced far fewer benefits than it should have. This is due essentially to the legacy of the GPP.

3. Driving Forces in the Process of Social Change

Conflict is generally not given its due place as a driving force in the process of social change. Instead, the idea of solidarity is held up as the hope for building convergence, agreement and consensus among social groups. Iglesias (1992, 171) asserts the need to move away from confrontation and begin practicing convergence and consensus. He then stresses the need to cement a new, very broad social pact. ECLAC (1992) insists that the most neglected, vulnerable groups must have opportunities to express themselves and thus be heard when the many agents of society clamor for the allocation and use of resources, be they physical, economic, cultural or involving exercise of power. It describes the political implications of this, claiming that the demands of these sectors should be present in party platforms, in the public debate, and in decisions involving policy formulation and the composition of public expenditure. Thus, the many groups bypassed by development would open their own channels of representation when demands are processed and decisions are made.

All this is very commendable; but how can it be achieved when society is undergoing a process of change that actually wrests power from those groups that make most of the decisions? What can be done to rein in the disruptive effects described by Kuznets (1980)?[1] We must never overlook the different forces that shape the process of social change: conflict (Marx), innovation (Schumpeter) and ideas (Keynes). These three forces vary from one occasion to another in terms of their relative importance and the degree of intensity with which they occur; but they determine the pace and characteristics of the process of social change. Thus, one of the great challenges is knowing how to accommodate them. Even though this problem is very complex, it must never be pushed aside. Much would be lost from such an attitude.

Many of the phenomena associated with the process of change carry an inherent component of conflict that cannot be avoided. This is not a new concept in economic analysis. For example, the Ricardo model long ago posited major conflict between agricultural producers, industrial producers and laborers. Thus the great challenges for economic policy is deciding how to make the desirable feasible.

---

[1] Kuznets says, "...while the new knowledge and technological innovations meant a potentially revolutionary expansion in productive power, they also had a variety of disruptive effects...Such attractive changes, as they may have been to those ready and capable of exploiting the new growth opportunities, were disruptive to those who lost relatively" (427).

4. Conditions Supporting State Reform

Certain positive features of economic policy, having to do with greater participation in the international economy, are often underrated. The opening of the economy offers much-proclaimed benefits associated with trade earnings and enhancements in the efficiency of factor allocation. It has other extremely important benefits as well, such as:

a) It creates conditions under which state reform becomes inevitable. In a GPP model, entrepreneurs have no interest in making the government more efficient. They enjoy a highly protected market, and when government inefficiency costs them money, they easily pass their additional costs on to the consumers, in the form of higher prices for goods and services. An implicit or even explicit partnership develops between business groups and bureaucratic and political groups, with consumers shouldering the costs.

When the economy is thrown open, this alliance cannot survive. Local entrepreneurs must compete with importers in the home market, and when they attempt to sell abroad, they must go head-to-head with products from other countries. They can succeed in neither unless they control their unit costs of production, which in turn requires an efficient public sector. A clash between the members of this alliance looms inexorably. Either the government reforms and local producers become competitive, or the whole process collapses because bureaucratic and political groups block change and local businesses are shut out of opportunities on the international economy, unable to meet the challenges of market opening.

b) Economic liberalization encourages the emergence of a whole new business class. The GPP and ISI models breed a parasitic entrepreneurial group (Roxborough, 1992)[1], specialized in obtaining rents. The new economic policy, by encouraging competition, forces entrepreneurs to become more productive, incorporate new technology, and seek new markets. Entrepreneurial groups need a deep mentality change, which will not occur by spontaneous generation; instead, it grows out of conditions created by the process of opening.

---

[1] Roxborough's position is: "Whereas the excessive state regulation and politicisation of ISI was inconsistent with the flowering of entrepreneurship, market-oriented reforms should provide the necessary conditions for available entrepreneurial talent to find investment outlets. This may well happen. However, to hope that a largely parasitic and state-dependent bourgeoisie will transform itself overnight into a group of competitive risk-taking entrepreneurs may turn out to be more ideological fantasy than empirical reality" (423).

c) Greater possibilities become available for achieving equity. The new economic policy can do much in this regard. For example:

   i) Macroeconomic stability eliminates the inflationary tax which generally hits low-income groups.

   ii) Because they need to be more competitive, entrepreneurs spend money to train human resources. This is the only way they can systematically incorporate new technology and raise productivity. As a result, workers encounter better employment possibilities and higher real wages.

   iii) Improved socio-political conditions attract more local and foreign investment. This also has a positive impact on employment and real wages.

None of the three publications studied herein acknowledges that the GPP model raises the costs of social change processes. There is no question that social groups accustomed to the GPP model cling to their privileges much more tenaciously than was imagined when structural adjustment programs were first implemented. This keeps the process of social change moving very slowly. The problem of the costs of adjustment demands more attention, and compensatory measures need to be larger and adopted over a much longer term.

5. Tax Reform

There is consensus on the need for tax reform as a way to bring more resources into public coffers. However, this important point still needs to be discussed in more depth. Several different points need to be aired:

First, in most of the countries of Latin America, "social" services such as education and health are highly inefficient and not very productive. Under such circumstances, allocating additional tax receipts without first making the services more efficient would merely waste resources.

Second, because of the way "social" systems are set up, lowest-income groups very often receive inadequate coverage and protection. Two cases in point are pension programs and systems for access to education. Before more tax receipts are poured into such "social" services, profound reforms should be carried out to guarantee benefits not only to the middle classes, but to low-income groups as well.

Third, the much-proclaimed concept of "regressiveness" and "progressiveness" in the tax system should be placed in its proper perspective. Taxes paid by the "poor" could quite possibly be more than offset by benefits received from public outlays. The "progressiveness" and "regressiveness" of public finances need to be examined in their full context, taking into account both taxes and fund allocation, instead of focusing merely on the tax system. The tax regime per se may well turn out to be "regressive," meaning that the "poor" pay the same taxes as the "rich" for the purchase of an automobile or a pack of cigarettes. In fact, this does not particularly matter. Rather, the effects of both tax collection and public expenditure need to be factored into the equation before studying distribution so that the Lorenz curve also reflects the impact of public finances.

Fourth, when tax systems are reformed, it is vitally important to adjust taxes in a way that will not distort the process of production and accumulation. As Kaldor[1] stated many years ago and Meade[2] reiterated, taxes should fall much more heavily on consumption (consumer taxes, sales taxes, value-added taxes) and on certain excessive forms of accumulation, and much less on the production process (business income tax) and factors of production (payroll taxes). This very trend has been observed in recent decades in the countries of western Europe[3]. In general terms, the tax system should avoid exerting a negative impact on production and accumulation, and public outlays should encourage greater equity. For each of these objectives (production and equity), a different instrument (the tax system vs. public expenditures) would be available.

6. Stabilization, Structural Adjustment, and Economic Growth

None of the three papers attempts to differentiate clearly among three basic concepts: stabilization, structural adjustment and economic growth. If is important to do this due to the dissimilar nature and origins of the problems, and the diverse

---

[1] N. Kaldor (1955). *An Expenditure Tax*. Allen and Unwin.
[2] Institute for Fiscal Studies (1978).
[3] J.A. Kay (1990), especially Table 2, 22.

Table 3
Stability, Structural Adjustment and Economic Growth

	Stabilization Program	Structural Adjustment Program	Economic Growth Program
Problem	Instability	Inefficient economic system	Unsatisfactory economic growth rate
Origin	Excess effective demand (inappropriate monetary, fiscal and exchange-rate policies).	Low productivity of factors of production due to distortions of GPP model	Low production levels due to bottlenecks resulting from poor quality of factors of production
Policy measures	Restrict effective demand.	Introduce openness, liberalization, deregulation, state reform, appropriate microeconomic setting.	Incorporate science and technology, invest in human resources.
Difficulties	Has a recessive effect on profits, wages and public outlays.	Change allocation of factors of production and production structure. Entrepreneurs and workers need to relocate and retrain.	Changes technology and structure of demand. Entrepreneurs and workers need to relocate and retrain.
Positive effects	Restores macroeconomic balances.	Improves productivity of factors of production.	Improves quality of factors of production.

Source: own compilation.

measures needed to address them. The difficulties each one poses and, consequently, the results policy will achieve also vary considerably, which is why they need to be examined separately. Table 3 summarizes the main points.

First, stability programs are designed essentially to restore macroeconomic balances; the purpose of structural adjustment is to shift the economy as close as possible to the production possibility curve; and the economic growth program seeks to displace this curve to the right. The stability program addresses issues of effective demand, while the structural adjustment program and the economic growth model are more closely associated with changes in overall supply.

Next to the design of the programs, their economic impact differs as well. Programs to restore stability generally spark recession, albeit temporarily. Structural adjustment and economic growth programs tend to alter relative prices, and consequently change the structure of production. As a result, both entrepreneurs and workers are often displaced and obliged to change jobs and geographic location.

Although the main policy approaches can be clearly distinguished conceptually, in reality, they do not separate easily. The problems addressed and the impacts of the different programs often overlap. Hardships caused by stabilization policies are frequently attributed to structural adjustment programs, while adjustment measures have an impact on stabilization. Due to these overlaps, at least in the case of Latin America, it is best to address the problems simultaneously. Accordingly, there can be no fixed policy sequence. When extreme instability reigns, priority should be given to measures that will restore macroeconomic balances. However, this effort cannot prosper unless production is growing at the same time. Clearly, the willingness of entrepreneurs, workers and politicians to make sacrifices and lend political support will vanish if, after a certain lapse, no light has appeared at the end of the tunnel, and production has yet to rebound. Thus, all three types of programs need to be launched in a broad front, with their objectives and policies reinforcing one another in a virtuous circle.

VI. A Few Final Thoughts

A few closing ideas should be added.

1. Economists readily offer agendas or action programs. Perhaps the most well known is the Meade program, *The Intelligent Radical's Guide to Economic Policy: The Mixed Economy* (1975).[1] However, seeking convergence and mustering consensus are much more time-consuming and tedious tasks, as they involve reconciling many viewpoints. In the case of economic policy in Latin America, major progress has been made in the area of objectives, instruments, high-priority issues, and underlying assumptions.

2. Another challenging task still lies ahead: putting desirable economic policy into practice. The difficulties and pitfalls are daunting, the problems and obstacles, numerous. There are at least two reasons for this: i) differences in preliminary conditions from one country to another (demographic characteristics, natural resources, geographic location, level of development); and ii) differences in each country's emphasis on economic policy objectives. As a result, every case needs to be considered separately. It can never be assumed that the experience of one country can be repeated in the others, or that a common economic policy can be developed for all. Instead, specific details of condition, nuance, emphasis – all this helps determine desirable economic policy.

3. Some issues need to be examined in more depth. Two in particular are worth mentioning. First, how can Latin American countries overcome the GPP model and force economic agents to become more competitive and efficient? Second, how can state reform come about? Finding satisfactory solutions to these two problems is an absolute precondition for speeding the region's economic development.

4. The consensus achieved so far is strikingly and disconcertingly silent about economic development theories that sparked wide discussion in Latin America during the 1950s and 1960s. Specifically, no mention is being made of such ideas as balanced growth, the big push, stages of development, economic take-off, circular causation, the demonstration effect, dependency, unequal terms of trade, disguised unemployment, the center-periphery, the domination effect, the polarization-propagation effect, or forward and backward linkages. All this is absent from the current debate. What has become of the wealth of ideas that grew up around these issues? Will they remain as mere relics on library shelves, of interest

---

[1] See Littlechild (1978) for a criticism of Meade's position.

only to students of the history of economic thought? Is there no need for a conscious effort to incorporate at least part of this reservoir of knowledge into the discussion for building consensus on Latin American economic policy?

5. Economic development theory seems to grow more complex with each passing day. This is due, above all, to the inescapable tendency to see economic development as part of the general process of social change, in which confrontation and conflict play a preeminent role. Because we live in such a complex world, we constantly try to simplify. A particularly telling example is the plethora of recent contributions to economic growth theory [1]. However, we must always be alert to the danger of over-simplification, lest our models become divorced from reality. No matter how much progress is made toward convergence and consensus, every common agenda will inevitably have gaps, inconsistencies, internal contradictions, and loose ends, leaving room for more than a few misunderstandings. At the same time, however, new avenues and openings constantly take shape, along with new possibilities and prospects. We must never forget, moreover, that any consensus or common agenda must be renewed constantly, as circumstances, knowledge, values and institutions change and shift. This is why whatever is unexpected, whatever is irrational, whatever is unpredictable will always occupy an important place in the unfolding of events. Ultimately, we find that Lewis was right when he stated that a country gets ahead only when it has the good fortune to be under the right leadership at the right time (1955, 418). Although his prescient statement says very little, it communicates much.

---

[1] See, for example, Scott (1991 and 1992) and Sala-i-Martin (1990).

Bibliography

Barro, Robert, and Xavier Sala-i-Martin. 1992. "Convergence." *Journal of Political Economy* 100 (2): 223-251.

Bator, Francis. 1958. "The anatomy of market failure." *Quarterly Journal of Economics* 72:351-379.

Bitar, Sergio. 1988. "Neoliberalismo versus Neoestructuralismo en América Latina." *Revista de la CEPAL* 34 (April): 45-63.

Cairnes, J.E. 1874. *Leading principles of political economy.*

Economic and Social Commission for Latin America and the Caribbean (ECLAC). 1985. *Bases y opciones estratégicas para reorientar el desarrollo.* Chap. 3 in *Crisis y desarrollo en América Latina y el Caribe.* LC/L.333 (sem.22/6), rev.1. (Also published in *El trimestre económico.* 1986. (Mar.): 75-209).

―――――. 1990. *Transformación productiva con equidad: la tarea prioritaria de América Latina y el Caribe en los años noventa.* LC/C.1601 (SES. 23/4).

―――――.1992. *Equidad y transformación productiva: Un enfoque integrado.* LC/G.1701 (SES.23/3).

Fajnzylber, Fernando. 1990. "Industrialization in Latin America: from the "black box" to the "empty box."" *Cuadernos de la CEPAL* 60.

Fischer, Stanley. 1991. "Growth, macroeconomics and development." *NBER Working Paper* no.3702.

Grindle, Merilee. 1991. "The new political economy: positive economics and negative politics." In Gerald M. Meier, ed. *Politics and policy making in developing countries: perspectives on the new political economy,* 41-67. International Center for Economic Growth.

Hayek, Friedrich. 1945. "The use of knowledge in society." *American Economic Review* (Sept): 519-530.

Hirschman, Albert O. 1980. "Auge y ocaso de la teoría económica del desarrollo." *El trimestre económico* (Oct.-Dec.):1055-1077.

Hume, David. 1752. "Of commerce." In David Hume *Writings on economics,* ed. E. Rotwine, 3-18. 1955. Nelson.

Iglesias, Enrique. 1992. *Reflexiones sobre el desarrollo económico: hacia un nuevo consenso latinoamericano.* Inter-American Development Bank.

Institute for Fiscal Studies. 1978. *The structure and reform of direct taxation.* Report of a committee chaired by Prof. J.E.Meade. Allen and Unwin.

Inter-American Development Bank. 1993. *Reforma social y pobreza: hacia una agenda integrada de desarrollo.* Mimeo. Preliminary version.

Kaldor, Nicholas. 1955. *An expenditure tax.* Allen and Unwin.

Kay, J.A. 1990. "Tax policy: A survey." *The Economic Journal* (March):18-75.

Kuznets, Simon. 1980. "Driving forces of economic growth: What can we learn from history?" *Weltwirtschaftliches Archiv:*409-429.

Lal, Depak. 1985. *The poverty of development economics.* Harvard Univ. Press.

Lewis, W. Arthur. 1955. *The theory of economic growth.* Allen and Unwin.

———. 1954. "Economic development with unlimited supplies of labour." *The Manchester School of Economic and Social Studies* (May):139-191.

Littlechild, S.C. 1978. *The fallacy of the mixed economy: An "Austrian" critique of economic thinking and policy.* The Institute of Economic Affairs. Hobart Paper. No.80.

Lucas, Robert E., Jr. 1988. "On the mechanics of economic development." *Journal of monetary economics* (22):3-42.

Marshall, Alfred. 1887. "A fair rate of wages." In A. Pigou, ed. *Memorials of Alfred Marshall* 212-226. 1925. Macmillan.

McCulloch, J.R. 1843. *Principles of political economy.* New edition.

Meade, James E. 1948. *Planning and the price mechanism.* Allen and Unwin.

———. 1975. *The intelligent radical's guide to economic policy: The mixed economy.* Allen and Unwin.

Nelson, Joan, ed. 1990. "Economic crisis and policy: The politics of adjustment in the Third World." Princeton University Press.

Nelson, Richard, and Edmund S. Phelps. 1966. "Investment in humans, technological diffusion and economic growth." *American Economic Review* 2 (May):69-75.

Pourgerami, A. 1992. "Authoritarian versus nonauthoritarian approaches to economic development: Update and additional evidence." *Public Choice* (Oct.): 365-377.

Robbins, Lionel. 1953. *The theory of economic policy in English classical political economy.* Macmillan.

———. 1968. *The theory of economic development in the history of economic thought.* Macmillan.

Roxborough, Ian. 1992. "Neo-liberalism in Latin America: limits and alternatives." *Third World Quarterly* 3:421-440.

Sagasti, Francisco. 1991. *Remarks on development thinking in Latin America.* Mimeo.

Sala-i-Martin, Xavier. 1990. "Lecture notes on economic growth." *NBER working paper.* No.3563.

Scott, Maurice FG. 1991. "A new view of economic growth: Four lectures." *World Bank discussion paper.* No.131.

———. 1992. "Policy implications of "A new view of economic growth."" *Economic Journal* (May):622-632.

Smith, Adam. 1776. *An inquiry into the nature and causes of the wealth of nations,* ed. Cannan.

Sunkel, Osvaldo, and Gustavo Zuleta. 1990. "Neoestructuralismo versus neoliberalismo en los años noventa." *Revista de la CEPAL* 42 (Dec.):35-53.

Toye, John. 1991. "Is there a new political economy of development?" In Christopher Colclough and James Manor, eds. *States or Markets? Neo-liberalism and the development policy debate,* 321-338. *IDS development studies series.* Clarendon Press.

Williamson, John, ed. 1990a. *Latin American adjustment: how much has happened?* Institute for International Economics.

———. 1990b. "The progress of policy reform in Latin America." *Policy Analysis in International Economics Series.* No.28. Institute for International Economics.

———. 1991. *Development strategy for Latin America in the 1990s.* Paper presented at a conference: Latin American Thought: Past, Present and Future, 14-15 Nov. Organized by the IDB in honor of Raul Prebisch, Washington DC.

———. 1992. *Democratization and the "Washington consensus."* Paper presented at a conference: Economic Liberalization and Democratic Consolidation, 3-4 Apr., SSRC, University of Bologna.

World Bank. 1992. *World Development Report 1991.*

Stabilization and Poverty in Latin America during the 1980s

Moritz Kraemer [1]

1. Introduction

Today, more than ever before, Latin American societies are predominantly urban ones. Outside Central America only Paraguay had a rural population that exceeded urban dwellers slightly in 1990. Venezuela and the Southern Cone States display urbanization rates of around 85%, followed by the population-richest countries in the region, i.e. Brazil and Mexico, where three out of four citizens live in cities. [2] These mere facts assign greater analytical emphasis on urban regions than in the past. The focus on cities should thus be equally essential in research on the poverty situation in the hemisphere. Regionally disaggregated poverty data underlines the growing significance of urban poverty in the 1990s in absolute as well as in relative terms. [3] Whereas the majority of the Latin American poor in 1980 were rural based (73 Mio. vs. 63 Mio. in urban agglomerations), this relation had been reversed by 1990. By then the absolute number of the rural poor has grown to 80.4 Mio. But the expansion of numbers of poor city-dwellers surpassed that growth rate easily and the number of people in cities living below the poverty line amounted to 115.5 Mio. The relative incidence has jumped in the same time span from 30% to 39% of the urban population. While in 1980 54% of all Latin American poor have lived in the countryside this number declined to 42% by 1990. Countrywise data is presented in Appendix Table 1 of Schinke's contribution to this volume. It shows that contrary to developments in other parts of the world urban poverty increased in virtually all Latin American countries between 1975 and the adjustment period in the 1980s. The exceptions are Panama, Colombia and Ecuador, where urban poverty rates remained at their far-above regional average rates between 36% and 40%.

---

[1] Economics Department, University of Göttingen, Platz der Göttinger Sieben 3, D-37073 Göttingen.
[2] World Bank (1992b, Tab. 31).
[3] CEPAL (1992) and Latin American Special Reports (1992).

The aim of this essay is attempting to unfold the reasons for these profound structural changes in the regional poverty profile. Internal migration movements may have played an important role, but can only partially explain the observed developments. The data presented in the preceeding paragraph suggests a yearly growth rate of 6.25% in the number of the urban poor, while the urban population encompassing the poor as well the non-poor has been growing at a much lower pace at around 3%, whereas overall population growth did barely reach 2%.

Section 2 will sketch within the framework of simple microeconomic reasoning the effects of the pursued stabilization policies on primary incomes of different poor or potentially poor subgroups of society. Empirical labor market evidence that supports the elaborated theses terminates the section. Sections 3 and 4 by contrast, will present data that is relevant to improve the understanding of the effects on poverty brought about by predominant adjustment patterns during the 1980s. Conclusions and a very brief discussion of the popular demand for social conditionality on behalf of the international financial institutions will close this essay.

2. Stabilization and Primary Income

2.1. Theoretical consequences of stabilization instruments on the labor market

2.1.1. The basic model with perfect labor markets

Inquiries concerning the effects of stabilization on urban poverty cannot be accomplished without centering on an economic analysis of the determinants of the primary income's evolution during the reform period. In the following model we assume - presumably not unrealistically - that capital income of the population below or close to the poverty line are equally negligible as are their rents from land ownership.[1] In this setting primary income is equivalent to the monetary rewards for offering labor on the factor markets, which is far more evenly distributed in society than are other factors of production. Therefore it appears unavoidable to concentrate the analysis on the effects on the domestic labor market, once a typical stabilization package has

---

[1] Fox/Morley (1991, 1-2).

been implemented. The latter is hereby defined as comprising expenditure reduction as well as expenditure switching elements, in other words fiscal austerity and a real devaluation of the domestic currency.

For analytical purposes the economy is divided into two separate subsectors, say N and T. In sector N only nontradables are produced, whereas the output in sector T is tradable.[1] Both sectors are characterized by the existence of decreasing marginal returns of all factors used in the production process. Since we are concerned only with a rather short run adjustment period we exclude the potential for technical progress. The partial production function of labor is therefore to remain unaltered during the adjustment period. Each sector's demand for labor (m_T; m_N) depends primarily on marginal value of labor in the same sector. The wage rate w is expressed in units of tradables and due to the assumption of perfect intersectoral mobility of factors Jeavons' law of one price applies in the national labor market. In other words, there is one uniform wage rate in all sectors of the economy.

As long as this wage rate w does not exceed m_T (m_N) the tradables- (nontradables-) sector increases employment. Workers are laid off whenever m_i in the sector i falls below the market wage. The easiest case is depicted in figure 1. $O_T O_N$ is the amount of labor available in the national economy. For now we presume that in the time horizon studied it is fixed and insensitive to changes in other variables, notably the wage rate. m_N and m_T are then the labor demand curves for the N- and T-sectors respectively. The equilibrium wage rate will initially be w_0 with $O_T C$ workers employed in the tradables-, and $O_N C$ in the nontradables sector.

Stabilization attempts regularly include real devaluations in order to reestablish the external equilibrium. This policy will lower the price P_N of nontradables relative to that of tradables (P_T). The correction of a distorted, usually overvalued, real exchange rate RER ($=P_N/P_T$) has complex effects on the domestic labor market. According to the Stolper-Samuelson-theorem the renumeration of the factor that is used relatively more intensively in the production of the good whose relative price increases due to the devaluation will rise. In the case of Latin America we allow for the commonly made assumption that the production of nontradables is relatively more labor intensive than

---

[1] Woodward (1992, 102-105) discusses critically the bipolarity of the tradable/non-tradable dichotonomy and concludes that "Tradability is largely a matter of degree, rather than a clear division of all goods into one group or the other." (103).

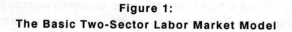

Figure 1:
The Basic Two-Sector Labor Market Model

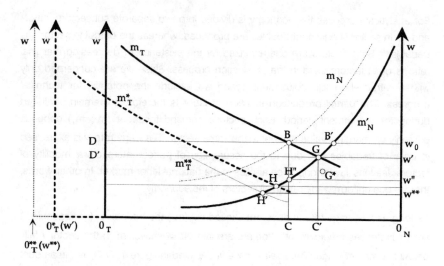

that of tradables.[1] The outstanding importance of the informal sector in the production of services seems to add further support to this assumption.[2] The marginal product that has been expressed in units of tradables will decline for nontradables due to an adverse change of the real exchange rate (or the internal terms of trade P_N/P_T) that accompanies the devaluation. Thus the m_N-curve shifts downward to m'_N and according to the sketched neoclassical labor demand function employers in the nontradables sector will hire less workers at any given price than before. Given the fixed supply of labor of $0_T 0_N$ the uniform real wage rate measured in tradables will

---

[1] In accordance to that Helleiner (1987, 1503) claims that "[t]he presumption must be that most non-tradables are highly labor intensive, e.g. construction, government and other services. Indeed, *'switching from tradables to nontradables'* may sometimes be seen as little more than a euphemism for reducing wages and employment in government and the organized service sector."

[2] Demery/Addison (1988, 12).

decline to w_1 and higher employment ($0_T C'$) in the tradables sector and reduced work opportunities ($C'Q_N$) in nontradables occur.

2.1.2. Variable supply of labor and structural rigidities

The basic model is easily criticised for its rigorous and admittedly rather heroic assumptions. These will now be lifted successively to discuss more realistic labor market conditions. One particularly rigid assumption has been the blunt statement that even in the light of reduced national wages from $0_T Dw_0 Q_N$ to $0_T D'w'Q_N$ the number of workers competing for jobs would remain unaltered. Various authors observed that this simplificating assumption hardly ever held empirically.[1] In particular it has been noted that the labor market participation rates of youths and especially women rose in the 1980s. Secondary school enrolment data in Costa Rica shows a drop which has been attributed to the growing need to contribute to eroding family incomes.[2] Quantitatively even more important has been the increased participation of women in the face of falling wage rates of their husbands. Whereas 18.83% of women worked in the beginning of the 1980s their participation has climbed to 22.03% by the end of the decade, while the renumeration of their new employment opportunities has been well below average.[3]

A lowered real wage rate of w' will thus broaden the width of the horizontal axis relative to a situation where w_0 prevailed. If the labor supply were, for example, boosted to $0_T *Q_N$ the demand curve for labor in the tradables sector m_T will shift leftward in line with the "left" vertical axis to $m_T *$.[4] The consequences of this would be a new equilibrium in H and an additional decline of real wages. According to the observed household behavior this may increase the supply of labor anew which leads to further wage drops and so on. However, sooner or later this process must come to a halt. Otherwise a near total participation rate with a wage rate close to zero would result, which is obviously a nonsensical outcome. Instead, a falling marginal propensity to look for jobs has to be taken into account. The lower the wage rate gets, the less new entrants

---

[1] Psacharopoulos/Winter (1992, 15); World Bank (1990b, 126) and Albanez et al. (1989, 24).

[2] Gindling/Berry (1992, 1610).

[3] Krawczyk (1993, 11).

[4] Alternatively we could draw a positively (negatively) tilted left (right) vertical axis to take the wage-dependent labor supply into account.

will appear in the labor market. This breaks the downward spiral and the dynamic self-feeding process stops at some point, let's say, arbitrarily, H'. The exact location of this point can not readily be identified without recurring to empirical case by case studies of household behavior that are not yet at hand. However, what can be said with certainty is that the new equilibrium wage rate, expressed as before in units of tradables, will fall even further than in the original scenario, in figure 1 down to w^{**}.

A further complication that has not been considered in the basic model is the - at least in the short run - undeniable prevailing of structural rigidities that prevent workers to change into a job in another sector easily. Several reasons are responsible for that. Some importance may be assigned to the time consuming retraining of workers laid off in the N-sector necessary in order to obtain qualifications specific to sector T. Besides it may take some time until reluctant and rightly cautious investors come up with the necessary investment in T in order to absorb the workers set free in N. This problem is aggravated if we consider that on a national intersectoral level capital is generally much less mobile than labor. Even if capitalists were willing to reinvest in the production of tradables, they cannot transfer their capital bound in N at a faster pace than the rate of depreciation. In the short run workers are therefore not able to move from the N into the T sector. The employment structure will therefore stay unaltered with $0_T C$ of the workers involved in the tradables production and $0_N C$ in that of non-tradables. Whereas the T-workers will, at least in the very short run, do not see their incomes fall, their colleagues in the N-sectors have to absorb a wage-drop from w_0 to w''. Since they are "trapped" in the N-sector no immediate equalization may take place. Instead there is a sectorspecific undershooting (to a point vertically below B) since the real wages fall even beyond the equilibrium G, that will eventually occur after all rigidities impeding instantaneous labor reallocation have been overcome.

If this model represents reality a devaluation will increase poverty, measured as the head count ratio, promptly if low income households concentrate their economic activity in the nontradables sector. This may well have happened in Chile, where the increased poverty can be identified as having arisen primarily in the informal sector, which is concentrated around all sorts of personal services. [1] The poverty index will in this case decline only very slowly along the process of the intersectoral migration of workers from the N to the T sectors, i.e. during the adjustment from point H" to point G, when nontradables wages recover. Were most of the poor just above the

---
[1] Demery/Addison (1987, 1494).

poverty line working in the T-sector, we would observe a different pattern of a slow but steady increase of the poverty head count ratio, since tradables-wages fall steadily from w_0 to w'.

2.1.3. Fixed real wages

In the aftermath of Keynes' *General Theory* debates on the presumed downward rigidity of real wages kept various generations of economists busy. In an economic environment where widespread indexation of nominal wages prevails, the flexibility of real wages is far from asserted. Where the wages are either explicitly or implicitly linked to price inflation of tradables, real wages would stay unaltered at w_0. Following a devaluation this would imply rapidly rising unemployment rates up to $BB'/0_T0_N$. In the absence of viable social security nets getting unemployed equals marginalization and falling below the poverty line. The price adjustment that has been prevented by prevailing indexation contracts is substituted by quantity adjustments in the form of higher unemployment. Usually wages are indexed not to a commodity-basket solely consistent of tradables, however, but the consumer price index (CPI), that contains a certain proportion of nontradables, too. The higher the percentage of tradables in the CPI, the higher the resulting unemployment in the economy will be.

2.1.4. Sectoral minimum wage legislation

Labor markets in developing countries are far from free and flexible and interventions as well as structural causes are responsible for their segmentation. One typically observed intervention of that kind is a minimum wage legislation that intents to prevent real wages from falling under a fixed floorlevel w^* set by public administrators. This may or may not be attributable to the heroic attempt of policymakers to reduce the impact of economic recessions on vulnerable sections of the workforce. As a matter of fact, however, it is quite common, that not all sections of the workforce benefit to the same extent. Typically the unionized and politically influential employees in the formal industrial sector gain substantially more than poorer workers in more informal workingplaces.[1]

---

[1] For a more detailed analysis of sectoral segmentation compare Lopez/Riveros (1989, chap.2). Their result is consistent with the implications of the present model, i.e. an increasing differential between wages in the formal and the informal sector.

In the following analysis the tradables sector is to be split up into two mutually exclusive subsectors X, where exportables are produced and M, the importables sector. In the importsubstituting industry M there is a legal minimum wage effective which is set at w_M^+. This may be due to the fact that until the recent backswing towards open market politics most Latin American countries pursued economic strategies that tended to favor manufacturing industries. The high and tariff-protected price level for these import-substituting goods allowed companies to pay the minimum wage imposed on them by the government. The labor market in the X- and N-sectors in contrast is unregulated and the interplay of market forces determines the equilibrium wage rate.

This scenario is depicted in figure 2, where the former tradables sector demand curve for labor m_T has been disaggregated into m_X and m_M as the labor demand curves of the exportables- and the importables sector respectively. The demand for labor in the M-sector will never exceed $0_T L_M$, since wages are prevented by law to drop below the minimum wage w_M^+. Thus the labor demand curve in sector M stops in point K and continues thereafter vertically down to L_M.

The demand curve for *both* tradables sectors (m_{X+M}) is for this very reason kinked in point B which corresponds with the minimum wage rate. From B onwards the slope of the tradables labor demand curve coincides with the slope of m_X (which itself is not shown in figure 2), since m_M runs vertically at lower wage rates than w_M^+ and thus no effective labor demand can be articulated. For simplification we assume that the original equilibrium rate w_0 coincided with the minimum wage rate. The market then starts off in point B.

The real devaluation of the domestic currency once again shifts the labor demand curve of nontrables producers downward to m_N. But this time no new equilibrium in G can occur, since the distortion in the importables sector resulted in the kinked m_{X+M} curve. The new equilibrium might instead be expected to be realized in G' with a lower wage rate w_2 in the free labor market segments of sectors X and N. But this is not to happen. The reason for this superficially surprising statement is that the wage differential ($w_M^+ - w_2$) will be a powerful incentive for mobile labor to migrate from sectors N and X to M, where more attractive incomes can be earned. If we include m_{N+X} into the figure (i.e. the joint labor demand curve of the two unregulated sectors) it will intersect

Figure 2:
Labor Market Model with Minimum Wage Legislation

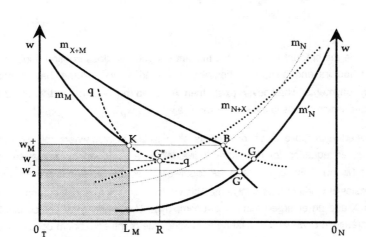

the labor demand curve of the regulated sector (m_M) in its vertical part at an unregulated wage rate of w_2. However, not $0_N L_M$ workers will choose to accept employment at this salary but - and this reasoning draws heavily from Harris' and Todaro's migration theory - may instead try to find a job in the better paid sector M.

A riskneutral worker will quit a position in the nonprotected sectors as long as, after taking into account the possibility of becoming unemployed, the expected wage in M exceeds the riskless wage w_2 he or she could earn in X or N. Since "migration" in this setting might include the sectoral swap of a job without the physical displacement of the workers it may be preferable to use the expression "transfer" instead. In the following, transfer costs will remain ignored. They may indeed be much lower than in the traditional migration theory, since the worker is not necessarily forced to move geographically into a different social setting. Given the labor demand curve m_M and the the minimum wage rate w_M^+, no more than L_M workers will ever get employment opportunities in M. If U persons are already looking unsuccessfully for a job in this sector, than the transfer of riskneutral workers will continue as long as

$$w_2 < \underbrace{\left(\frac{L_M}{L_M+U}\right) w_M^+}_{\kappa} ; + ; \underbrace{\left(\frac{U}{L_M+U}\right) R}_{\lambda} ,$$

where R is the amount of money the migrant will get if he does not find a job in the desired sectors and becomes unemployed instead. If we assume that no social security payments whatsoever exist, then R would equal zero and λ could be eliminated which results in the simpler formula $w_2 < \kappa(U, w_M^+)$.

The dotted hyperbolic curve qq depicts all possible points, where this condition becomes an equation for riskneutral individuals in a world without social security benefits ($w_2 = \kappa$).[1] For all points to the southwest of qq the "<"-sign is prevalent and the transfer of workers thus continues. This will lead directly to a loss in employment in N or X and an enlarged number of unemployed U competing for scarce M-jobs. This increase in U will lead to a falling right hand side of the equilibrium condition and therefore to a movement towards and finally back to qq. The new labor market equilibrium will set at point G" with $w_1 > w_2$ and voluntary search joblessness of $L_M R$.

Unemployment benefits, i.e. positive Rs, can easily be integrated and lead to a growing right hand side of the equation (λ). This leads to a flatter qq-curve still passing through K (where $U=0$) and an intersection with m_{N+X} to the northeast of G". The resulting pool of unemployed will thus exceed $L_M R$ that prevailed in the absence of unemployment benefits and the free wage rate rises relative to the base case scenario with $R=0$ in the N and X-sectors will lie between w_1 and the minimum wage in sector M.

If workers are risk-averse rather than risk-neutral they will stay with the old job in the X or N-sectors where the secure wage of w_2 can be earned even if $\lambda+\kappa$ were to exceed w_2 slightly. The equilibrium condition defining the qq-curve would have to be reformulated to

---

[1] The qq-curve can formally be derived by isolating U. If R is set equal to 0 we obtain $U = L_M (w_M^+ - w_2) / w_2$.

$$V(w_2) = \frac{L_M}{L_{M+U}} V\left(w_M^+\right) + \frac{U}{L_M+U} V(R)$$

with the second derivatives of the utility functions V(.) being negative, i.e the existence of diminishing marginal utility of income. For simplicity set $R=0$, because the effect of dole money has already been discussed in the preceding paragraph. The risk averse attitude will lead to a steeper qq-curve since an expected wage after transfering to the M-sector equal to the safe wage (w_2) in N and X would be regarded as inferior, due to the fact that the risk involved (i.e. becoming unemployed and earning less than the present w_2) is not being compensated for by some extra expected renumeration. Indifference is occurring only at a point where $w_2 = \kappa+\lambda+\mu$ ($> \kappa+\lambda$) with μ being the premium necessary to induce the risk-averse worker to take on the risk involved with the transfer. The new equilibrium will be located south-west of point G" of the benchmark case ($R=0$ and $\mu=0$). The resulting unemployment in the M-sector would fall short of $L_M R$, since (ceteris paribus) fewer workers would search for new jobs than in the risk-neutrality case. Since less workers leaving the free sectors N and X the pressure on wages increases and an unregulated wage of $w<w_1$ will occur.

On the other hand the "risk premium" μ for a risk loving individual would be negative and the qq-curve flatter which leads to unemployment higher than $L_M R$ and a less depressed free wage of $w>w_1$. Of course, the geometrical result of this case (equilibrium north-east of G") is comparable to the scenario with risk-averse workers in a world of social payments.

It can be concluded that the more riskloving workers are (the more negative μ), the higher the wage differential ($w_M^+ - w_2$) and the more generous unemployment benefits R are, the more severe the joblessness situation will become. It will then also be more probable, that urban poverty will augment rapidly. This is even more likely as the majority of the privileged employees in M will belong typically to the better-off middle classes. [1]

---

[1] This model specification seems to be applicable to the Argentinean labor market. Whereas employees in services (that is N), accounted for roughly a third of poor Argentineans, this proportion has grown to near 50% by 1989. Commerce and general services, generally regarded as sectors with comparably low entry-barriers, have suffered most (Morley 1992, Tab.1). ILO-data (1992, Tab. 10 B) for Argentina and Venezuela show, that the unemployment situation worsened above average for former employees in service sectors (sectors 5-9 by ILO classification).

2.1.5. Reductions in Public Employment Opportunities

In Latin America, as elsewhere, did not only external disequilibria occur that had to be addressed by expenditure-switching measures such as devaluations during the 1980s, but policy makers had to cope with inflationary tendencies as well that could be attributed to excessive domestic absorption. This called for expenditure reduction policies that consisted typically of the need to eliminate growing public sector borrowing requirements and monetary restraint.[1] Fiscal reforms aimed at reducing public deficits incurred in many cases dramatic austerity measures, a point to which we will be returning when discussing public social spending behavior. Along with spending cuts in almost every area of public activity went the attempt to reduce the State's payroll. This happened by laying off public employees directly or by privatizing state-owned enterprises, which typically leads to massive labor redundancies as well. While it must be admitted that civil servants do usually not belong to the poorest population, the State's rationalization effort usually hits the lower strata working in lower levels of the vocational hierarchy particularly hard, since they have usually been the first to be made redundant.[2] Some of the laid off can thus easily fall below the poverty line, since not having earned very much while still having the job, savings that could be run down after being fired will typically be very modest.

The widespread and severe collapse of public investment affected the poorest segments most adversely, too, since e.g. the construction of buildings or physical infrastructure generally represents a major source of demand for unskilled workers.[3] Keeping this in mind the expected effect on urban poverty will be more significant than the aggregate numbers of fired government workers would suggest. Since state institutions are typically concentrated in the cities and first of all the capital, most of the adverse changes had to be absorbed by the urban population. Thus we expect poverty in cities to have suffered particularly under the austerity measures that have been chosen. Scarce empirical data appears to back the impact on the cities. The percentage of urban workers employed in the public sector declined between 1980 and 1990 in most of the countries in the hemisphere. In Chile the number declined from 11.9 to 7%, in Colombia from 13.8 to 10.6% and in Venezuela from 35.6% down

---

[1] The monetary aspect of stabilization will not be considered in this model, because its distributional impact is highly country-specific and not transmitted primarily via labor markets.
[2] Demery/Addison (1988, 30).
[3] Woodward (1992, 29)

to 22.6%.[1] Notable exceptions however were Argentina and Mexico. But with respect to Argentina the long overdue fiscal adjustments pursued after 1990 by the Menem administration certainly reversed the trend of increasing state employment.

These dramatic changes in the role of the public sector reduces not only the demand for labor in sector N (e.g. administrative services) but also in T (reduced employment in state-owned firms). The State's employment could be regarded as having been politically induced rather than oriented along lines of the logic of setting marginal productivity equal to marginal returns, which is particularly difficult for the public sector anyway, because it provides many public goods, for which "prices" are not easily determined. If we were to disaggregate the sectoral labor demand curves m_i (i=T,N,X,M), the public demand curves would be far steeper than the private sector's, if not vertical. In contrast to the original setting without expenditure reduction measures both sectors' labor demand curves will now be stripped of a substantial part of the wage-inelastic public component. This shifts the m_i-curves towards the respective vertical axes and a point G* to the south of G in figure 1 is realized. In other words, wages will be compressed even further and fall to a level below w', which was the result obtained in the original scenario (without sectoral minimum wage legislation).

2.1.6. Theoretical Conclusions

A model has been presented under certain assumptions that are likely to reflect Latin American realities in the 1980s. In section 2.1 it was suggested that nontradables are more labor intensive since they are often produced in the capital starving informal sector. In accordance with the Stolper-Samuelson proposition we derived a reduced real wage rate following a devaluation and thus a change in relative factor prices takes place. Since labor is the sole productive asset that the urban poor tend to possess, wages are their only income source and the poverty situation worsens. When we include the possibility of imperfect labor markets, different categories of labor have to be distinguished. Whereas some groups suffer from undershooting of their wages or unemployment other labor market segments are isolated from the adverse changes. The more unequal the adjustment burden is distributed on the labor market, the wider the poverty gap will become.

---

[1] Latin American Special Reports (1992, 6).

Of course, in alternative settings the model can derive quite different results. If we were to suppose that tradables rather than nontradables were more labor intensive, then the ratio of factor prices will change in favor of labor and he nationally aggregated wage bill will actually grow. In itself, this would almost certainly help to reduce poverty, but this positive effect might nonetheless be counterbalanced by austere fiscal measures taking place simultaneously, which shifts both the m_T and m_{NT} labor demand curves downward. The exogenous assumption about the relative labor-intensities is therefore crucial for the effects on poverty in general and urban poverty in particular.

Furthermore, reduced *individual* wages can be compensated for on the *household* level by increased labor market participation of women and other family members that had formerly not worked in the market. If women are forced to look for a job, the obvious danger occurs of minors, especially girls, being withdrawn from school in order to compensate for their mothers' reduced non-market production in the household. This reaction tends to perpetuate poverty in the families affected over generations, since the human capital stock of the young cannot be built up sufficiently. Even if household incomes were to stay constant, the welfare level would still fall, since less time can be allocated to nonmarket activities and free time, which in turn will reduce household utility. Dropping wage levels will therefore harm poor households under all conceivable circumstances.

In order to estimate the welfare changes of a household the consumed basket of commodities is of primary importance. Whenever the marginal propensity to consume nontradables equals 1, a reduction in wages (measured in tradables) will not affect the household's consumption possibilities adversely. The higher the proportion of tradables in the consumed set of goods (e.g. internationally traded food items) the higher the drop in welfare and the deepening of the poverty gap.

The model has therefore to be used cautiously. Without reliable quantitative information on factor intensities of various product groups, the factor endowment and consumption patterns of households at different income levels and institutional peculiarities of labor markets, no certain results can be obtained. Strictly speaking even the income- and price-elasticities of potentially poor households would have to be known in order to assess distributional and poverty impacts, since the change in relative prices will result in complex substitution processes. While this empirical nirvana is not likely to be arriving anytime soon, we have to rely very much on common sense- and plausibility assumptions. The results of this procedure are by no means automatically worthless if the underlying assumptions are made explicit to the reader.

2.2. Empirical Labor Market Evidence

Two indicators are of particular interest in investigating changed factor incomes of the poor. Thus the rate of unemployment reveals the magnitude of the proportion of workers without access to any kind of paid activity, whereas the wage level can be used as an indicator for the economic situation of the population that succeeded in getting a job. However, unemployment data ought to be treated with particular caution. First, especially in the poorer countries with nonexistent or only marginal unemployment benefits open unemployment is not a very common feature, since the majority of workers in many countries are not entitled to receive official unemployment benefits. Rather more frequently, adversely hit workers switch over to "enterpreneurship" in the informal sector, where they face an uphill struggle of economic survival. The informal sector in Latin America did indeed swell significantly from 25.6% in 1980 to 30.8% in 1990. Especially in countries with low increases in open unemployment rates the labor market crisis can be identified by the "dynamics" of informal activities, which for a good proportion account for de-facto unemployment. Thus official unemployment figures do not take into account the qualitative change of a worker formerly employed in the formal sector now being forced to sell chewing gum and cigarettes in the streets or wipe windscreens at traffic lights. Mexico may be a good illustration. In the decade under consideration the proportion of the total labor force that is self employed in the informal sector grew by over two thirds from 18 to 30.4%. Less dramatic but still decisive were developments in Argentina and Brazil.[1] The drop-out of workers out of the formal labor market reduces their income flows quite considerably and is therefore, other things being equal, poverty increasing.[2]

---

[1] Latin American Special Reports (1992, 6).

[2] Fox/Morley (1991, 13) present data indicating that the formal/informal income differential oscillated between 3.25 and 2.5 in the 1980s.

Secondly, definitions of unemployment are seldom chosen to reflect the core of what joblessness really means. A worker in Mexico, for example is considered unemployed, whenever he is working less than one hour weekly and has taken "acciones concretas" - whatever that means - to change his or her employment situation.[1] Colombia is another example where working for more than 60 minutes a week is sufficient to classify a worker as "employed".[2] In the theoretical extreme when all full time jobs were to be reduced to only 10 minutes daily in a six day working week, official unemployment figures would not change at all. The underlying problems of work dissatisfaction and declining household incomes is therefore hardly ever captured by unemployment figures.

Thirdly, unemployment figures do not tell the researcher a great deal of which subgroups of the society were hardest hit by shrinking labor demand. While due to lacking data no comparative analysis is feasible, household surveys in Chile "show that it was essentially the heads of households of the lowest income quintile that bore the brunt of unemployment: in that group 25% were unemployed, compared to 9% in

Table 1
Unemployment Rates in Latin America (1981-1989)

	1981	1983	1985	1987	1989
Argentina	4.50	4.20	5.30	5.30	7.30
Brazil	4.30	4.90	3.40 (1988)	3.70	3.90
Bolivia	9.70	14.20	18.00	20.50	20.00
Chile	11.30	14.60	12.10	7.90	5.30
Costa Rica	8.30	8.10	6.10	5.60	3.90
Colombia	8.10	11.80	14.10	..	..
Mexico	4.20	6.80	4.40	3.90	3.00
Peru	10.40	13.90	17.60	..	..
Venezuela	6.40	10.10	13.10	9.20	9.20

Sources: ILO (1987 and 1992), van der Hoeven (1987) for Colombia and Peru, and Gindling/Berry (1992) for Costa Rica.

.. Data not available

---

[1] Jarque (1993).
[2] Montenegro (1993).

the lower-middle-income quintile and 2% in the highest-income quintile. Also, unemployment hurt the lower income groups the most because they had fewer income earners per family."[1]

Despite the severe setbacks of unemployment figures a trend of increased employment problems can be observed in various countries of the region. According to table 1 the situation improved slightly in the second half of the decade, most notably in Chile and Costa Rica.

Figure 3 illustrates that not all workers made identical experiences with respect to the second labor market indicator relevant for assessing urban poverty, i.e. the development of real wages. In the majority of cases a decisive erosion of wages was the predominant pattern, however. The impression of figure 3 may actually underestimate the worsening primary income situation of poor and nearly poor households. Real wages in sectors where low qualified poor workers are typically employed dropped even further as wages in manufacturing. According to data presented in Albanez et al. real wages in construction and the informal sector in Latin America fell 2.5 and 3.5 times faster respectively.[2] The apparently positive development of wages on the Costa Rican labor market (Table A1) is at least partly due to the fact that the country has been sliding into economic crisis some years earlier than the rest of Latin America. The increase in wages therefore partly reflects compensation for prior losses.[3]

Advocates of wage restraint as a mean to stabilize the economy claimed that lower wages "could even have favorable implications for some poverty groups (such as unemployed workers and workers in the informal sector) by increasing employment in the formal sector.[4] Unemployment rates and real wages do not appear to be connected causally. It may be claimed that the depression of real wages contribute to avoid large losses in employment. The examples of Venezuela and Peru, however, seem to suggest that reduced real wages do not guarantee a stable employment situation automatically.

It has frequently been argued, that the urban poor have found their consumption possibilities cut additionally, because a large part of the commodities consumed

---

[1] Bourgignon et al. (1991, 27).
[2] Albanez et al. (1989, 19). Compare also Liuksilia (1992, 41).
[3] Real wages in Costa Rica fell by 27% between 1980 and 1982 (Morley 1992, 18).
[4] Heller et al. (1988, 9).

Figure 3: <u>Index of Real Wages in Latin America 1980-90 (1981=1)</u>

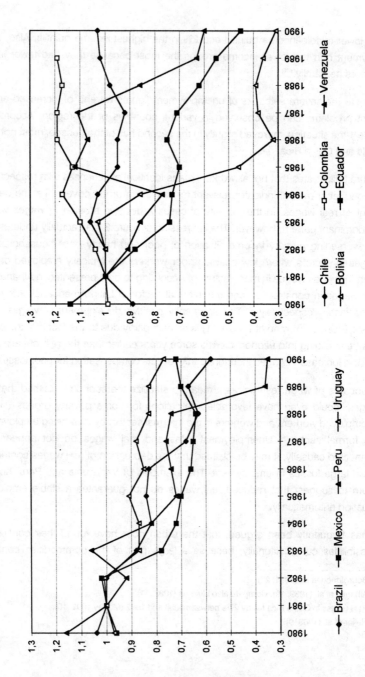

Sources: Albanez et al. (1989), Banco de Mexico (1992), ILO (1987, 1992), ECLAC (1992)

consists of basic foodstuffs, whose prices are supposed to increase even further than the CPI, that is commonly used for discounting nominal wages in order to examine real wages.[1] Due to their differing consumption pattern the poor would therefore be hit even more than is suggested by the wage data in figure 3. This hypothesis has been defended by claiming the fact that due to the large tradability of staples expenditure switching policies tend to raise their prices as do expenditure reduction policies that lead to price hikes in foodstuff via cut subsidies.[2] Theoretically the argument seems impeccable. Table A2 however shows, that the food price index (FPI) augmented in no more than 3 out of 8 Latin American countries systematically faster than the CPI. Empirically the argument thus does not hold.

But even leaving this additional complication aside the presented data made it quite clear that the primary incomes of poor household have suffered considerably by the macroeconomic adjustment processes most countries had to adopt during the 1980s. The following section tries to answer the question, whether the poor could compensate partly by increasing their entitlements to transfers that may offset the adverse changes. It thus investigates the development of the poors' secondary income positions after implicit and explicit redistributive measures of the state sector.[3]

3. Social Spending and Stabilization

3.1. The Role of the State in Fighting Poverty

A potent government has several measures at hand to influence the income distribution patterns in a society. On one hand direct tax and spend redistribution appears a feasible path, while subtler instruments include subsudised investments in human capital and provision of public goods with the aim of improving the factor productivity of vulnerable social groups. In an economic environment where fiscal consolidation programs directly led to harshly curtailed public spending, fiscal support for the poor

---

[1] Woodward (1992, 33), Helleiner (1987, 1503), Albanez et al. (1989, 18 and 23) and Cornia (1987, 27).

[2] Heller et al. (1988, footnote 29), in contrast, argue that "in countries with severe external imbalances, the poor usually do not have access to all tradable goods at official prices. Consequently, poverty groups are forced to purchase some of these goods in parallel markets at prices that exceed official prices. Although a depreciation of the exchange rate may result in a large increase in official prices of tradable goods, its impact on actual prices paid by the poor may be relatively small or even negative."

[3] A review of different "entitlements" to purchase life-sustaining goods can be found in Sautter (1992).

seems to have been particularly problematic and unlikely. Table A3 indicates that virtually all Latin American economies went through the same process of a dwindling relative weight of public expenditure. If it is accepted that public expenditure are less progressive than private ones the contracting activity of the state in the national economy leads per se to an inequality-increasing redistribution of national income.[1] Since public sector demand for goods and services is predominantly urban based the consequences of fiscal contraction will hit urban poor even more than other groups in the society.[2] Despite shrinking public expenditures past financing decisions forced governments to come up with enormous interest payments to foreign creditors that ceased to be financable in the Euromarkets as it used to happen in the 1970s and early eighties. This heritage of merrier times reduced the potential for social programs even further. In a fiscal surrounding as the one that haunted Latin American finance ministers through pretty much all of the eighties only exceptional commitment could have isolated non-interest spending programs. If this necessity of fiscal restructuring effects the absolute level of social spending that might help fighting poverty, the worsening primary income situation of the poor will rather be accentuated instead of offset. Thus changes in government spending policies may actually result in an economic situation of the poor even more dramatic.

One category of government spending that has the potential to ease the plight of the needy are subsidies, especially for basic foodstuff. These subsidies have regularly been criticized by development economists for their lack of concentration on the poorest strata of the population. While this assertion is justified in most cases, the uncompensated elimination of food subsidies will certainly make lifes for the urban poor more difficult, since lower wages are eroded by higher food prices. Food subsidies have hardly ever been sustained in the adjustment process. This is partly due to the weak financial position of the governments involved, but partly to explicit demands by the Washington based international financial institutions. Unfortunately data on the changes in spending behavior in the realm of food subsidies is scattered. Colombia cut its subsidies by 29% between 1980 and 1982 and eliminated them altogether later on. Mexico's tortilla-subsidies were reduced by 27% in the first half of the decade, while Brazil reduced its food subsidies by no less than 81%. This led to a decline food subsidies' proportion at overall government spending in Brazil (Mexico) from 5.56 to

---

[1] Helleiner (1987, 1492).
[2] Demery/Addison (1987,1505).

1.65% (3.71 to 2.59%).[1] This reduction does not necessarily mean that the poor are worse off than before. Better targeting to the needy could compensate for the absolute drop in government outlays.[2] This holds equally, perhaps even more true for the expenditures that will be discussed in the next paragraphs, namely such categories as social security and welfare, education and health.

3.2. The Evolution of Social Expenditures

3.2.1. Expenditures on Health and Education

Public spending on promoting the educational and health-situation are one way to increase the productivity and thus the primary incomes of the chronically poor population in the longer run. While it is undeniable that these social programs do not instantaneously alleviate the economic predicament in which many poor find themselves trapped in, they do however offer valuable insights in government priorities. Where investments into human capital remain very low or are cut above average to protect other spending programs such as military or administrative services, the commitment to fight poverty of the policymakers in charge is hardly sufficient to cope with social problems. Figures A1 and A2 in the appendix illustrate the evolutionary development of central government expenditures as percentage in gross domestic product in ten countries during the 1980s.

The overall trends appear to be inconclusive. But the general downward trend of overall government activity relative to GDP combined with the occasional restructuring of the budget to the disadvantage of health and education led to a lamentable decline of the latters' importance relative to GDP in most countries. Since the economic recession actually led to negative GDP growth rates in various countries while the population expanded, the absolute *per capita spending* fell more sharply than figures A1 and A2 would suggest.[3] We can observe a worrying asymmetry of health and education spending behavior in economic upswings and downswings. While in the prosperous

---

[1] Pinstrup-Anderson (1987, Tab. 3.8 and 3.9). Lustig (1992, 86-87) stresses that the Mexican authorities tried to improve the targeting of subsidies towards the poorer strata of the population. The real support experienced by the poor declined nonetheless. Bienen and Gersovitz (1986) offer a good survey on the political dangers of cuts of food subsidies.

[2] For examples consult World Bank (1990b, 112-117) and Ribe/Carvalho (1990).

[3] For absolute data consult Albanez et al. (1989, 29).

years of 1978-1980 these social expenditures per capita grew more slowly than total central government outlays excluding interest payments (+7% vs. +10%) they were reduced more sharply between 1980 and 1985 (-18% vs. -16%).[1] The health sector was somewhat better protected than education. But in health, too, only Ecuador and Uruguay accomplished higher percentages at the end of the decade relative to the early eighties.

This aggregate data, while interesting in itself, has to be interpreted under various caveats. *First*, no comprehensive and comparable data for the activities of subordinate regional or local governments has been considered. They might account for a substantial part of health and educational expenditure, especially in the bigger federal nations. This lacking information is particularly important, where decentralization efforts were core concepts in the ongoing structural adjustment process. While data is generally not easy to obtain and accuracy often unreliable, state or local expenditure for social purposes as a percentage of total government spending appears to have increased slightly in several cases. The proportion has grown significantly in Argentina between 1982 and 1984 from 56% to 65% in the educational sector and from 78% to 80% in health spending. Data for Chile suggest a more stagnant picture, since in the three years following 1982 state and local spending remained at 48% in health services, whereas it rose slightly from 44% to 46% in education.[2] In Mexico, by contrast, the states' educational spending actually *sank* from 14.6% of total public education expenditure in 1981 to a mere 10.6% in 1988. This decline reinforced the reduction in federal governments' proportions in the same period additionally. A similar effect has been observed concerning the Brazilian states.[3]

The limited collection of information does not allow for the assumption, that local governments systematically compensated for drops in central government educational and health spending, since they usually faced similar budgetary restraints as federal finance ministers did. Although changing patterns of the spending behavior of subordinate governments are of great importance, their impact on the urban poor has so far not been studied comprehensively. Where enhanced decentralization assigns more responsibilities to the regional level, as in Argentina, this process needs to be accompanied by sufficient revenue raising devices. Otherwise poorer states are not

---

[1] According to data of The World Bank (1990b, Tab.7-5).
[2] Ebel (1991, Tab.15).
[3] Ebel (1991,.50).

able to finance the additional cost intensive investments and current expenditures in the spending programs. Consequently interregional imbalances would be exacerbated and poverty increased.

Second, the structure of the cuts within health or education budgets have to be examined. Typically the deepest cuts took place within investment programs, whereas current expenditures were much better protected. This implies that the negative impact of fiscal austerity on the actual services have been cushioned, at least in the short run.[1] If we take the longer view the dramatic fall in investment will jeopardize the human development of the poor in later years, since aging infrastructures have not been replaced timely. This will accentuate the hardship of the lower classes in the nineties rather than in the early crisis years themselves. In the health sector the curtailment of hard currency inputs like drugs and imported medical equipment was a priority cut in order to avoid a further dramatization of the balance of payments situation. That may hurt the poor considerably less than alternative cuts in less sophisticated treatments.[2] The general cut in wages of teachers, nurses and doctors could encourage especially the most qualified among them - according to availability - to adopt either another job and leave altogether or to assume other privately paid activities during regular work hours, which might include the sale of public medical supplies to private pharmacists. Those who generate the highest income from "unofficial charges" and corruption practices in contrast have incentives to stay on.[3] In both cases the quality of the service suffers and those segments of the society that are not in a material position to offer extra side payments or bribes are once again the most disadvantaged.

Third, the data presented does not tell us a great deal about the recipients of the services. In most countries, more than 80% of public health spending flows into construction and maintenance of hospitals, whose services are directed to higher income groups.[4] This bias in favour of the urban upper classes is equally prevalent in the education sector. In Argentina, for instance, two thirds of all heavily subsidized university students belong to upper class families. "The rich benefited five times more than

---

[1] Albanez et al. (1989, 18-30) and World Bank (1990b, 141).
[2] Woodward (1992, 213-214).
[3] Woodward (1992, 132-133 and 224).
[4] Albanez et al. (1989, 31). World Bank (1993, 66) remarks that the decisive restructuring of health spending in the favor of hospitals in Brazil "leads patients to seek care in hospitals; up to 80% of the cases crowding hospital emergency rooms could be treated as effectively, but more cheaply, at the primary level."

the poor from publicly provided education. [...] About US$1bn could be made available for alleviating poverty by simply eliminating or reducing the social benefits currently going to the richest 20%."[1] Equally disturbing is the fact that in Chile, Costa Rica, Uruguay and in the Dominican Republic more than half of all subsidies for higher education end up in the richest quintile.[2] A more efficient targeting of expenditures could make an overall cut and better support for the poor coexist simultaneously. Unfortunately, this pattern did not occur in many countries. At least in the first couple of years after the outbreak of the crisis did governments slash budget cuts not across the board, but in a manner that protected services of relatively irrelevant use for the poor (such as universities and hospitals) much more effectively than measures with a far higher poverty alleviation potential.[3] In Mexico the health expenditure programs aiming at directly benefiting the poor had been cut about twice as much than the budget of the Ministry of Health, who offers its services to the better-off population.[4]

3.2.2. Expenditures on Social Security and Welfare

Even more relevant in the short run for fighting acute poverty than spending on health and education that aim to improve the recipient's productivity are outlays for social security and welfare. These transfers offer direct and immediate support to the purchasing power of vulnerable population groups. Since the absolute number of the poor augmented heavily in the "lost decade", a mere stagnation of welfare payments would constitute a noticeable per capita loss. Therefore an increase at least in line with the growth of poverty would be needed, if the secondary income levels were to decline less rapidly than the primary ones. Lamentably, this was once more not the case. As Table A3 in the appendix clarifies only few of the eight countries for which comparable data is available actually experienced positive growth rates as shares of GDP at all. And in the case of Ecuador the qualification has to be made that this line of spending was and still is of only marginal importance, which leaves Costa Rica (and,

---

[1] Latin American Special Report (1992, 5).
[2] World Bank (1990, 85). Costa Rica receives some praise, however, in World Bank (1993, 70) for directing 30% of government spending for health to the poorest 20%.
[3] Cornia (1987a, 28).
[4] Cruz Rivero et al. (1991, 9-10).

to a lesser extent, Argentina) as the sole success story.[1] The targeting of monetary or in-kind transfers involved is obviously a matter of foremost importance, perhaps even more crucial than in the spending categories discussed in the previous paragraph. Since the used data is highly aggregated and virtually no comparable research on the distributive incidence of all categories of social security and welfare disbursements is available, the argument will not be followed any further.

4. Poverty Indicators During Stabilization

4.1. Nutrition

The discussion of the previous sections revealed the limitations of clearcut causal relations between the social spending policies or human capital investments of central and subordinate governments on the one hand and the consequences for poverty profiles on the other. An alternative procedure to assess the effects on poverty lies in analyzing the development of so-called output indicators of social conditions.[2] They cover problems that usually go hand in hand with and can even be regarded as prototypical facets of individual states of economic deprivation. This study considers only indicators that can be assumed to react rather rapidly to external shocks and are therefore able to identify short term changes in the population's welfare situation.

Possibly the most important and certainly the most obvious indicator of all is the evolution of the nutritional status of the populace, first of all the calory- and protein-supply. The average daily per capita calory consumption in the pre-crisis decade (1969-71 to 1979-81) augmented by a yearly rate of .48%, while the protein supply rose by slightly less (.33% p.a.). This positive development of nutritional indicators was stopped if not reversed during the crisis years (1979-81 to 1987-89), when calory supply stagnated at .07% p.a. and protein supply even descended by a yearly rate of

---

[1] Since small welfare programs, such as the Ecuadorian one, cannot exploit economies of scale in administration, their anti-poverty impact is even less relative to bigger ones, as the mere comparisons of numbers would make believe. In 1980 Ecuador's administration thus absorbed 23.7% of all social security and welfare programs. The proportion in countries like Chile, Argentina or Uruguay lie between 4 and 6.5% only (Mackenzie, 1988, 509).

[2] The advantage of using poverty indicators rather than economic data like per capita GNP lies in the tendency of the latter to be less sensitive with regard to distributional measures. Social indicators replace the inherent "one dollar - one vote" problem of GNP figures with "one man - one vote" procedures. Improvements for the rich are therefore less likely to compensate losses incurred by the poor.

-.03%. This bleak picture is coherent with what would have been expected after the discussion of changes in primary and secondary incomes. In the late 1980s neither the calory-, nor the protein supply in Chile, Peru and Argentina reached levels equal to those that had been achieved as early as 1970 (Tab A4).

Since the numbers presented are simple means of country values, they do not take into account the widely differing populations of Latin American countries. A more representative picture can be obtained by weighing each country's growth rates of the indicators by its populace. This has been done in table A4 using population data of 1980. The declining growth rate thus becomes even more striking. While in the eighties the average Latin American citizen experienced a yearly augmentation of growth rates in calory supply of a meager .08%, this number had dropped from a tenfold level of .81% in the precrisis decade. An equivalent decline from .47% down to .04% was observed in the evolution of average protein consumption.

The Latin American nutrition data therefore appears to document the skid mark of the crisis years' adjustment burdens. In one out of two countries the per capita provision with calories actually *shrunk* while this holds true for protein for 5 out of the 12 country sample. Especially alarming is the fact, that the adverse trends could be observed in the poorest countries in the region, which have started off from very low levels of consumption in the first place. Bolivia is a point in case, where, as a result of the nutritional decline, the absolute number of undernourished children grew from 609,000 to 760,000 between 1981 and 1987.[1]

There is some reason to suspect the used FAO-data to even underestimate the real decline of household expenditure for food during the eighties. Poor people tend to substitute superior foodstuffs for cheaper ones in order to maintain their calory intake.[2] A recent investigation in the Mexican city of Guadalajara confirms this microeconomic adjustment pattern. If the actual consumption bundle is compared with the minimum one, the result is striking. While 171% (137%) of the minimal amount of pasta (resp. corn tortillas) were consumed on average, the quota for fruit and

---

[1] Musgrove (1993, 26).

[2] Albanez et al. (1989, 11). The poorest households however have no choice but to throttle their calory intake once a recession affects their income level, since they have already consumed exclusively inferior food before their economic clouds got darker.

vegetables stood at a bare 25%, for eggs at 38.5% and for meat at 36%.[1] Similar research results exist for Guayaquil in Ecuador.[2] While this strategies may be successful in keeping the energy intake of the household constant, the danger of vitamin- or mineral deficiencies is more than obvious. The appearances of these nutritional disturbances harms children in a particularly damaging way. While they are in their growing age, the health hazards can also include the suboptimal development of their cognitive capacity, which affects the return on investments in human capital adversely and thus reduces their future capability of escaping poverty by their own means.

4.2. Social Indicators

Among the wide range of social indicators of development two are probably of primary importance if poverty related issues are to be addressed. The first is an educational indicator, the enrollment ratio in primary schools, and the second is a health indicator expressing acute poverty, the infant mortality rate. The enrollment ratios in Latin America are by international comparisons with other developing regions highly satisfactory. While this is true, the positive trend of the past has been reversed during the debt crisis years and fell actually by about .5% a year (cf. table A5 in the appendix). If the country specific rates are weighed by their population once again, the picture looks slightly better. This effect can easily be traced back to encouraging developments in population rich Brazil. The weighted average rate still indicates stagnation, but considering the fact, that nearly full enrollment is common in most of the countries of the region, this fact is not particularly alarming. It remains slightly disturbing, however, that in more than half of the countries of the sample, the probability of primary enrollment for a child actually *fell*, although remaining on a rather high level.

While the thesis of growing infant mortality[3] has frequently been advanced, empirical evidence sheds serious doubt on the simplistic crisis-mortality causation. Aggregated data presented in table A5 proves, that the improvements in this important indicator

---

[1] Del Castillo (1992, 11). Lustig (1992, 87) reports that a survey found "that the majority of families with incomes lower than twice the minimum wage experienced a decrease in consumption of all food products except tortillas. In addition there was clearly a substitution away from animal proteins."

[2] World Bank (1990b, 126).

[3] Infants are defined as comprising all newborn babies until the age of one.

even accelerated in the years under study. To sound the all-clear signal would be premature, however. A closer look at the available more detailed data has some disturbing insights in store. While Mexico's aggregate indicator improved even above the regional average, poverty related mortality rates among infants increased rapidly. Anemia, which is caused by low levels of food, grew by nearly a fifth between 1981 and 1985. This increase was second only to nutritional deficiency itself, which increased by 35%! This significant change in the structure of death causes among infants was less marked in the cities than in the countryside.[1] The deteriorating food availability among the poor also promotes infectious diseases, which accentuates the impact of declining nutritional levels even further. While the picture is bad enough for infants, it might look even worse for children over one year of age. The reason for that proposition is the assumption that parents tend to concentrate their feeding and education effort on the very young children, while the older ones are expected to be less vulnerable and more self reliant and therefore enjoy less parental care.[2] While in Mexico the percentage of infant deaths caused by nutritional deficiencies as percentage of total infant mortality rose from 1% to 5.2% between 1980 and 1988 the same percentage rose even faster for preschool mortality (1.5 to 9.1%).[3] There is reason to believe that causes of mortality of the adult population changed in comparable patterns during the crisis years, paying a tribute to deteriorating nutritional and hygienic environments.[4] Perhaps the most spectacular and most heavily publicized example among those "deaths by poverty" is the re-emergence of a cholera epidemic, to which approximately half a million persons fell prey and of which an estimated 5000 people died by the end of 1992. The origin of this new wave of a previously nearly extinct disease is thought to have been squatter settlements at the outskirts of Lima, where the poorest of the poor live.

These remarks may suffice to disturb observers that might fell tempted to lean back in comfort referring to the rosy picture drawn by the superficial appearance of the aggregated social indicators. They reflect reality in a highly distorted manner, since they tend to brush over more relevant developments on the household level.

---

[1] Cruz Rivero et al. (1991, 22-27). Woodward (1992, 139) reports that hospital admission for child malnutrition more than doubled in Jamaica between 1978 and 1985.
[2] Cruz Rivero et al. (1991, 23) report of a study of analogous findings in Brazil.
[3] Lustig (1992, 88, Table 3-10).
[4] Latin American Special Report (1992, 3).

5. Conclusions for Policy Making

The essay presented a labor market based theoretical framework to explain the nearly twofold rise in urban poverty in one single decade, the 1980s. This two-, respectively three-sector model provides a useful tool to analyze economic settings different from the Latin American context, too. Different assumptions concerning institutional arrangements in the labor markets, factor mobilities and -intensities as well as the design of social security systems will render different conclusion about the distributional impacts and thus the poverty issue. Although the available data on governments' social expenditure are somewhat difficult to interpret, since they are not sufficiently detailed in order to enable us to evaluate their effects on various social subgroups, the scattered incidence available alludes to a pattern where the secondary incomes of the most vulnerable population decreased at an even faster pace than their primary labor income. The curtailing of public social spending is in per-capita terms even more dramatic than in absolute ones, since due to the economic recession a rapidly swelling number of poor compete for them. The worsening or stagnating nutritional indicators are documenting the results of this process. The question arises quite naturally, whether this human suffering due to economic restructuring could not have been prevented by altering the typically prevailing adjustment recipes and what the role for the international community could have been.

The international financial institutions have been frequently criticized for not paying sufficient attention to the social disruption inherent in the severe adjustment recession which followed neoliberal reform recipes of opening markets and fiscal stabilization. The IMF however has continuously rejected this reproach by arguing that it can hardly be considered the doctor's fault if the patient falls sick. Besides the Fund claims that it is not responsible for social decline because "although the Fund assists in the design of the appropriate macroeconomic framework, the social choices that are inevitable in this process are left to the countries themselves."[1] And furthermore the Washington based institutes defend their policies by observing that the countries that did not follow orthodox reform measures have had rates of increasing poverty outstripping those of the reform countries.[2] Thus World Bank and IMF present themselves indirectly as the advocates of the interest of the socially deprived, at least in the long run, by pushing for market based reforms.

---

[1] Gupta/Nashashibi (1990, 12).
[2] World Bank (1992, 2-11) and Glewwe/Hall (1992, 11-12).

The relevant question that has to be discussed is a somewhat different one, however. The choice of policies is not a bipolar one between old fashioned and socially blind orthodoxy on the one hand and macroeconomically irresponsible populism on the other. The 1990 World Development Report estimated the poverty gap in Latin America at a mere 1% of GDP. Even if this estimate may appear somewhat optimistically low, since it is based on a poverty HCI of only 19%, it becomes obvious that Latin American poverty is basically a distributional issue. It is not so much a lack of resources (like e.g. in Subsaharan Africa or South Asia) that is responsible for the prevalence of poverty, but the rudimentary existence of entitlements for an unacceptably high proportion of the population. Therefore not only distributionally unaware orthodoxy and distributionally obsessed and self defeating populism are viable options, but a third possibility could lie in adjustment programs that assist the negatively affected popular masses to a much greater extent than it has happened in the 1980s. The so-called Social Investment Funds that have sprung up across the continent in the early 1990s can play an important role in achieving this goal, although much needs still be done to improve their targeting precision and operational efficiency.[1]

The popular demand for "social conditionality" on behalf of the IMF and the World Bank has therefore quite naturally elapsed and is repeated in the literature at least since financial fragility forced ever more countries into policy negotiations with these organizations. Picking up the metaphor, the doctor must not be neutral to the choice of the cure and must not let the patient choose a treatment that burdens the already weakest organs additionally. This misperceived abstinence in the face of the actual power distribution in the countries leads to an unintended coalition with the political forces of the elite that have no interest in a socially more equitable adjustment path, since the latter might undermine the own dominance of large sectors of state and economy.[2] It has been rightly argued that this social conditionality would infringe the national sovereignty of the states involved even further. This is certainly a valid argument, and the IMF should not work as an economic pseudo-legislator. But the strong influence on policy making in countries under economic pressure is at least since the early eighties an undeniable fact. In the "new world order" after the dissolution of

---

[1] For a recent survey see Sautter/Schinke (1994) and Olschewsky/Witt (forthcoming). My own article on Mexico's *Pronasol* in this volume offers some in-depth analysis of the may be most comprehensive social program in the region.

[2] Betz (1990, 30), Cornia et al. (1987, 132), Altman (1990, 124) and Helleiner (1987, 1499-1500 and 1510).

east-west antagonisms questions of enforcement of human rights and human living conditions became the focus of the attention of the international community's agenda. In this world order assistance granted does no longer have to go to the strategically important, but should be better channeled to the politically and economically weak and underrepresented. In a world where raising voice (and purse) against social injustice is to become the humanitarian ideal the need for an institutional leverage to protect the deprived manifests itself. It is no longer sufficient to *suggest* how the vulnerable could be at least partly isolated from painful adjustment pressure, but firmer insistence on a more equitable burden sharing is required by the creditors. The proposed social conditionality that limits disbursements to countries that present viable and credible protection devices for the poor in their adjustment plans would exactly allow that. Since without the *d'accord* of the World Bank and - most important - the IMF bilateral and private sources of international financing usually dry up, too, the governments would have economically hard times to protect the elites rather than lower income groups.

The IMF is by its statutes not yet allowed to pursue this path openly, although its more recent annual reports it increasingly stressed the complementary nature of economic adjustment and social programs. At the World Bank, on the other hand, the focus has shifted remarkably to the poverty issue. While this is encouraging in itself the changes are not always sufficiently fundamental. While increased disbursements for poverty fighting projects and improving the targeting of social programs are equally welcome, they are no substitutes to the imposition of social conditionality at structural- or sectoral adjustment loans. Rather, they are logical complements. Considered in isolation, the new initiatives can only stem the tide of the countervailing decline in living standards of the poor caused by conventional adjustment patterns. An integrated attempt to eliminate poverty would need to adopt a congruent strategy, where the negative effects of economic reforms on the poverty situation is minimized in the first place.

A reduction of choices in the development process would actually facilitate the job of socially aware governments to impose the elimination of subsidies and tax breaks for the wealthier classes. Their politically powerful die-hard opposition would be diverted to the doorsteps of the IMF and the World Bank, since the government could insist that it has been forced by these institutions to make the adjustment more equitable. "Good governance" could be helped by isolating policy-makers credibly from certain influences by national interest groups. While some middle- and upper-income groups would certainly be furiously against the measures, it is not very likely that a fierce opposition against the Bretton-Woods institutions would upsurge immediately, since the latter have long been regarded as allies by the higher income groups. Besides it is much harder to lobby (or bribe) well paid international officials far away in Washington D.C. than to buy support of national politicians, who are - due to their own uncertain political and economic future - much more prone to be open to "incentives" provided by some special interest groups. Politically destabilizing social unrests in the case of mass-depriving adjustments could therefore equally be defused as obstructive and unproductive rent-seeking activities by the middle classes that oppose cuts in their own preferential treatment.

The valuable scapegoat function of IMF and World Bank would thus be extended beyond conventional economic conditionality. Assisting governments to enforce more social justice facing elitist interests should be interpreted as one of the basic services that the international financial institutions have to offer their member states. We must not hope that by a reform along the proposed lines all poverty could be eliminated in a decade or so. Economic adjustment will always affect at least some of the poor in a negative way. However, a gain in coherency of economic and distributive policies could be obtained and an important first step towards a "new world order", where international involvement in affairs that have formerly been regarded as "internal" would have been accomplished. Whether the Bretton-Woods institutions in the way they are structured at present and still lacking a clear political mandate are the appropriate organizations to take that precarious step of social conditionality remains dubious at best. A greater involvement of United Nations organs with a higher extent of legitimacy among a much broader set of countries appears to be one alternative path. The contribution of Hermann Sautter in the present volume differentiates the problems of what has fashionably been dubbed "Global Interior Policy", within which pro-poor interventions infringing conventional sovereignty of states by multilateral organizations would have to be embedded. Whatever the institutional design might be, the improvement in the economic outlook in numerous countries, first of all in Latin America itself, offers an opportunity to concentrate analytical competence on elaborating proposals of institutional reforms that would ease the burden of widespread human suffering once a new adjustment crisis strikes.

References

Albanez, Teresa, Eduardo Bustelo, Giovanni Andrea Cornia, and Eva Jespersen. 1989. "Economic Decline and Child Survival: The Plight of Latin America in the Eighties." *Innocenti Occasional Papers*. No.1. Florence.

Altman, Jörn. 1990. "IMF Conditionality: The Wrong Party Pays the Bill." *Intereconomics* 25(3):122-125.

Bourguignon, François, Jaime de Melo, and Christian Morrison. 1991. "Poverty and Income Distribution during Adjustment. Issues and Evidence from the OECD Project." Country Economics Dept. *WPS*. No.810. The World Bank. Washington D.C.

Banco de Mexico. 1992. *Indicadores Económicos*. México D.F.

Betz, Joachim. 1990. "Soziale Auswirkungen der Sparprogramme von Weltbank und IWF in Entwicklungsländern." *Aus Politik und Zeitgeschichte* 40(30-31): 24-31.

Bienen, Henry S., and Mark Gersovitz. 1986. "Consumer Subsidy Cuts, Violence, and Political Stability." *Comparative Politics* 19(1): 25-44.

CEPAL. 1992. *Notas Sobre la Economia y el Desarollo*. No.536 (November).

Cornia, Giovanni Andrea. 1987a. "Economic Decline and Human Welfare in the First Half of the 1980s." In G.A.Cornia, Richard Jolly, and Frances Steward, eds. *Adjustment with a Human Face*. Oxford.

———. 1987b. "Adjustment Policies 1980-85: Effects on Child Welfare." In G.A.Cornia, Richard Jolly, and Frances Steward, eds. *Adjustment with a Human Face*. Oxford.

———, Jolly, Richard, and Frances Steward. 1987. "An Overview of the Alternative Approach." In G.A.Cornia, Richard Jolly, and Frances Steward, eds. *Adjustment with a Human Face*. Oxford.

Cruz Rivero, Carlos, Rafael Lozano Ascencio, and Julio Querol Vinagre. 1991. "The Impact of Economic Crisis and Adjustment on Health Care in Mexico". *Innocenti Occasional Paper*. No.13. Florence.

del Castillo, Gustavo. 1992. *Mexico and the United States: The Politics of Free Trade and the Loss of Mexican Options*. mimeo.

Demery, Lionel, and Tony Addison. 1993. "The Impact of Macroeconomic Adjustment on Poverty in the Presence of Wage Rigidities." *Journal of Development Economics* 40:331-348.

———.1988. *Die Linderung der Armut während der Strukturanpassung*. Weltbank. Washington D.C.

———. 1987. "Stabilization Policy and Income Distribution in Developing Countries." *World Development* 15(12):1483-1498.

Ebel, Beth. 1991. "Patterns of Government Expenditure in Developing Countries during the 1980s: The Impact on Social Services." *Innocenti Occasional Papers.* No.18. Florence.

ECLAC. 1992. *Economic Survey of Latin America and the Caribbean 1990.* Vol.II. Santiago.

Edwards, Sebastian. 1988. "Terms of Trade, Tariffs, and Labor Market Adjustment in Developing Countries." *World Bank Economic Review* 2(2):165-187.

FAO. 1990. *Production Yearbook.* Vol. 44. Rome.

Fox, Louise M., and Samuel A. Morley. 1991. *Who Paid the Bill? Adjustment and Poverty in Brazil, 1980-95.* Background Paper of the World Development Report 1990. WPS No.648. World Bank. Washington D.C.

Gindling, T.H., and Albert Berry. 1992. "The Performance of the Labor Market During Recession and Structural Adjustment: Costa Rica in the 1980s." *World Development* 20(11):1599-1616.

Glewwe, Paul, and Gillette Hall. 1992. "Unorthodox Adjustment and Poverty in Peru." *Finance & Development* 29(4):10-13.

Gupta, Sanjeev, and Karim Nashashibi. 1990. "Poverty Concerns in Fund-Supported Programs." *Finance & Development* 27(3):12-14.

Helleiner, Gerald K. 1987. "Stabilization, Adjustment and the Poor." *World Development* 15(12):1499-1513.

Heller, Peter S. et al. 1988. "The Implications of Fund-Supported Adjustment Programs for Poverty." *IMF Occasional Paper.* No.58. Washington D.C.

ILO. Various years. *Yearbook of Labour Statistics.* Geneva.

IMF. Various years. *Government Finance Statistics.* Washington D.C.

Jarque, Carlos M. 1993. "Evolución Reciente del Desempleo en México." *El Mercado de Valores* 4 (February 15). México D.F.

Krawczyk, Miriam. 1993. "Mujeres en la region: los grandes cambios." *Revista de la CEPAL* 49.

Latin American Special Reports. 1992. *Poverty: an issue making a comeback.* Latin American Newsletters. London.

Liuksila, Claire. 1992. "Colombia: Economic Adjustment and the Poor." *Finance & Development* 29(2):40-41.

Lustig, Nora. 1992. *Mexico - the Remaking of an Economy.* Washington D.C.

Mackenzie, G.A. 1988. "Social Security Issues in Developing Countries. The Latin American Experience." *IMF Staff Papers* 35: 496-522.

Morley, Samuel A. 1992. *Macroconditions and Poverty in Latin America.* Department of Economic and Social Development. Inter-American Development Bank. mimeo.

Musgrove, Philip. 1993. "Feeding Latin America's Children." *The World Bank Research Observer* 8(1):23-45.

Olschewski, Roland, and Matthias Witt. Forthcoming. *Soziale Nothilfe- und Investitionsfonds in Lateinamerika.* Arbeitspapiere der EZE.

Pinstrup-Andersen, Per, Maurice Jaramillo, and Frances Steward. 1987. "The Impact on Government Expenditure." In Cornia, Giovanni Andrea *Adjustment with a Human Face.* Oxford.

Psacharopoulos, George, and Carolyn Winter. 1992 "Women's Employment and Pay in Latin America." *Finance & Development* 29(4):14-15.

Ribe, Helena, and Soniya Carvalho. 1990. "Adjustment and the Poor." *Finance & Development* 27(3):15-17.

Sautter, Hermann. 1992. "Armut in Entwicklungsländern - Ein wirtschaftsethisches Problem." *WISU* 5(92):421-428.

———, and Rolf Schinke. 1994. "Die sozialen Kosten wirtschaftlicher Reformen - ihre Ursachen und die Möglichkeiten einer Abfederung." *Discussion Paper.* No.63. Ibero-America Institute for Economic Research. Göttingen.

Woodward, David. 1992. *Debt, Adjustment and Poverty in Developing Countries. Vol.2.* Save the Children (UK). London.

World Bank. 1990a. *Making Adjustment Work for the Poor.* Washington D.C.

———. 1990b. *Weltentwicklungsbericht 1990.* Washington D.C

———. 1992a. *Poverty Reduction Handbook.* Washington D.C.

———. 1992b. *Weltentwicklungsbericht 1992.* Washington D.C.

———. 1993. *World Development Report 1993: Investing in Health.* Washington D.C.

Annex

Table A1:

Index of Real Industrial Wages, 1980-90 (1982=1), discounted with CPI

	Arg	Bra	Chi	CR	Col	Mex	Per	Uru	Ven	Bol	Ecu
1980	0.86	1.04	0.89	..	0.99	0.96	1.16	0.97	1.14	..	1.14
1981	**1.00**	**1.00**	**1.00**	..	**1.00**	**1.00**	**1.00**	**1.00**	**1.00**	..	**1.00**
1982	1.08	1.00	1.00	**1.00**	1.04	1.02	0.92	1.01	0.91	**1.00**	0.88
1983	1.53	0.88	1.06	1.21	1.10	0.78	1.06	0.87	0.86	1.03	0.74
1984	1.70	0.82	1.03	1.40	1.17	0.72	0.82	0.87	0.77	0.86	0.73
1985	1.42	0.84	0.95	1.49	1.13	0.70	0.72	0.91	1.12	0.46	0.70
1986	1.58	0.83	0.95	1.46	1.19	0.66	0.74	0.85	1.07	0.32	0.75
1987	1.38	0.68	0.92	1.73	1.19	0.65	0.76	0.88	1.11	0.38	0.71
1988	1.37	0.63	0.98	1.59	1.17	0.64	0.74	0.83	0.86	0.39	0.62
1989	0.99	0.67	1.02	1.56	1.19	0.70	0.36	0.83	0.63	0.36	0.55
1990	1.08	0.58	1.03	1.56	..	0.72	0.35	0.77	0.60	0.31	0.45

Sources:
Calculated on basis of data in Albanez et al. (1989, 20),
Banco de México (1992), ILO (1987 and 1992) and ECLAC (1992)

Note:
[..] : Data not Available

Table A2:

Food Price Index Divided by Consumer Price Index, (1982=1)

	Arg	Bra	Chi	CR	Col	Mex	Per	Uru
1980	0.98	0.88	1.11	0.89	1.03	1.05	1.07	1.14
1981	0.98	0.87	1.06	0.89	1.00	1.03	1.07	1.07
1982	**1.00**	0.84	**1.00**	**1.00**	**1.00**	**1.00**	**1.00**	**1.00**
1983	0.99	0.96	0.99	1.00	1.00	0.94	1.07	1.04
1984	1.01	**1.00**	1.00	0.97	1.00	1.00	1.05	1.13
1985	0.95	1.03	0.98	0.95	1.06	1.01	0.99	1.07
1986	0.99	1.07	1.02	0.94	1.07	1.01	1.04	1.16
1987	1.00	0.94	1.05	0.93	1.14	1.00	0.92	1.13
1988	1.01	0.96	1.04	0.92	1.17	0.98	<u>0.76</u>	1.10
1989	0.98	0.87	1.07	0.93	1.16	0.99	..	1.10
1990	0.80	0.78	1.07	0.93	1.13	0.98	..	1.15
1991	..	0.73	1.11	0.91	1.13	0.95	..	1.05

Sources: ILO (1986 and 1992)
Note: [..] : Data not available

Table A3:

Social Spending of Central Government
(in % of total expenditure)

	Arg	Bol(2)	Bra(1)	Chi	CR	Ecu	Mex(3)	Per	Uru	Ven(4)
Population in 1980 (millions)										
	28.2	5.6	121	11.1	2.3	8.1	70.4	17.3	2.9	15
Expenditure for Social Security and Welfare										
1975	27.5	3.4	38.6	24.0	26.5	1.04	24.7	0.2	45.1	5.8
1980	26.1	1.0	33.0	32.3	7.1	1.27	16.0	..	47.7	5.8
1981	26.0	0.9	34.6	38.0	10.3	1.19	14.7	0.0	51.6	4.7
1982	30.0	..	34.9	41.8	11.2	1.03	10.5	0.0	54.2	6.9
1983	33.6	..	34.1	42.7	14.5	1.50	10.3	0.0	52.1	7.0
1984	37.9	5.8	31.2	41.8	11.2	1.12	9.3	0.0	47.8	6.4
1985	32.6	..	23.4	39.0	14.5	0.91	9.7	0.0	48.5	5.7
1986	32.3	24.8	22.7	38.0	19.2	1.21	8.2	0.0	49.4	6.9
1987	31.7	18.7	23.7	34.5	11.3	1.35	6.8	0.0	51.2	..
1988	40.5	11.4	20.2	29.8	13.3	1.16	7.6	..	50.8	..
1989	..	14.3	19.9	..	13.2	2.18	9.4	..	49.6	..
1990	..	17.7	..	..	13.8	1.91	12.4	..	50.8	..

	Arg	Bol(2)	Bra(1)	Chi	CR	Ecu	Mex(3)	Per	Uru	Ven(4)
Expenditure for Education										
1975	10.6	23.7	6.8	12.1	28.8	27.1	18.2	20.5	11.5	17.2
1980	8.8	26.6	3.4	14.5	24.6	34.7	17.9	11.1	8.7	21.4
1981	7.3	24.4	3.8	14.4	23.7	28.0	18.2	11.3	7.7	18.3
1982	6.7	13.6	4.7	14.8	22.6	26.5	13.1	16.4	7.7	15.7
1983	7.4	26.9	3.6	13.8	19.4	29.0	10.9	15.2	6.5	19.8
1984	9.5	11.6	3.1	13.1	18.4	27.7	12.4	15.9	5.9	19.1
1985	6.0	n.a.	3.0	13.2	18.8	24.5	11.6	16.2	6.4	19.7
1986	6.0	18.4	3.3	12.9	16.2	25.1	9.1	21.4	7.1	19.6
1987	6.9	24.8	4.8	12.0	22.1	24.9	8.3	15.6	7.8	..
1988	9.3	20.7	4.2	10.1	18.6	23.4	9.1	20.7	7.9	..
1989	..	20.3	5.3	..	17.1	21.1	11.8	21.1	7.6	..
1990	..	18.0	..	..	19.0	18.2	13.9	16.2	7.4	..

	Arg	Bol(2)	Bra(1)	Chi	CR	Ecu	Mex(3)	Per	Uru	Ven(4)

Expenditure for Health

Year	Arg	Bol(2)	Bra(1)	Chi	CR	Ecu	Mex(3)	Per	Uru	Ven(4)
1975	2.5	8.4	6.5	7.0	..	7.3	4.2	5.1	3.9	9.1
1980	1.7	..	6.5	7.4	28.7	7.8	2.4	4.5	4.8	8.7
1981	1.4	7.2	7.4	6.4	29.7	7.8	1.9	5.3	3.8	7.3
1982	1.1	2.0	7.6	6.8	32.8	7.7	1.3	5.2	3.3	7.6
1983	1.3	3.1	7.2	6.0	22.5	8.2	1.2	5.4	3.4	8.7
1984	1.8	1.5	7.4	6.2	24.5	8.3	1.5	5.8	3.7	8.7
1985	1.3	..	6.4	6.1	22.9	7.3	1.4	6.0	4.1	9.0
1986	1.9	1.9	6.1	6.0	19.4	7.3	1.3	6.2	4.8	10.0
1987	2.1	9.0	9.5	6.3	20.2	11.1	1.2	5.5	4.3	..
1988	2.0	7.7	6.1	5.9	24.7	9.8	1.3	7.0	4.5	..
1989	..	6.6	7.2	..	27.2	11.4	1.5	5.6	4.8	..
1990	..	2.3	..	..	26.3	11.0	1.9	5.1	4.5	..

	Arg	Bol(2)	Bra(1)	Chi	CR	Ecu	Mex(3)	Per	Uru	Ven(4)

Expenditure of Central Government in % of GDP

Year	Arg	Bol(2)	Bra(1)	Chi	CR	Ecu	Mex(3)	Per	Uru	Ven(4)
1980	28.2	9.0	24.6	28.7	25.2	12.8	18.9	19.4	22.2	26.2
1981	25.6	9.3	27.3	30.3	20.7	16.1	21.9	18.4	25.2	35.7
1982	23.0	25.0	27.9	31.2	18.4	15.5	31.6	17.6	30.4	33.2
1983	28.3	14.4	30.8	30.4	23.8	13.3	26.7	19.4	25.6	28.2
1984	19.9	33.0	31.9	31.9	23.1	13.1	23.9	18.4	24.1	22.5
1985	28.3	n.a.	31.6	31.6	22.0	15.1	25.9	17.4	22.9	22.9
1986	23.1	11.4	29.3	29.3	26.6	15.8	29.0	16.1	23.1	24.1
1987	22.2	10.9	28.5	28.5	27.6	15.5	31.0	14.8	23.3	25.8
1988	15.8	12.4	28.8	28.9	25.1	13.7	27.2	11.9	25.0	27.2
1989	..	13.1	..	..	26.6	13.8	24.2	10.2	25.6	22.6
1990	..	14.3	..	..	26.3	14.4	..	..	..	..

Sources:

IMF (Government Financial Statistics [GFS], var. years). Most of the data used from GFS 1991
GFS 1987: Welfare and health spending in Costa Rica 1980-81 and percentage of total government spending as GDP-percentage in Ecuador 1980 and Bolivia 1980-81. GFS 1985: Welfare and education expenditure in Ecuador 1975 and 1980. Population Data from FAO Production Yearbook 1990

Notes:

Numbers in italics are preliminary.Underlined numbers indicate, that comparability ends in this year.
Twice underlined numbers are calculations derived from GFS-yearbooks country tables
[..] : Data not available.
Since 1987 Costa Rica's numbers include social and medical welfare institutions as well as
  public universities in central government budgets. (GFS 1991, p.647).
(1) The conceptual change after 1981 is irrelevant for the present analysis (GFS 1991, p.635).
(2) Since 1983 social security funds are included in central government budget (GFS 1991, p.633)
(3) The conceptual change after 1985 is irrelevant for the present analysis (GFS 1991, p.696).
(4) From 1983 on not only the Instituto Venezolano de las Seguros Sociales is included in the budget, but operations
  of other social funds, too. Since 1985 130 public authorities were excluded. (GFS 1991, p.745-6)

Table A4:

Nutritional Indicators in Latin America 1969-1989

	Arg	Bol	Bra	Chi	CR	Ecu	Jam	Col	Mex	Per	Uru	Ven	Average
Population in 1980 (in millions)													
(1)	28.2	5.6	121	11.1	2.3	8.1	2.1	26.9	70.4	17.3	2.9	15	25.93
Calory intake per capita per day													
(2) 1969-71	3265	1947	2498	2649	2403	2126	2532	2165	2620	2278	2997	2344	2485
(3) 1979-81	3187	2092	2703	2670	2566	2297	2623	2489	3014	2203	2772	2670	2607
(4) 1987-89	3110	1968	2722	2553	2791	2518	2622	2571	3048	2244	2697	2620	2622
(5) Annual growth 1970s (%)	-0.24	0.72	0.79	0.08	0.66	0.78	0.35	1.40	1.41	-0.33	-0.78	1.31	0.48
(6) Annual growth 1980s (%)	-0.31	-0.76	0.09	-0.56	1.06	1.15	-0.00	0.41	0.14	0.23	-0.34	-0.24	0.07
(7) Population-weighted average annual growth in the region (1977-82; in %)													0.81
(8) Population-weighted average annual growth in the region (1982-89; in %)													0.08
Protein consumption per capita per day (in grammes)													
(9) 1969-71	103.4	49.1	60.5	69.3	56.6	49.9	65.7	48.6	66.8	60.9	90.6	58.4	64.98
(10) 1979-81	106.1	54.4	59.8	73.1	62.2	48.0	62.5	53.6	77.7	57.7	83.3	67.3	67.14
(11) 1987-89	100.3	53.8	60.4	69.2	64.0	51.7	64.7	57.0	77.9	58.7	81.9	64.3	66.99
(12) Annual growth 1970s (%)	0.26	1.03	-0.12	0.54	0.95	-0.39	-0.50	0.98	1.52	-0.54	-0.84	1.43	0.33
(13) Annual growth 1980s (%)	-0.70	-0.14	0.12	-0.68	0.36	0.93	0.43	0.77	0.03	0.22	-0.21	-0.57	-0.03
(14) Population-weighted average annual growth in the region (1977-82; in %)													0.47
(15) Population-weighted average annual growth in the region (1982-89; in %)													0.04

Source: FAO Production Yearbook 1990, vol.44, Tables 3, 106 and 107 and own calculations

Table A5:

Social Indicators in Latin America

	Arg	Bol	Bra	Chi	CR	Ecu	Jam	Col	Mex	Per	Uru	Ven	Avg.
Population in 1980 (in millions)													
(1)	28.2	5.6	121	11.1	2.3	8.1	2.1	26.9	70.4	17.3	2.9	15	25.93
Primary School Enrollment (1)													
(2) 1977	110	80	90	117	111	101	97	103	116	110	95	104	102.83
(3) 1982	119	86	96	112	106	114	99	125	121	114	122	105	109.92
(4) 1989	111	81	105	100	100	118	105	107	114	123	106	105	106.25
(5) Annual growth 1977-82 (%)	1.59	1.46	1.30	-0.87	-0.92	2.45	0.41	3.95	0.85	0.72	5.13	0.19	1.35
(6) Annual growth 1982-89 (%)	-0.99	-0.85	1.29	-1.61	-0.83	0.49	0.84	-2.20	-0.85	1.09	-1.99	0.00	-0.47
(7)	Population-weighted average annual growth in the region (1977-82; in %)												1.33
(8)	Population-weighted average annual growth in the region (1982-89; in %)												0.01
Infant Mortality Rate (2)													
(9) 1978	44	158	92	55	28	66	20	98	60	102	46	40	67.42
(10) 1983	36	123	70	40	20	76	28	53	52	98	38	38	56.00
(11) 1989	30	106	59	19	17	61	16	38	40	79	22	35	43.50
(12) Annual growth 1978-83 (%)	-3.93	-4.88	-5.32	-6.17	-6.51	2.86	6.96	-11.6	-2.82	-0.80	-3.75	-1.02	-3.08
(13) Annual growth 1983-89 (%)	-2.99	-2.45	-2.81	-11.7	-2.67	-3.60	-8.91	-5.39	-4.28	-3.53	-8.71	-1.36	-4.86
(14)	Population-weighted average annual growth in the region (1978-83; in %)												-4.43
(15)	Population-weighted average annual growth in the region (1983-89; in %)												-3.78

Remarks:
(1) Ratio of pupils in relation to population in primary school age (usually 6-11 years). Since some pupils are younger or older than official primary school age may the proportion exceed 100%. Data for 1977, 1983 and 1989 from World Development Reports 1980, 1985 and 1992.
(2) Number of infants born in a certain year dying before their first birthday relative to 1000 births of living babies.
Data for Argentina and Peru early seventies instead of 1978 (World Bank: Social Indicators of Development 1991-92).

Sources:
Data for 1978: World Development Report (WDR) 1980, for 1983: WDR 1985; for 1989: WDR 1991. Population Data: FAO (1990)

Figure A1: Central Government's Health Expenditure as percentage of GDP, 1980-90

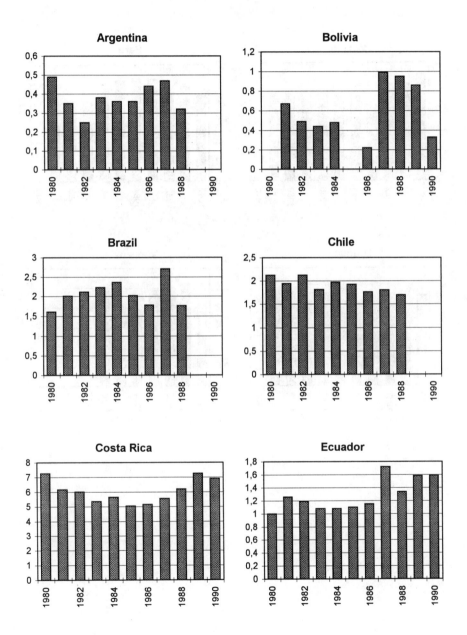

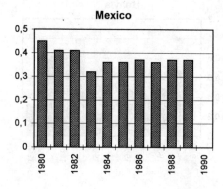
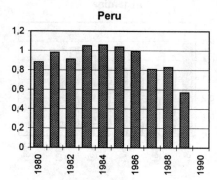
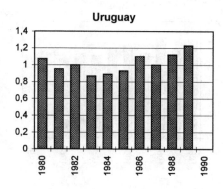
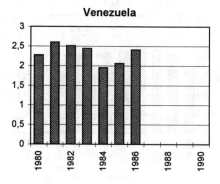

Figure A2: Central Government's Education Expenditure as percentage of GDP, 1980-90

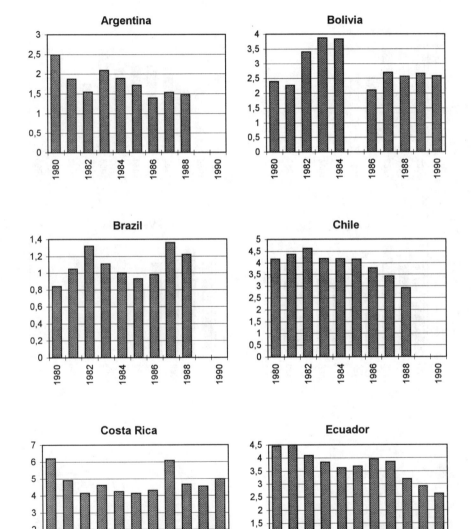

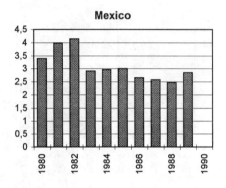
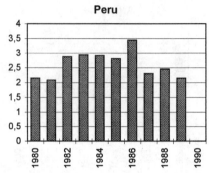
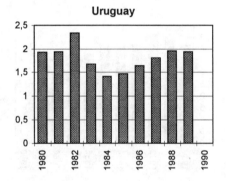
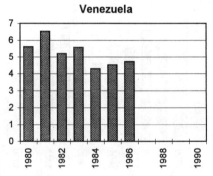

Figure A3: **Central Government's Expenditure for Social Security and Welfare as percentage of GDP, 1980-90**

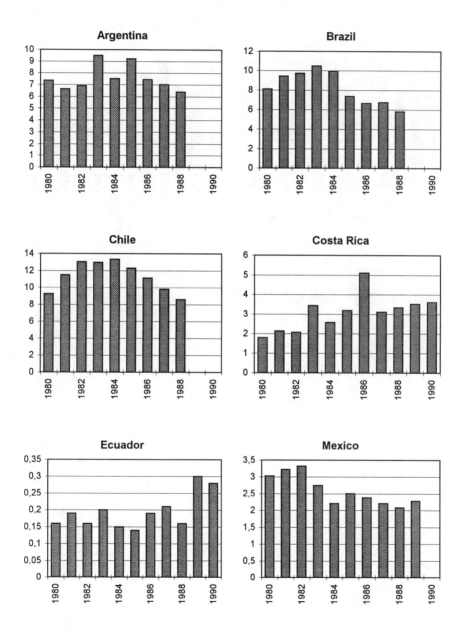

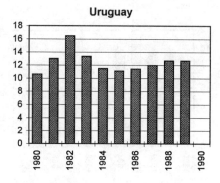
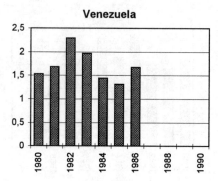

Programa Nacional de Solidaridad - Poverty and Power Politics in Mexico

Moritz Kraemer [1]

1. Introduction

More than any other country of the western hemisphere during the 1980s Mexico followed a consistent and uninterrupted path of economic adjustments and restructuring in order to overcome the problems that kept the nation in their grip. Finding quick solutions for the economic predicaments was unpostponable after the outbreak of the Mexican debt crisis in 1982 that almost immediately spilled over to the whole of Latin America. The Mexico we face today is at least economically a drastically more open and market-oriented country than the one that tumbled from the oil boom into the debt bust in the early 1980s. And even in political terms there is now a lively and ongoing debate on the degree of liberalization and competitiveness that has taken place, especially during the Salinas *sexenio* that is coming to an end in December 1994.

However, new problems have soared as a result of the ongoing economic transition effort. Foremost the spread of poverty among the numerous losers of the adjustment process is a disturbing feature. While this is by no means a complication specific to the Mexican adjustment experience, it is certainly the concomitant that blurs the rosy economic success stories the most. However, official policy did not remain unresponsive to rising demands for a social policy that would help Mexicans to struggle their way out of utter misery. Far from being paralyzed by the shock of the desastrous and unprecedented decline of electoral support for the prevailing corporatist system with the hegemonic *Partido Revolucionario Institucional* (PRI) as the centerpiece, the incoming Salinas administration immediately felt the need to accommodate potential

---

[1] Economics Department, University of Göttingen, Platz der Göttinger Sieben 3, D-37073 Göttingen.
The author wants to thank Ann Craig at the Department of Political Science at the University of California San Diego, José Vergarra, Guillermo Carranza and Juan Pluma Morales at Pronasol Headquarters in Mexico City and Alvaro Urreta Fernandez (Delegado de SEDESOL in Morelos) for valuable discussions and information. I am also indebted to Hermann Sautter whose constructive comments on an earlier version proved to be as unerring as usual.
The final version of this paper was written in July 1994 (before the presidential election).

social unrest by preventive action on the social policy front. Any emerging powerful social resistance against the decline in living standards could be politically perilous and thus jeopardize the road to economic modernization envisaged by the technocratic elites in Mexico City. As a device intended to avert the feared backlash to the deepening economic reforms the *Programa Nacional de Solidaridad* (Pronasol), inaugurated in December 1988, was paramount to any other. Meanwhile it has become the flagship of the Salinas government and numerous analysts consider it as a symbol of the rebirth of the PRI's political dominance in the electoral arena after the heavily disputed presidential election in summer 1988. Pronasol's effects were from the very beginning not confined to poverty alleviation alone but - being a highly symbolic and publicized instrument - was bound to spill over into politics in one way or another, whether this was a prior intention of Salinas's team or not. Since the program affects tens of millions of Mexicans directly or indirectly it is also likely to have some influence on the perspectives of political liberalization and democratization in the country.

This paper aims to investigate therefore not primarily the poverty alleviation potential of Pronasol, but also to estimate its relevance for the reform of the political system. The next part of the paper will present an overview of poverty trends and the development of social indicators in Mexico since the crisis has struck. This will shed some light on the colossal challenge facing Pronasol and the immense importance of any policy measure aiming at combating poverty.

Part three will present the main mechanisms of how Pronasol works, which kind of programs are pursued and what the achievements have been after almost half a decade of experience, including a critical assessment of its efficiency in solving poverty-related problems. The fourth part will discuss the tangled interdependencies between Pronasol on the one hand and the political environment on the other with causalities pointing into both directions. Concluding remarks summarize the main arguments and appraise the future of Pronasol concerning its effectiveness in combating poverty as well as its longer term significance for Mexican political culture and thus its potential to support or hinder further political liberalization.

2. The Incidence of Poverty in Mexico

The decades after World War II were characterized by remarkably high and stable economic growth rates and rapid modernization. Even during this long honeymoon of import substituting industrialization poverty increased in absolute numbers.[1] However, poverty was held at bay in relative terms which was achieved by general and untargeted subsidies[2] for all kinds of publicly provided goods and services that increased the purchasing power of a great number of Mexicans and also by simply relying on the trickle down of growth to the lower social strata. When the "Mexican Miracle" stumbled upon well-known problems of deepening import substitution beyond the easy phase of lower quality consumer goods in the early 1970s the discovery of vast oil reserves saved the beleaguered development strategy. But not for long. After the López Portillo government went deep into debt with the country's oil richness as a corollary and Euromarket interest rates rose at the same time as the terms of trade deteriorated and the demand of a world economy in slump declined an overwhelming foreign exchange crisis dictated painful and immediate adjustments in economic policymaking.[3]

Being cut off from international lending the de la Madrid administration taking over in late 1982 had no choice but to pick up the pieces left over by its predecessors and commence a major change in public expenditure structure. In order to fulfill its contractual obligations concerning external debt service due[4] the government had to curtail all other budget titles, including social expenditures. Although a vicious recession hit Mexico after 1982 (between 1981 and 1983 per capita income growth fell by 12.5 percentage points to -7.5%) central government expenditures for Social Security and Welfare, for education and for health all fell from a combined share of national product of 7.9% in 1982 over 6% in 1983 to hit the floor with 5.5% in 1984. The per capita cuts are much deeper still, since GNP fell in the same period and the number of the needy increased in line with the economic downturn.

---

[1] Compare Provencio (1990, tables 2 and 3).

[2] The lack of targeting was not only prevalent in general food, transportation, energy and other subsidies, but even in programs that supposedly supported the poor exclusively. Méndez et al. (1992, 64) state for COPLAMAR, a plan explicitly directed towards the most marginalized groups (hence the -MAR in the acronym) in the country: "de 459 municipios que recibieron apoyos, solamente 196 se consideraban marginados [...]."

[3] For details about the developments that led to the Mexican crisis and the adjustment efforts between 1982 and 1992 compare Kraemer (1992).

[4] The country's net transfer received from abroad was more than $5bn in 1981 and turned *negative* to almost $9bn per year in 1984 and 1985.

Wage earners had to cope with a depressed labor market that kept their real incomes throughout the 1980s at a level that was on average 30% lower than they used to be back in 1981/82, with the minimum wage dropping even faster. Others did not find any work at all with the open unemployment rate more than doubling to 14.7% between 1980 and 1985.[1]

The effects of the adverse developments of the labor market and shrinking social expenditures on the living conditions and welfare levels of the population were quite predictable: a general decline spared almost nobody except for the ultrarich which gained heavily by engaging in capital flight and financial speculation against the overvalued peso. Muñoz Ledo, Senator for the left wing opposition of the PRD (*Partido Revolucionario Democratico*) probably put it more drastically than anyone else by declaring that the government policy was "a degradation of the species, a genocidal policy."[2] Are these strong words covered by the evidence observed? There is a widespread agreement that poverty has indeed increased quite considerably during the 1980s and was no longer confined to be a mere rural problem, but the growth rate of the urban poor even exceeded the one in the countryside. The differing trends of urban and rural poverty can be traced using the data presented in appendix table 1 in Rolf Schinke's contribution to this volume, although his data does not coincide with the one used in this article. The channels through which adjustment policies are leading to rising urban poverty via labor markets are theoretically discussed in my second contribution to the present anthology.

Due to methodological singularities poverty indices can usually not be compared across studies. The government reported an increase of Mexicans living in extreme poverty (defined here as a standard of living that does not meet 60% of the requirements for a minimal level of well-being) from 13.7 to 17.3 millions between 1981 and 1987. Since during the same time span the number of the "moderately" poor increased also from 18.4 to 24 millions the combined number of all poor grew twice as fast as the population as a whole (4.3% vs. 2.2% p.a.).[3] A recent joint study of Mexico's statistical agency (INEGI) and CEPAL found a turning point in the poverty trend as late as 1989 when at least the presence of extreme poverty could be curtailed (Table 1). Extremely poor are by this definition individuals whose income lies below

---

[1] Mexico Service (1991, 11).
[2] Cited in Centeno (1991, 36).
[3] Calculated from data in Jiménez Badillo (1992, Cuadro 1).

the threshold, which is the critical amount necessary to purchase a basic set of goods. But even in 1992 the relative share, let alone absolute numbers, of the poor and extremely poor still exceed the indicators observed in 1984, which was immediately following the probably worst year of the "lost decade".

Table 1
Percentage of Mexicans living in Poverty
(abs. numbers in millions in brackets)

	Extreme Poverty	Moderate Poverty	Not Poor
1984	15,4 (11,0)	27,1 (19,4)	57,5 (41,0)
1989	18,8 (14,9)	28,9 (22,9)	51,2 (41,3)
1992	16,1 (13,6)	27,9 (23,6)	55,8 (47,1)

Source: González Amador (1993, 16).

Whatever the chosen poverty line, "the incidence of poverty is *unambiguously* higher among rural households compared to urban households"[1], even if rural-urban food price differentials are taken into account. Using the Foster-Greer-Thorbecke index for 1984 it was estimated, that two thirds of the extremely poor inhabit rural areas, if we set the weight $\alpha = 0$ (and thus obtain the standard head count index). If we weigh the poorest of the extremely poor more ($\alpha = 2$) the index rises to 76%. "This indicates that not only is most of the extremely poor population concentrated in rural areas, but *the poorest of the extremely poor are in rural areas*."[2] It is interesting to spot some socio-demographic characteristics of the poorest segments of the population using 1984 household data disaggregated on a decile level.[3] Contradictory to conventional wisdom, for example, the percentage of households headed by women is considerably lower among the lowest deciles than for the nation as a whole, which still lacks a convincing explanation. The facts that rural households are less likely to be headed by women than the on average better off urban ones (12.3 vs. 16.9%) and that the poorest deciles are disproportionately rural can only partly elucidate this result, since

---
[1] Lustig (1993, 8). Italics in original text.
[2] Banamex (1993b, 144). Italics in original text.
[3] For the following compare the statistical annex in Lustig (1993).

the percentage of woman-headed households of the two most destitute deciles is even lower (9%) than what could be expected if the ultrapoor were exclusively rural. According to expectations we find that household size is greater in the lowest deciles, where we observe also the highest dependency ratio. This is the reason why "most of the population in extreme poverty are minors in rural areas."[1] Despite rising labor market participation of poverty-stricken women and children during the adjustment crisis the ratio of income earners relative to household size for the lowest quintile is still only about two thirds of the national average.

At the same time the relation between individual educational achievements and the position in the income distribution could hardly be more clear cut: while 57.2% of all Mexicans have had no formal instruction at all or have not finished Primary School level, the proportion for individuals in the lowest decile is nine out of ten and for the deciles II and III about eight out of ten. Furthermore agricultural workers and self-employed are the most likely to fall into the category of the "hard core poor" as Lustig calls them.

Accentuating the augmentation of poverty, the already highly unequitable distribution of national income worsened even further during the crisis with *everyone* except for the richest 10% losing relatively (Figure 1). Thus, even in years with modestly positive per capita growth rates (such as 1984-85 and 1989-92) it was basically the best off that benefited and it is likely that for the poor the positive effect of rising national income was more than compensated by the declining shares of this enlarged pie accruing to the weakest social groups. Hopes for a rapid and beneficial trickle-down of growth towards the poor are therefore clearly unfounded.

Recent CEPAL data suggests that the income distribution may actually have worsened further after 1989 with the top ten percent earning not less than 41.4% of national income and the percentage of households earning less than the national average increasing from 74% to 76% between 1989 and 1990.[2] Since the Gini coefficients are higher in agricultural sectors than in other areas[3] the distributional problem is particularly acute in regions where the incidence of poverty is the highest anyway.

---

[1] Banamex (1993b, 145).

[2] Chávez (1993).

[3] Lustig (1993, Table 6).

Figure 1:
Income Distribution by Deciles 1984 and 1989
(in percent per decile)

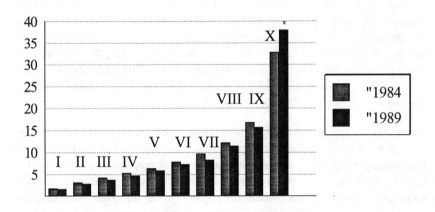

Source: Acevedo Pesquera (1993).
Note: I denotes the poorest decile and X the richest decile.

How do those abstract distributional and poverty measures translate into social indicators that shape the poors' everyday life experience? For our purpose it may be sufficient to simply enumerate some of the severe deficiencies in living conditions that can be witnessed today. [1] The nutritional intake fell during the crisis years (1981-88) with the per capita consumption of corn and beans declining by 42 and 44% respectively! Faced with dwindling household incomes families tend to substitute nutritionally more valuable foodstuff (vegetables, eggs, meat) with cheaper one (usually tortillas) in order to maintain the desired calory intake. But as a consequence they consume less vitamins, protein and nutrients. [2] The results of this nutritional change are dramatic with one out of two children suffering from physical or mental defects caused by malnutrition while one child out of 20 dies in the first years following complications from insufficient food intake. While infant mortality declined throughout

---
[1] For the following see Mexico Service (1991, 12-14).
[2] del Castillo (1992, 11) and Moguel (1992, 42-43).

the adjustment period the death toll of diseases caused by malnutrition rose against that trend.[1] Every third death in Mexico could be prevented if better medical care were available. Almost two thirds of all houses in Mexico are considered overcrowded, and it is again the poorest who suffer most from the housing shortage: while on the national average 2.8 persons share one room the numbers for the two lowest deciles are 5.1 and 4.5 (data for 1984).[2] While interpreting aggregate indicators like the preceding ones it must not be forgotten that living conditions differ widely from region to region and are usually less favorable in the countryside. While for example 99.2% of households in the Federal District dispose of electricity this proportion is only 66.8% in poor rural Chiapas. This holds equally true for sewerage systems where the respective proportions are 93.7% and 41.1%.[3]

These remarks may suffice to underline the urgency with which policy makers had to address the poverty problem that plagued the country and still does so, even if some encouraging signs seem to suggest that the worst may be over. Whether the progress achieved is regarded impressive not only by foreign governments sending missions to Mexico with the intent of copying Pronasol in their own countries[4], but also by the supposed beneficiaries must be doubted, especially after just in the poorest state of the Federation - which should have gained the most from Pronasol - an armed upsurge of impoverished peasants shook the fragile political stability on New Year's Day 1994.[5] In the following the essay will identify some of the reasons, why governments tend to be much more excited about schemes like Pronasol than some members of the target group.

---

[1] Between 1981 and 1985 the incidence of anemia rose by 18% and that of death by malnutrition itself by 35%, a trend particularly accentuated in the countryside. Cruz Rivero et al. (1991, 22-27).

[2] Lustig (1993, Table 8).

[3] González Gómez (1992, Cuadros 2 and 4).

[4] Among those delegations representatives of countries as diverse as Brazil, Costa Rica, India and China could be found. Compare *El Nacional* (March 31, 1993, 1) and Moffett (1993, 1).

[5] Even the rebellion of the *National Zapatista Liberation Army* (EZLN) in Chiapas was used as a proof that Pronasol works efficiently in combating the roots of poverty. According to the *Gaceta de Solidaridad* (1994, 3), Pronasol's official newspaper, Salinas paradoxically claims success, since the conflict was limited to four municipalities, whereas the remaining 2403 municipalities in the country are amidst a process of establishing "new hope" thanks to Pronasol!

3. Pronasol as a Poverty Alleviation Strategy

3.1. Basic Concepts of Pronasol

Representatives of the Salinas government were from the very beginning eager to admit that improving distributional and poverty related indicators could not be improved by simply waiting for some trickle down, especially as recent Mexican economic history does not suggest that this effect will ever materialize to any appreciable degree, at least if the reduction of the absolute number of the poor is the goal.[1] Lifting all the *extremely* poor of 1984 above the cutoff-income that separates the poor from the extremely poor with this hands-off approach would take half a century if we assume that the per capita growth rates of about 1% p.a. observed during 1988-90 would continue forever.[2] This estimate is overly optimistic since the numbers of the extremely poor actually increased after 1984 (Table 1) and the poor benefit only less than proportional from economic growth (Figure 1). Waiting for better times to arrive will thus clearly not do the job. At the same time the pressing need to reduce the government's fiscal deficit in order to avert the threat of hyperinflation made the recourse to traditional measures of letting general subsidies raining down on all kinds of goods and services obviously unfeasible and furthermore ideologically incompatible with the market driven economic reforms.

The alternative strategy would be an efficiently targeted social welfare program that addresses the most pressing needs of the poor - and the poor only. Pronasol was introduced as the measure in order to achieve exactly that. Progress in poverty alleviation for each peso spent was to be maximized by following four basic principles:[3]

- **Respect for Initiatives and Decisions of the Target-Group Communities.**
  Pronasol is not supposed to define what the needy lack most urgently or to dictate solutions to identified problems. Instead, the potential beneficiaries are to articulate

---

[1] Carlos Rojas Gutiérrez who became the head of Pronasol is quoted in Centeno (1991, 28) stating that "[e]conomic growth [through the 1970s] by itself did not bring about a redistribution of wealth; in fact, it helped increase inequality... Mexico enjoyed five decades of economic growth prior to the crisis, and yet the distribution of wealth did not become more equal." The Secretary of Pronasol's *Consejo Consultivo*, Enrique Tiburcio (1992, 7) agrees: "Nuestra práctica nos reclama que no se puede dejar el bienestar simplemente a los impulsos del crecimiento, se requiere de nuevos tejidos sociales y nuevas formas de acción pública que sustenten y accompañen al crecimiento económico."

[2] Lustig (1994, 3).

[3] PRONASOL (1993, 12-13), Rojas Gutiérrez (1992, 441), Tiburcio/de Alba (1992, 190).

their demands, to chose themselves the concrete projects to be undertaken and the strategies of realization. The exploitation of the superior decentralized local knowledge of what is needed and how it can be achieved is intended to reduce wasteful projects with unsatisfyingly high cost-benefit ratios that plagued traditional top-down planning.

- **Participation of the Communities at all Stages.** Pronasol intends to keep local communities involved in planning, decision making, implementation, control and evaluation of projects (the so-called "social control"). The extent of participation is most obvious in the implementation phase, since the benefiting community has to raise 20% of total funds itself [1] to complement Pronasol's resources by either providing unpaid direct labor input, monetary savings or local materials. This sacrifice is supposed to ensure that only those projects are pursued that are actually most desired by the poor themselves.

- **Shared Responsibility.** For each project an accepted and public agreement specifies the contributions, responsibilities and duties of the involved parties, i.e. the community and Pronasol.

- **Transparency and Honesty.** The public funds are entrusted to the community that is fully accountable and has to proof scrupulously that it has used them efficiently in the agreed project. [2]

These four principles are considered sufficient to secure that public funds are channeled directly and with minimum leakages to the poor and that abuse and corruption are kept under control. Since the initiative for projects supported by Pronasol resources is to come from the poor population itself there is a quasi-automatic guarantee that the projects chosen are perceived to have the highest utility for the very neighborhood. Not everything is possible, however. Pronasol statutes limit support to small-scale projects with a total value of no more than roughly US$30,000. They must be completed within one fiscal year and the funds should go toward physical investment projects only, i.e. demands for coverage of current expenditure of already existing infrastructure would *not* be eligible. [3]

---

[1] Bailey (1994, 19).

[2] The communities have to agree to prepare quarterly reports (even monthly until 1993) on the progress of project implementation (Bailey 1994, 18).

[3] Bailey (1994, 19).

3.2. Programs within Pronasol

Pronasol is subdivided into three separate spheres of action, *Solidarity for Social Well-Being, Solidarity for Production* and *Solidarity for Regional Development,* enumerated in descending order of their quantitative importance with the first one regularly absorbing well above half of the total budget. [1] Each of the three contains again a large and continuously growing number of subprograms.

- **Solidarity for Social Well-Being.** [2] This most important and best-known segment of Pronasol pursues productive projects that promise immediate alleviation from the most pressing social deficiencies. Typical measures - mostly provision of labor-intensive infrastructure - are found in sectors like health care (creating or improving medical units and hospitals), education (construction or renovation of schools and scholarship programs for potential drop-outs), food and distribution (establishment of stores and dairy outlets), potable water supply and sewerage systems (building, extending and repairing, especially in urban agglomerations), electrification, streets- and sidewalk-paving and -resurfacing, regularization of unresolved legal land ownership and the like.

- **Solidarity for Production.** In this field of activity Pronasol is supporting marginalized agricultural producers with low yields due to unfavorable production conditions or unexploited productive potential. Special funds are available for the support of indigenous communities (mainly in the south), for agricultural day laborers (mainly in the north) and sectoral programs assist projects for coffee growers, small scale miners and fishermen. Since 1992 marginalized entrepreneurs can also benefit through *Empresas en Solidaridad*, a program that channels risk capital into small firms without access to commercial bank credit. [3]

- **Solidarity for Regional Development.** This heading comprises a heterogeneous collection of long-term development projects in regions that have a high productive potential. Most of the projects are realized in the poorer southern states. [4]

---

[1] Tiburcio/de Alba (1992, 179) and Molinar Horcasitas/Weldon (1994).
[2] For a more detailed presentation of the separate programs consult Presidencia de la Republica (1992, 151-159), PRONASOL (1993) or *Consejo Consultivo* (1994).
[3] Olguín (1993) and Moffett (1993, 1).
[4] The comprehensive list in Consejo Consultivo (1994, cuadros 12 and A1).

3.3. Organization of Pronasol[1]

When Pronasol was created in December 1988 it started off being administered by the Planing Ministry (SPP) before being revalorized by being allocated as it's centerpiece to the newly created Ministry of Social Development (SEDESOL)[2], headed by Luis Donaldo Colosio, formerly the PRI's president and until his assassination in March 1994 his party's presidential candidate for 1994. But even under his successor in the presidential race and Colosio's former campaign manager - Ernesto Zedillo - who is likely to win the presidency until the year 2000, the personal preoccupation and presence of the head of the executive - known from Salinas[3] - is likely to continue and will keep Pronasol on top of the government's political agenda. Formally, the *Comisión del Programa Nacional de Solidaridad*, which is led by the President himself, is the highest executive body in which representatives of major federal ministries define strategies and general guidelines to be followed by Pronasol. The *Comisión* can draw on advice and expertise of the *Consejo Consultivo*, a "think tank" in which representatives of the states, indigenous groups, the social sectors and prestigious social scientists discuss the experience with the programs and strategies and formulate reforms in order to improve their functioning. The president signs an agreement with each of the state governors in which the details of the distribution of responsibilities among the different levels of government are laid down.[4] The *Comité de Evaluación* is responsible for the realization of studies on the social and economic impact of the implemented investments. SEDESOL maintains field offices (Delegaciones) in each of the states with a *Delegado* coordinating Pronasol's activities in the very state.

---

[1] Rojas Gutiérrez (1992, 442) and PRONASOL (1993, 15-19).

[2] The acronym of the <u>Se</u>cretario del <u>De</u>sarrollo <u>So</u>cial should be SEDESO. The final "L" makes SEDESOL sound similar as PRONASOL thus underlines semantically the central position of the latter within the former.

[3] Although the Pronasol "ad blitz nearly as extensive as the program itself" never mentions Salinas's name, "virtually all of the nearly-weekly trips he takes around the nation are wrapped around Solidarity projects" (Spencer 1993, 7). Salinas visited more than 250 projects in 177 municipalities between December 1988 and January 1992 alone (Méndez et al. 1992, 64-65).

[4] In fact Pronasol enters since 1989 as a special section into the more broad based Joint Development Agreements (*Convenios Únicos de Desarrollo,* CUD), which are a major document settling the relations between central and state governments.

The institutions which are at the heart of Pronasol and the real innovative ones are the *Comités de Solidaridad* (CS), in which the poor organize in order to plan and implement themselves the projects to be funded by Pronasol. The CS comprise on average eighty participating persons [1] and the more than 150,000 *comités* [2] are supposedly organized in a democratic manner with all representatives (president, secretary, treasurer) being elected by a public neighborhood assembly. However, not each single CS is a creation of ordinary citizens or autonomous grassroots activists, but it has been observed, that municipal authorities, local *caciques* or party functionaries frequently create committees themselves which they consequently preside and dominate [3], while other CS are existing in government files only and do not work at all. [4] Even if it is furthermore acknowledged that a substantial proportion of Solidarity Committees arose from previously existing community groups [5] and at times not much more than relabeling former organizational structures may have taken place in order to be able to draw on federal funds distributed through Pronasol, the mobilization effort following the introduction of the program is still substantial. It is the Solidarity Committees that handle all of the project work and exercise the "social control" once their proposals have been approved by the local SEDESOL delegation. [6] The Salinas administration gives this concept praise not only because it allegedly fosters democratization and decentralization (both claims will be discussed in the following chapter), but also because Pronasol is thus able to accomplish a substantial investment program without creating yet another inefficient and possibly corrupt bureaucracy which reduces dramatically the government's administrative outlays and is highly desirable in the light of the ongoing reforms of curtailing the public sector in general.

Since the use of Pronasol money is controlled not only by the Federal Audit Office (*Secretaría de la Controlaría General*) but also more directly by the vigilance of the

---

[1] Contreras and Bennett's (1994, 6) case study on the northern border area.

[2] This is the most recent number used in Salinas de Gortari (1993, 33).

[3] "Conviene mencionar la posibilidad de la existencia de varios CS por municipio presididas por Presidentes Municipales." Méndez et al. (1992, 61). Compare also Echeverría (1992, 40).

[4] Moguel (1992, 44-45).

[5] A case study of three border cities found that less than half (42%) of the surveyed CS were really newly established groups, with only one out of five committees not being a successor of a previous organization in Mexicali (Contreras/Bennett (1994, Table 15.1). However, since especially the state of Baja California is notorious for its extensive prior organizational experience this relabeling-frequency may well be much lower in Mexico as a whole.

[6] A detailed description of the application process and the project life cycle can be found in Bailey (1994, 16-20).

Solidarity Committees themselves (that would be directly hurt by the embezzlement of funds) the existence of illegal leakages or the misuse of public resources is probably less common than for traditional investment programs which improves the program's effectiveness even further. However, in the evolution and diversification of Pronasol more and more programs have been included that do not demand CS as a precondition for disbursements.[1] The neighborhood-oriented approach thus becomes diluted and the organizational concepts used progressively blurred.

Whether the organizational design with its emphasis on the role of community groups can really be considered as a major breakthrough on the road to a more participatory society in an increasingly decentralized political environment is not guaranteed, however. We will have to return to this question in the next chapter, when the political impact of Pronasol will be scrutinized.

3.4. Spending and Achievements of Pronasol

The Salinas *sexenio* will perhaps be remembered as the years when social expenditures of the Mexican state finally rose again. Table 2 summarizes some of the most important data of the big changes that occurred after 1988. While Pronasol was still not much more than 10% of all central government social spending it's share of GDP grew even faster (by 140% between 1989 and 1992) than social spending as a whole (+50%). The relative weight of Pronasol is even underestimated by those numbers, since the proportion of funds financed by the states grew from 29% to 37% during the same period and this rising amount has to be added to the federal government's outlays. The surge in social spending in general and of Pronasol in particular is even more astounding if we acknowledge that the share of the public sector in national economic activity actually shrunk at the same time. The positive development can therefore only be explained by a massive restructuring of the public expenditure pattern. Social expenditure absorbs today indeed more than half of the programmable federal budget (excluding debt service). This has been made possible by the drastic reduction of the country's debt burden brought about by lower interest rates and a major debt renegotiation deal in March 1989 under the Brady initiative.[2] While debt service payments more than doubled social spending as recently as 1989 this

---

[1] Bailey (1994, 14-15) mentions among others the programs for coffee growers and migrant workers, *Empresas de Solidaridad* and basically all regional programs.
[2] For details consult Kraemer (1991).

Table 2:
Indicators of Social- and Pronasol Spending

Year:	'83	'84	'85	'86	'87	'88	'89	'90	'91	'92	'93	'94
Social Expenditure/GDP [%]	6.7	6.7	6.9	6.6	6.2	6.0	6.1	6.4	7.8	9.0	9.5^F	10.2^F
Social Expenditure/ Programable Budget [%]	28.0	27.6	31.1	30.7	30.6	32.0	35.6	37.6	44.9	50.9	51.6^F	53.9^F
Social Inv./Social Expend. [%]	14.7	15.7	12.6	15.4	14.5	10.6	10.4	14.6	17.2	17.3	..	..
Soc.Expend./Debt Service [%]^A	..	..	..	0.38	..	0.33	0.47	0.64	1.29	1.94	..	..
Federal Pronasol Expenditure (bn. Pesos) [%]	..	..	..	..	..	..	1.6	3.3	5.2	6.8	7.6^B	8.8^E
Growth Federal Pronasol Expenditure [%]	..	..	..	..	..	..	..	106	58	31	12	16
States' Pronasol Spending/ Fed. Pronasol Spending [%]^D	..	..	..	..	..	..	0.29	0.32	0.31	0.37	..	..
Pronasol/Soc.Expend. [%]^C	..	..	..	..	..	..	7.4	11.1	11.3	12.3	..	..
Pronasol/GDP [%]^C	..	..	..	..	..	..	0.45	0.71	0.88	1.08	..	..

Sources: Peón (1992, Gráficas 1,2,4); ^{A} Rojas (1992, Cuadro 1); ^{B} Salinas de Gortari (1993, 33); ^{C} Lustig (1994, Tab. 5.3); ^{D} own calculation using Lustig (1994, Tab. 5.4); ^{E} Cano (1994, 39); ^{F} Aspe (1994, Gráfica 17).
.. Data not available.

relation has virtually been reversed since the government gained more financial breathing space. At the same time the poverty fighting effectiveness of each peso spent in the social sectors has improved since the share of new investment rose dramatically, which is at least partly due to Pronasol. With only 11% of all social spending in 1991 Pronasol contributed no less than 45.5% to aggregate social investments, thus providing a much greater number of new anti-poverty infrastructure in formerly discriminated poor areas than any other social program.[1] Critics point to the fact that not all of the funds were used productively in order to alleviate the incidence of poverty in Mexico, but a considerable percentage has been diverted into administration of the program and costly public relation efforts. Brushing through the vast number of publications and considering the presence of painted Pronasol

---
[1] Tiburcio/de Alba (1992, 188).

symbols in the streets[1] the casual observer finds it hard to disagree that this might indeed be the case. Even after insisting on the question of the proportion of funds absorbed by administration in Pronasol's headquarters in México D.F. the author could get no precise information. Officials conceded, however, that the proportion is probably unacceptably high. But this had been due to the fact that, being a new instrument, Pronasol's need to make itself known and therefore invest in PR activities had been extraordinarily high in the first years. The unsatisfying ratio of administration costs relative to total spending would disappear automatically once the intentions and functioning of Pronasol are widely understood.

But monetary indicators do only tell part of the story and Pronasol's weight in social policy may well be more important since a significant part of investment costs does not appear in the budget of either the state- or central government.[2] This is especially true for the provision of unpaid self-help by the communities themselves that contributes to creating assets but is "free" for the public sector. "Because citizen participation minimizes labor costs and reduces waste, the program's price tag [..] is far less than what the government would have paid to do the work itself."[3] Road building project costs could thus be reduced to 70% of earlier outlays and school repair costs to a mere 60%. Some social progress conducted by Pronasol does furthermore not require any own funds at all and other agencies cover the costs, such as the more than one million acts of regularization of land property rights.[4] From a poverty alleviation point of view, critical arguments like comparing the superficially higher real social expenditures in the early 1980s with the ones in the early 1990s have to be interpreted with caution[5], since neither improvements in targeting nor the importance of complementary resources is taken into account.

While the input (money) into Pronasol may still appear modest, the output's share (infrastructure) is probably much more significant due to the "hidden taxation" of the poor and to efficiency gains. According to official sources the money for the projects

---

[1] A Pronasol-painting does not always mean that the building has actually been created or renovated with SEDESOL-funds. The author was visiting a school in Ocotlán de Morelos (Oaxaca) in March 1994 with "Escuela Digna" and "Solidaridad" written on its walls in massive letters. Asking the schools employees they contested that any Pronasol activities apart from the paintings had taken place.

[2] "The increasing visibility and scope of Pronasol suggest that it operates with a much larger pool of resources than those presented in the public account." Dresser (1991, 5).

[3] Moffett (1993, A1).

[4] Méndez et al (1992, 62-63).

[5] Moguel (1992, 42).

does stem from curtailing other state expenditures, especially interest payments and the divestiture of public enterprises.[1] The government keeps on stressing the latter in order to make the socially risky privatizations more acceptable to the poor public. Since there is no information available whether there exists any formal earmarking mechanism that links Pronasol expenditure to privatization revenues, this claim can be declared to be merely rhetoric and without any real substance. And this is a good thing, too. An explicit privatization-Pronasol link would reduce social policy to a residual variable connected to an absolutely unrelated income source. A minor part of the funding does also come from donors abroad, most notably the World Bank.[2]

Without getting lost in too much details a quick look at the achievements so far underscores the impact Pronasol has had until 1992.[3] The *Escuela Digna* program that built and maintained 74,000 educational facilities has thereby helped 12 million pupils, whereas 750,000 children from low income background obtained money- and in-kind support in order to prevent their dropping out of school (Niños de Solidaridad). By building 1,110 rural medical units Pronasol increased capacity by 50% relative to 1988. 1,7 million families that have settled in areas with unclear property rights obtained land titles while an additional 13.5 million (11.5 million) Mexicans have today access to safe drinking water (drainage systems) and 16 million more have electricity. While there is absolutely no way to check whether these numbers are a gross exaggeration, Pronasol's achievements are certainly by no means minuscule, even if scepticism leads one to discount the administration's self-praise.

Can the reduction in poverty between 1989 and 1992 ascertained by the INEGI/CEPAL study (Table 1) be attributed to Pronasol or do we observe an example of "good luck rather than good policy"? There are some arguments beyond the mere quantitative boost of real social expenditures and better control of the use of the funds that seem to support this connection between Pronasol activities and poverty reduction.

---

[1] Tiburcio (1992, 4) and Presidencia de la República (1992, 151).

[2] The Bank made US$350m available (roughly 1bn Pesos) between 1990 and 1993 conditional to additional US$700m to be raised by the Mexican government and the investment of those funds in the four poorest states (Oaxaca, Chiapas, Hidalgo and Guerrero). *La Jornada* (Sept. 1, 1993).

[3] Almost all official publications concerning Pronasol boast with the positive effects that are said to be brought about by the program. The most recent one (Salinas de Gortari 1993, p.33) is used here. For a more detailed list compare PRONASOL (1993, 20,22,24 and 27) and somewhat differing *Consejo Consultivo* (1994, Cuadro A2).

* **Self Targeting.** Most of the projects require some input by the beneficiaries themselves, usually labor. This "cofinancing" device can work as a mechanism introducing an element of self selection that directs the funds automatically towards the poor, since the implicit taxation in terms of the value of the "lost" time (absorbed by activities in the project) is higher the higher the wage of the respective individual. Pronasol is therefore particularly attractive to people with low or no opportunity costs of time, e.g. the poor, unemployed or seasonally underemployed campesinos.

* **High Investment Share.** The extraordinary high share of investment in total Pronasol expenditure relative to conventional social programs means that under its auspices a great number of *new* facilities have been built. Since the richer states are already comparatively well equipped and therefore incur basically current costs rather than investment the latter will mainly occur in marginalized and rural areas. The distribution of health posts, schools etc. is thus likely to have improved.

* **Regional Targeting of Federal Subsidies.** The amount of transfers of federal resources depends on the per capita income of the recipient states. While the poorest states receive up to three fourths of the total project costs, the richer state have to provide half of the costs themselves by making state money and community resources available.[1] This link between subsidies and income level leads to a situation in which the regions where the need is greatest receive, *ceteris paribus*, a relatively more generous share than richer states. While *ex ante* nothing can be said about the distribution of benefits *within* each state, the *inter*state distribution of Pronasol funds makes an effective onslaught on poverty feasible.

3.5. Criticism of Pronasol

This is only one side of the story, of course. Other arguments maintain that by the way Pronasol is designed important drawbacks are incorporated and it is therefore no effective instrument to face the challenge of poverty reduction. Some of the most commonly pronounced criticisms however do not really address Pronasol itself, but at their core point at something else. Some critics, for example, reject Pronasol not for its own features, but rather because they see it as a measure connected with the

---

[1] Spencer (1993, 7) and Gershberg (1994, 4).

neoliberal economic strategy which they condemn on its own behalf.[1] This is not a criticism of Pronasol as such. The argument that Pronasol funds are too small to make any real dent will not be followed further either, since the mechanisms of Pronasol are quite unaffected by the total amount of funds flowing into the program (which, as we have established above, are anyway higher than the budgetary incidence might suggest). There are nonetheless a large number of critical judgments that should be taken more seriously and some of them will now be briefly analyzed.

- **Pronasol Doesn't Reach the Poorest**[2]. Even if it were accepted that Pronasol projects are generally efficient in eradicating poverty and funds are targeted into the most depressed regions and states it is by no means certain, that the very poorest communities get the assistance they need. The initiative for projects has to come from the community and it appears at the least dubious, whether the neediest groups are the ones that have a comparative advantage in easily organizing and applying for Pronasol support. Considering that "more than a third of adults in recent years have been classified as functionally illiterate"[3] and that achieved educational levels are lowest among the ultra-poor[4] it must be doubted, whether the most marginalized neighborhoods are always in a position to fight their way through the formal application process and project implementation. On the other hand, since most of the projects are non-marketable investments rather than cash transfers it is at least unlikely that the unequal intrahousehold distribution[5] leads to an usurpation by the best off family members (usually male household heads), leaving the poorer family members as miserable as before. Instead, the poorest of all groups, i.e. minors, cannot be excluded from the positive effects. Thus, while it is not clear whether the poorest households benefit from Pronasol at least the poorest in the households that do benefit will gain.

---

[1] The argument that Pronasol is of a merely compensatory nature has been put most eloquently by Denise Dresser (quoted in Smith, 1992, 11): "Just like the wife of the industrialist who organizes soup kitchens to benefit the poor that her husband creates, the Salinas government distributes selective subsidies to the population its economic policies impoverish." Cf. also Moguel (1992, 41-42) and Bailey (1994, 3) for the example of Pronasol's production fund for coffee growers, and Peniche (1992, 23) de la Peña Valencia (1992, 88: "Aspe los hace y Rojas los redime. Sólo que el de Hacienda es más rápido y eficiente que el de Pronasol") for a general critique.

[2] Lustig (1994, 16).

[3] Mexico Service (1991, 13).

[4] Table 9 in Lustig (1993).

[5] Banamex (1993b, 146).

On the other hand, if the poor households are reached by some of the projects in the first phase it must be doubted, whether the benefits distributed among the most deprived groups - e.g. by the installation of social infrastructure - can be sustained in the longer run. In Pronasol's Chalco showcase the introduction of electricity, drainage and other services led to a situation where the most marginalized groups were incapable to pay the related fees and had no choice but to move once more as invaders to places that resembled very much the place Chalco had been before the program arrived there. [1]

Since in it is not uncommon for Mexican neighborhoods that very poor and rather prosperous people coexist pretty closely, the socioeconomic structure in the Solidarity Committees tends to be equally mixed. In this surrounding it can be supposed that the intellectually more adequately prepared better-off people more or less control the decisions of the community. Meeting a CS in Cuernavaca in March 1994 the author found the group under the firm leadership of a few middle class families. This resulted in a decision to pave the street connecting the community with the main road rather than installing lacking basic infrastructure such as drainage or sanitary installations in the squatter-homes of the poorer neighborhood members.

- **Technological Problems.** Some projects may be unsuitable for untrained communities. The construction of many investments does require special technical skills that may not be prevailing among the poor. Therefore money is wasted due to unqualified implementation and the effect of each peso spent is therefore much lower than it could be if the investment were contracted to a specialized individual or firm. [2] But these efficiency losses need not be too substantial since the local know-how and innovative potential even among untrained people should by no means be underestimated. Furthermore the costs will be reduced when the community moves down the learning curve and in aggregate they are unlikely to outweigh the efficiency costs caused by unmotivated and corrupt administrators that would be present in alternative program designs.

---

[1] Cano (1994, 40).

[2] "Turning teachers, clerks and cooks into a construction crew wasn't easy, however. When they first tried mixing cement, they used an entire 50-pound sack for just a short stretch of sidewalk, and the sidewalk soon crumbled." Moffett (1993, A6).

- **Structural Causes of Poverty are not Tackled**[1]. According to some critics, Pronasol cannot efficiently eradicate the incidence of poverty, since the main causes are not addressed. This is only half right. While population pressure, labor markets, social discrimination or austerity measures do indeed play no part in the concepts used, other structural reasons are considered. The achievement of a more equal access to educational or health services, for example, is imminent in core programs of Pronasol. There are various measures intended to raise labor productivity and thus the income of the poor.

- **Immediate Effect on Poverty is Negligible.** Pronasol has been accused of not doing enough to reduce the immediate impact of poverty. Most projects create social infrastructure that may increase the poor's productivity and self help potential, but transfers in order to offer short term relief has been the exception to the rule. For that reason some critics demand that programs like *Niños en Solidaridad* that provides scholarships for poor children should be expanded, since they combine the advantages of immediate relief with a more long term productivity effect. On the other hand, the claim that Pronasol created very few job opportunities[2] needs not be perfectly true. Since the introduction of Pronasol has increased the percentage of physical investment within social spending programs (cf. Table 2, line 3), the backward linkages to the construction sector can be considerable.

- **The upper limit of project size is too small.** The Solidarity Committees will not be granted any support for projects whose costs exceed the peso equivalent of about US$30,000 or which take more than one year to complete. Accepting Pronasol's basic philosophy that the communities ought to know best what is needed in order to ease their burden it appears slightly arbitrary to impose that the most pressing needs may not cost more than the upper limit or take longer to realize. Some high priority projects are thus out of reach and the average poverty eradication potential of Pronasol projects may therefore be artificially depressed. There are some good arguments in favor of the ceilings however. The first one is the pragmatic reasoning that smaller projects allow to spread given funds among a larger number of communities.[3] Unlimited funds might furthermore tempt

---

[1] Dresser (1991, 12).
[2] Lustig (1994, 15).
[3] Cano (1994, 40).

communities to ask for conspicuous, but economically suboptimal projects such as hospitals instead of primary health care units.[1] Besides, bigger projects are more complex and difficult to handle. Only a few neighborhoods would possess the managerial skills necessary to efficiently administer and implement much bigger projects. Since the poorest communities are not very likely to dispose of these skills the first criticism mentioned above appears even more relevant. More important, the limit is not valid for all types of projects in the same way. Some "big ticket" programs like potable water and sewerage systems or regional programs do apparently exceed the capacity of a single Committee.[2] Where a CS application is not preconditional, the US$ 30,000 ceiling does not hold and more ambitious endeavours can be aimed for.

- **Urban Bias.** It has been claimed, that "la preocupación por los sectores pobres es mucho mayor en las zonas urbanas que en las rurales y es muy bajo el número de reuniones con los sectores indígenas."[3] If that were true Pronasol would indeed care mainly for people not living in the poorest, i.e. rural, areas. This "urban bias" has been derived by analyzing the kind of projects personally visited by Salinas, of which 57% were urban, 27% rural and only 5% concerned with the particular needs of the indigenous. This interpretation is highly misleading, however. Practical travel reasons may well account for this disequilibrium. Besides it is not the President's presence that matters but rather the funds disbursed. An empirical analysis of the statewise distribution of Pronasol funds in 1991 actually found exactly the opposite. There was a significant *negative* correlation between the percentage of the population living in metropolitan areas (more than 100,000 inhabitants) and Pronasol spending, while a higher share of a state's indigenous population actually *increased* per capita disbursements.[4] For the *Escuela Digna* subprogram (which absorbed 8% of the total Pronasol budget in 1992)[5] it has been found that having a large population in middle sized cities (between 2,500 and 100,000 inhabitants) increases Pronasol spending, whereas a large proportion of the state's population living in large cities (>100,000) reduces funds availability.[6] States with middle sized urban agglomerations may therefore be

---
[1] Lustig (1994, 16).
[2] Bailey (1994, 15).
[3] Méndez et al (1992, 65). Also Peña Valencia (1992, 85).
[4] Molinar Horacitas/Weldon (1994, Table 7.7).
[5] Jiménez Badillo (1992, Cuadro 5).
[6] Gershberg (1994, 15 and Table 13.2).

favored relative to others. This is a mild version of urban bias, but the state level studies do not allow any valid conclusions on *where* the funds are invested on the micro level, i.e. the investment may take place in rural areas of predominantly urban states and vice versa. In the subprogram *Fondos Municipales* (1992: 6.6% of total budget), for example, a clause exists that ensures, that an urban bias on the micro-level is impossible: "Only a maximum of 25% can be spent in the municipal seat, unless that community has at least two-thirds of the municipality's population, in which case it can receive up to 40% of the money."[1] The available evidence backing a preference for the (better off) urban agglomerations to the detriment of poor rural communities is therefore pretty shaky, if not undefendable.

- **Implicit Taxation of the Poor.**[2] It can be argued that the positive effects on the poor's welfare is much lower than it appears by brushing through the government's enumeration of physical achievements. The reason lies in the regulation that the poor have to pay directly a part of the cost in the form of free labor, materials or cash. While this may be considered as a voluntary decision (although social pressure in the Committees may occasionally force a minority to accept agreements "voluntarily" that make them personally even worse off), it still remains an implicit form of taxation whenever the opportunity costs exceed zero - which they usually do. While no estimates on this effect do yet exist, it may suffice to stress that the distributional incidence of "Do-it-Yourself"-antipoverty programs like Pronasol can be less favorable than they superficially appear.

4. Pronasol and the Mexican Political System

4.1. How the Political System influences Pronasol

From the very beginning it was clear, that Solidaridad was the brainchild of the inner circle around President Salinas himself and at least partly designed in order to restore the damaged legitimacy of Mexico's one party democracy after the 1988 presidential elections that brought him to power. In order to appreciate Salinas's political strategy followed with Pronasol it is worth reading his academic thesis about the connection

---

[1] Bailey (1994, 19).
[2] Lustig (1994, 12).

between public investment and support for the system in rural Mexico, in which he concludes that "[t]he fact that the State granted [..] resources without having been asked for them meant that the public works program [...] could not inspire attitudes of support for the system. [...] [A] State which does not permit the participation of its citizens runs the risk of losing not only instrumental efficiency, but also its very legitimacy."[1] However, he also recognized the danger, that participation and local leadership may actually undermine support for the system by creating a more self conscious and politically aware population. The task ahead was therefore twofold: to restore legitimacy by increasing participation in everyday politics without destroying the fragile and dwindling support for the PRI-dominated hegemonic political system. Pronasol was and still is a major strategic tool in order to circumvent this policy dilemma. One obvious way of trying to combine legitimacy-saving participation with resurging support for the political status quo (i.e. the PRI) is by linking expenditures to electoral events and indicating in a subtle way that the communities owe support for the party in exchange for the material reward of Pronasol projects. While the government avoids to openly equate Pronasol with the ruling party and Salinas prohibited any PRI rallies at his weekly tours of visiting Pronasol projects, more indirect ways to let Pronasol popularity work for the party are followed. It is not only Salinas's massive involvement that secures higher support for presidentialism and the prevailing structure as a whole, since people perceive that if not the PRI itself than at least its most important politician is responsible for the material blessings.[2] A more symbolic link is established by letting the Pronasol logo resemble very much the one of the PRI, both using the colors of the Mexican flag. Thus a symbolic melange of national pride, social justice and the party is created with identifying the latter (which might be considered as negative by many) with the former two (sentiments which are fullheartedly supported by most Mexicans).[3]

The strategic task for the party in power is to maximize support with the given Pronasol resources. Since popular backing of the party is not equally important at all points of time, but should first of all be high at times of elections many analysts maintained that the temptation to follow a political budget cycle (with statewise spending being boosted if state elections for governors are coming up and being lower in states where elections are still far away) must have proofed irresistible. As we will see in the

---

[1] Salinas de Gortari (1982, 40 and 42).
[2] Basáñez (1991, 4).
[3] According to a 1991 poll 76% are "very proud" to be Mexican (Basáñez 1991, 5).

next section the central government has indeed the discretionary power to distribute funds in that manner if it would chose to do so. Earlier evidence of this partisan manipulation in the literature consisted basically of anecdotes of particular projects, most frequently referring to the Chalco 2000 electrification and water project in México State, heavy Pronasol activism before the state elections in the left wing stronghold of Michoacán (12% of all spending in 1992 was directed to that state comprising only 4% of the population) and the international bridge (called "Solidarity"!) linking Nuevo Leon with the US.[1] The fact that the head of the newly created Social Development Ministry (SEDESOL) which is responsible for Pronasol's management came straight from being the PRI's president enhanced the suspicion that partisan abuse of public social spending is widespread. The *dedazo* in late 1993 in which Salinas chose Luis Donaldo Colosio as the PRI's presidential candidate and thus his likely successor has to be interpreted in this light as well. Picking Colosio further enhanced the Party-Pronasol link and was nothing less than an inherent promise to continue Pronasol policies all over the country during the coming *sexenio*. It is interesting to note, however, that the perception of the Mexican people of Pronasol as a concept used for electoral ends has decreased constantly and only a negligible proportion of those surveyed in late 1992 still mentioned this aspect.[2]

While all those arguments are highly speculative in nature there has been some empirical research that tries to establish this suspicion econometrically. The earliest and still unsophisticated attempt has been pursued by Piñeyro (1992), whose tendentious chapter headings ("PronaPRI", "Pronapopulismo") made quite explicit what result he wanted to find. His thesis that conspicuous and visible programs were particularly expanded before the august 1991 federal elections are actually partly contradicted by the data he presents himself. He explicitly mentions water and sewerage projects and *Escuela Digna* as electorally effective subprograms. However, his data indicates that the number of works in both programs grew at a *lower* rate from 1990 to 1991 than Pronasol's budget as a whole. Besides he doesn't let the reader know, why he considered the mentioned subprograms as particularly prone to partisan manipulation. On the other hand his remarks concerning the road infrastructure program are extremely interesting. While in 1989 and 1990 the mileage of

---

[1] Compare Dresser (1991, 23 and 1994, 13-14, 17-18), Scott (1992), Moffett (1991) and Ward (1994, 13-14). Dresser (1991, 24) remarks that "cheap" benefits were also very popular with the government: "[T]wo weeks before the midterm election of August 1991, Salinas toured Mexico and personally handed out in less than ten days as many land titles as distributed by the Mexican government over the past fourteen years."

[2] Banamex (1993a, 78).

maintained and newly constructed roads were more or less equal, this relation changed dramatically in 1991, when the latter, far more conspicuous, exceeded the former by almost 350%! This sudden gap narrowed again in 1992 once the crucial midterm elections were over. [1]

Contradictory results are also obtained by Gershberg's (1994) analysis of the *Escuela Digna* program, using 1990 data. In an inter-state OLS regression he finds support for the thesis that states received more money if there was higher support for Cardenas' PRD in the 1988 elections. Thus the claim that the PRI tries to bribe those states and buy votes off the (illoyal) opposition. Due to the inherent weakness of interstate studies concerning the distribution on the microlevel, Gershberg's second regression on the *municipal* distribution of *Escuela Digna-* and *Niños en Solidaridad*-money within Mexico State is better suited to test the hypothesis that the funds are used for partisan reasons. Interestingly the result sharply contradicts the interstate regression and is more significant, too. On the more relevant municipal level Pronasol appears to *punish* oppositional communities by (*ceteris paribus*) reducing spending instead of trying to buy their votes! The relation between oppositional strength and social investment is therefore not as clear as maintained by many analysts.

Probably the most thorough empirical research on the hypothesized political motivation of Pronasol spending has been conducted by Molinar Horcasitas and Weldon (1994). Their interstate regressions analyze spending in 1990 for Pronasol as a whole and the three subprograms separately. While most of the political variables do not come to be statistically very significant the authors find some interesting results, which partly help to explain Gershberg's inconsistent findings. Infrastructure spending within the Pronasol budget thus correlated positively with PRI support in the 1988 elections (i.e. loyal supporters reap benefits) as long as no state elections were due in 1991. If that was the case, however, the PRI-loyal states received *cet. par.* less (i.e. among states with upcoming elections money was channeled into opposition strongholds). Analyzing total spending of all Pronasol categories in 1990 the authors derive an astonishing result. PRD strongholds were generally lightly punished if no state-governor elections were due in 1991, but bribed if there were elections (Table 7.9 and 7.10). The spending pattern was different when it came to states where the conservative *Partido de Acción Nacional* (PAN) could gather substantial support in 1988. While no significant relation between the PAN's showing in 1988 and Pronasol

---

[1] *Consejo Consultivo* (1994, figure A13).

spending exists if no state election was due in 1991 PAN-states were heavily punished by Pronasol's withdrawal of funds if elections were due. According to the theory of a political budget cycle this means that if elections were coming up Pronasol redirected its support from PAN and PRI states to PRD states. Molinar Horcasitas and Weldon conclude that "[a]ccording to that strategy, PANistas are not as easily converted as Cardenistas, especially since many of the latter had once voted for the PRI, while the former have long voted for the opposition. It is much more efficient to try to reconvert to the official party those who were recently lost."[1] In other words, the PRI tries to maximize the marginal return in terms of voter support for each Pronasol peso spent and perceives that it is higher in PRD states like Estado de México or Michoacán rather than in northern PAN strongholds.[2] Since the typical PAN voter is better off middle-class and thus not directly benefiting a lot from Pronasol projects it makes perfect sense to redirect money towards PRD voters whose probability to live in poverty is much higher. Besides the PAN has proofed to be an opposition loyal to the PRI in a sense that it embraces similar economic ideologies and frequently supported the government's proposals in congress. "Buying" PANistas is therefore not only more costly than bribing PRDistas, but the consequences of a state lost to the PAN would also be less dramatic for the PRI than if the aggressive opposition of the PRD could take over a governorship.

Was this flexible strategy successful? In a second set of regressions the same authors claim that Pronasol strategies contributed significantly to the PRI's electoral recovery in the *federal* elections of 1991. In states with no gubernatorial elections in 1991 the marginal effect of Pronasol spending on electoral support was slightly *negative* (!), but the relationship becomes highly positive where *state* elections were due. The authors offer no explanation how this difference may come about. It is not apparent at all why the marginal return in terms of votes (in federal elections) of a Pronasol peso should be significantly different - and even have a different sign! - between states with simultaneous state elections on the one hand and those without on the other. A similar unexplained paradox can be observed in the analysis of determinants of the change in support for the PAN, while the regional distribution of Pronasol funds in 1990 did not have any measurable effect on the vote for the leftist Cardenista opposition (PRD). While the electoral calendar seems to influence Pronasol's spending behavior, Molinar

---

[1] Molinar Horcasitas/Weldon (1994, 13).

[2] Dresser (1994, 17) observes that "assisted by Pronasol funds, the PRI spent nearly twice as much to combat the PRD in Michoacán as it did to run against the PAN in Chihuahua."

Horcasita's and Weldon's conclusion that "there [is] strong evidence to support the claim that Pronasol is not only electorally driven, but that is also electorally effective"[1] has to be interpreted with some caution.

That the strategy of bribing the population in oppositional states and thus "buying" their vote is not as efficient as the PRI could have hoped for becomes pretty clear if it is considered that "in the gubernatorial elections in Michoacán [...] each vote for the PRI cost US$70 compared with just over $2 per vote for the PRD."[2] What are the possible reasons that could explain, why the electoral effect of Pronasol's regional spending pattern is more ambiguous than the evidence of an existing electoral budget cycle?

One explanation may be that the population, despite of the Public Relations battle on Pronasol's behalf, does not at all recognize that it is benefiting from a Pronasol project and has therefore no reason to thank the PRI by voting for it. Especially in states governed by the PAN the misperception concerning the source of the funds may even induce the population to vote for the PAN instead of the PRI if the former gets credit for what the latter's politicians actually distribute. In the border area, for example "due to a lack of precise information on the projects and how Solidarity works, a very low proportion of direct beneficiaries know that the improvements under way in their immediate surroundings [...] are being carried out by Solidarity. [...] Only 25% knew that there were Solidarity projects in their neighborhood."[3]

A second reason for the unclear relationship between spending and support lies in the perception that different socioeconomic groups hold of Pronasol. While it appears to be popular with almost everyone there are interesting differences if we disaggregate for certain demographic characteristics.[4] Surprisingly, while 57.7% of peasants and unemployed judge Pronasol as "good" the proportion of businessmen, employees and persons in leading positions is much higher (between 66 and 71%)! In other words, the actual or potential beneficiaries feel the least positive about the program, while Mexicans belonging to the upper (that are most unlikely to gain directly by any of Pronasol's projects) show the strongest support. Even if they identify the projects going on as Pronasol ones, the direct beneficiaries are therefore less likely to

---

[1] Molinar Horcasitas/Weldon (1994, 17).
[2] Ward (1994, 14).
[3] Contreras/Bennett (1994, 9).
[4] This paragraph uses poll data published by *Este País* (Oct. 1991, 9-11).

exchange funds for votes than the non-poor. Thus the pattern of regional distribution is of lesser influence determining the PRI's share of votes than assumed by proponents of the "regional spending-regional support" hypothesis. If non-recipients react electorally most sensitive, it is not as decisive *where* Pronasol invests, but rather *how much* it invests. Another interesting finding of the 1991 poll is that the perception of Pronasol gets better as further north we look. The north-south divide could mean, that the perceived identification of Pronasol as a PRI program is not very strong. Whereas the PRI is stronger in the south, only 59% judge Pronasol there as "good", while in the northern states, where the PRI had continuous electoral troubles, 74% have a positive opinion of the program. Similarly, while PRI voters are on average older than the national average [1], Pronasol support decreases with age. While Salinas himself is certainly strongly identified with Pronasol his party in contrast may not be successful to translate the agreement with social investment into partisan support, since the PRI is not perceived to be responsible for the progress.

4.2. How Pronasol Influences the Political System

The preceding arguments were mainly of a short- or medium-term nature. There is a considerable potential that Pronasol could be able to shape the way the Mexican political system will look like in the longer run. The influence is therefore mutual. This section discusses how this change in various aspects of the political environment could be brought about.

- **Promotion of the Civil Society.** The fact that tens of thousands of Solidarity Committees have sprung up is in the government's view an impressive proof that Mexico is heading towards a more participatory and politically open society. According to the official belief the direct democracy practiced in the Solidarity Committees will finally spill over into the realm of "real" politics and hence transform the country's political environment into a liberal democracy. The head of the *Consejo Consultivo*, Enrique González Tiburcio for example claims that thanks to Pronasol "la sociedad se hace más activa y participativa, y con ello se inicia la demanda de un nuevo sentido para la política social"[2], whereas Carlos Rojas,

---

[1] Arroyo Alejandre et al. (1988, Cuadros 10 and 11).

[2] Tiburcio (1992, 4). Compare also Scott (1991) and Tiburcio/de Alba (1992, 192-193): "En nuestro país [...] se ha tratado de dar cuerpo a una nueva relación con la sociedad civil. [...] El programa asume sus consecuencias inmediatas: movilización y participación, exigencia al gobierno y vigilancia creciente."

Pronasol's General Coordinator goes even further in stating that "se contribuye [...] al desarrollo de la cultura política en el país."[1] But whether or not the mobilization involved with the Solidarity Committees is a precursor of a more democratic, politically aware and active society depends on several caveats.[2]

First of all, very little is known about how the decisions are actually made within the CS. While the Pronasol guidelines scheduled perfectly democratic procedures for the Committees, the real power structure can look different. The heroic one-man-one-vote assumption will never occur in its pure form. Instead influence and control will always be unequally distributed according to rhetoric and managerial skills or economic power. It would therefore be crucial to know, *who* typically controls the CS. From the empirical results of Salinas' own academic work we know that there exists some awareness among the ruling politicians that higher participation of the population is likely to backfire politically: "The State confronts a dilemma: if it wants to increase productivity and efficiency in the rural sector through collective participation, it may have to do so at the expense of political support."[3] The poor are generally less active in politics than their better off compatriots. Since risk aversion towards change is - for obvious reasons - highest among the poor they tended to give at least their electoral support to the ruling party, if they do not abstain. Even though some degree of discontent may prevail it appeared for many among the poor less unattractive to vote for a continuation of the known grievances than to risk facing unknown new ones that might harm them even more. Scattered evidence seems to support the thesis, that the poor tend to support the PRI more than the national average.[4] If the Solidarity Committees introduce more participation and political awareness this could lead to the situation that the formerly passive poor recognize that autonomous political organizations - rather than PRI paternalism - is sometimes more advantageous for them. For the first time they may get the impression that there exists a choice for them while before they might have taken the party's near monopoly in political mobilization for

---

[1] Rojas Gutiérrez (1992, 443).

[2] The stereotype perception of Mexicans as phlegmatic and unpolitical citizens is an erroneous one anyway. During the 1980s political activism soared. The proportion of Mexicans that have either signed a petition, followed a boycott, participated in demonstrations/unofficial strike activities or occupied production plants/public buildings is now as high as in Canada (16%) and well above the figure for the U.S.(12%) *(Este País* Julio 1993, 17, figure 8).

[3] Salinas de Gortari (1982, 40).

[4] An investigation for the metropolitan area of Guadalajara found that "respecto al ingreso, los porcentajes más altos en favor del PRI se encuentran en grupos económicos muy polarizados: entre la población con ingresos más bajos (que ganan por debajo del salario mínimo) [...] y aquel sector de la población con los ingresos más altos." Arroyo Alejandre et al. (1988, 7).

granted. This leads to a reduction in electoral support of a substantial group of traditional PRI voters. The party, of course, will try to circumvent this dilemma by dominating as many CS as it possibly can. The party's organizational and personal capacity and the still overwhelming political strength on the local level [1] seem to make this strategy feasible in most cases. While no nationwide studies are yet available the evidence seems to suggest, that the PRI has followed that strategy with some notable degree of success. Municipal authorities (the vast majority consist of PRI affiliates) frequently take the initiative to create Committees which they subsequently preside. [2] In three northern cities more than one-fourth of all CS have explicit links to a political party, with the vast majority (90.4%) to the PRI. [3] More than one-third of all Committee presidents are members of a political party and an additional 27% in trade unions. While the data is not specific about party affiliation, it is more than likely that due to its massive membership and leadership experience most of those leaders will belong to the PRI or sympathizing unions.

The positive effect on the development of a civil society is further hampered by the fact that the majority of Solidarity Committees arose from preexisting community organizations. [4] This indicates that there exists a danger that the need to form a CS in order to be formally eligible for funding actually *undermines* social mobilization because autonomous grassroots organizations that have been created from below are frequently transformed into Solidarity Committees that depend on (PRI dominated) local governments and SEDESOL delegations. [5]

Some analysts further observed that since most of the Committees are not of a permanent nature, but usually dissolved after a project has been finished, the lasting political impact of these purely instrumental Committees is minimal. [6] While this may be true in some cases, the CS do usually have a life span that exceeds the construction phase of social infrastructure since "once projects are completed, the municipal

---

[1] In 1990 the PRI still held 95% of all municipal governments. Cornelius/Craig (1991, 61).

[2] Méndez et al. (1992, 61) and Albarrán de Alba (1994, 39).

[3] Contreras/Bennett (1994, Table 15.1).

[4] Contreras/Bennett (1994, Table 15.1).

[5] "Los Comités de Solidaridad [...] no deben competir con las organizaciones sociales que han sido construidas *desde abajo* y con el esfuerzo de años de pobladores urbanos y campesinos." Moguel (1992, 47). *El Uniersal* of Feb.18, 1992 writes: "El Programa [...] logró su objetivo de inmovilizar políticamente a la sociedad del Valle de Chalco, que desde su fundación en 1979 se caracterizó por ser luchadora por sus derechos. Así lo afirmó Alejandro Tapia González consejero político del [...] PRI." Cited in *El Cotidiano* 49, Julio-agosto 1992, 47.

[6] Méndez et al. (1992, 62).

government turns each over to its neighborhood committee, which then administers and maintains the project."[1] The institutional preconditions for a more sustained assistance to civil society are therefore given. Whether the potential can be used fruitfully or not depends primarily on the local existence of politically ambitious and autonomous leadership personalities. While many of the CS are still under the firm grip of party officials and autonomous grassroots NGOs are yet bought off with Pronasol funds, this presence is not all too likely. Colosio's insistence that the radical societal transformation has already been accomplished may therefore be regarded as premature at best.[2]

However, there are also encouraging signs. While it is true that just over a meager 13% of the beneficiaries directly participate actively in the projects and three out of four Committees only have a minimal organizational structure[3], forwarding proposals as well as effective decision making usually occur in the assemblies.[4] This means that democratic procedures are generally followed within the Committees. But this holds much less true for areas where prior social mobilization outside the PRI-corporatist structure is lower than in the studied sample. "In contrast [to Tijuana], in the context of Mexicali, where committees were created without the pressure of intense political competition and where PRI-controlled federal agencies and organizations exerted strong influence, the result is greater official control. This inhibits Solidarity's potential organizational impact. [...] Most initiatives [...] come from the leadership, neighborhood assemblies participate only marginally in decision making."[5] In such a surrounding of the communities' dependence on its leader it is possible, that authoritarian Committee presidents degenerate into a new generation of *caciques* that are as local power brokers hardly ever accountable elected bodies and subject to virtually no social control.

- **Decentralization.** The official view sees Pronasol as an important tool to foster more decentralized decision making, which in itself is considered to be imperative

---

[1] Bailey (1994, 18).
[2] "Hoy los supuestos del estado paternalista y asistencial están totalmente superados." Colosio (1992, 5).
[3] Contreras/Bennett (1994, 18 and 22). Nationwide the proportion of the minimalistic CS is presumably much higher, since in the case study the heavy weight of atypical Tijuana with its deep-rooted popular movements strongly biases the results. In Mexicali and N. Laredo in contrast 87.5 and 96.8% of all CS respectively did not comprise any subcommittees.
[4] Contreras/Bennett (1994, Table 15.6 and 15.7).
[5] Contreras/Bennett (1994, 24).

for political modernization.[1] Taking into account the large numbers of people involved in the program the decentralization thesis seems to be impeccable. But a closer look reveals that Pronasol is actually more likely to strengthen centralized and especially presidential powers.[2] This is not only due to the fact that the program's general guidelines are decided upon in Mexico City but more importantly that the power to distribute funds regionally remains completely at the central government's discretion. There is no formal rule concerning the determination of where the money should be spent.[3] Rather, SEDESOL negotiates budgets with each of the states and it is again SEDESOL field offices that have a decisive stance in deciding which municipalities within the states receive Pronasol money. And SEDESOL delegations have the final word about approval or rejection of concrete project applications by communities. SEDESOL has therefore an extraordinary amount of decision making competence and can force the spending outside the locations usually preferred by governors and local bosses, i.e. state capitals and municipal seats. Bailey calls the ongoing process "deconcentration" instead of decentralization, since federal ministries delegate the decision making to their own field offices that remain under direct central supervision and authority instead of handing competences over to lower levels of government like governors and municipal presidents (which would be called decentralization). The deconcentration process followed by Pronasol affects decentralization particularly adverse if the states' money is involved, while decision making remains concentrated within federal agencies. This is a relevant argument, since the cofinanced share of the states actually increased since the introduction of the program (Table 2). This way the lower levels of government lose progressively the decision making competence over their own resources.[4] Originally the envisaged degree of centralization (and simultaneous deconcentration) was even more pronounced,

---

[1] "Estas transformaciones requieren mecanismos de redistribución de las capacidades de decisión entre el gobierno central y los otros niveles de gobierno y la sociedad organizada. [...] Las experiencias que se diseñan y operan en forma centralizada han sido por lo general frustradas" (Tiburcio/de Alba 1992, 203 and Rojas Gutiérrez 1992, 443).

[2] "Because it is created and directed by the president, without any congressional input or judicial counterweight [historian Lorenzo Meyer] says Solidarity «strengthens the authoritarian nature of the Mexican presidency.»" Scott (1992, 4). For the following argument cf. Bailey (1994).

[3] This is why the suspicion arose that Pronasol is abused for partisan reasons in the first place.

[4] "With the arrival of Pronasol to a particular state, suddenly 30% or more of the governor's or municipal president's budgets must be redirected to Solidarity projects." Dresser (1994, 15). Municipal presidents of the PAN in Baja California claim that this interference with the competence of local decision makers had been used selectively by SEDESOL with preferential treatment (including lower cofinancing requirements) for Mexicali, the only PRI-governed city in the state (Albarrán de Alba 1994, 39).

since Pronasol officials intended to disburse money directly to the Solidarity Committees. Only after protests of local politicians the program's architects conceded to let the *municipios* getting involved in the financial transactions. [1]

- **Modernization of the Corporatist System.** The almost proverbial stability of the traditional corporatist structure in Mexican politics started to crumble under the adjustment burden of the 1980s. Especially organized labor - until then the most important and reliable pillar of the system - started to turn its back towards the PRI, which was progressively identified with the austerity measures leading to worsening employment opportunities and rapidly eroding wage rates. Similarly the campesino organizations were taken aback by deteriorating living conditions in the countryside, at least partly caused by the PRI government's agricultural pricing policies. The corporatist fabric that served hegemonic stability so well for decades fell into pieces. At the same time new and independent structures of representation emerged that went hand in hand with an ever more powerful opposition movement on the left. The challenge for the PRI was nothing less than modernizing corporatism and transforming it from a type that relied on the three broad sectors of the past (workers, peasants and popular sector) into one that takes the increasing social differentiation process into account and that must be capable of integrating the independent and for the most part disobedient organizations. A parallel structure to the established corporatist model would necessarily introduce a heavy dose of competition among different representative organizations that must, in the ruling party's eyes, reduce dramatically the maneuverability and governability of the Mexican society. Therefore the new groups must be integrated and brought under central control.

The discretionary and not yet institutionalized spending power of central government agencies leads directly to a high degree of uncertainty concerning the resources that a particular state will be able to dispose of in the near future, which in turn jeopardizes far-sighted and coherent planing on the local level. [2] Carlos Rojas' perception that Pronasol is a big leap forward in realizing the constitutional demand of establishing

---

[1] Gardy (1992, A11).

[2] While, for example, the states of Guerrero and Baja California both enjoyed an increase in Pronasol spending of about 75% between 1989 and 1990, they both would have been wrong in expecting that this growth would continue or that their budgets would develop in line. While the former's funds grew by 129%, Baja had to accept a *reduction* of 5% in the following year! In the same period Durango's Pronasol growth rate dropped by no less than 170%points! Peniche (1992, 22).

"free municipalities" can therefore easily be dismissed.[1] Pronasol is more likely to have curtailed competences of local governments further and even on the state level the SEDESOL *Delegados* have at times been nicknamed "co-gobernadores", which may in fact be not too far from the truth if their connection to the almighty presidency is more harmonious than the governor's.[2] The general public also looks to the central government rather to the governor if it asks for help, since it gets the perception that only the former gets things going via Pronasol. This bias of popular expectations also results in a further concentration process.

By re-coopting the population as consumers of public services and support instead of social classes (defined around factors of production) the party has strengthened its power base by exploiting the collective action problems that commonly prevent powerful consumer interest groups from arising. The renewal of the system was successful by building "a new coalition of support by denying the concept of class as an organizational factor of political life."[3] Potential left wing populists have been co-opted by offering them upward mobility within Pronasol's ranks: "It should be no surprise that Pronasol programs are designed and/or executed by individuals whose professional backgrounds lie in left-wing political organizations, including members of the Mexican Communist Party and the Unified Socialist Party."[4] It can be concluded that Pronasol's "divide, buy off, and conquer"[5] strategy has been pretty successful. It proves once more the amazing flexibility of the political elite and the capability of the PRI to weather even the worst political storms, still retaining power. But the political turmoil in Chiapas during January 1994 reminds us that the new corporatism is still very fragile and by no means the same guarantee of stability as the more traditional sort of corporatism proved to be during several decades until the differentiating societal structures went increasingly out of line with prevailing patterns of class representation.

- **Corruption and Caciquismo.** The concept of "social control" introduced by the integral involvement of the target groups in the form of Solidarity Committees led to the expectation that corruption and arbitrary abuse of power on the micro level

---

[1] Moguel (1992, 45).

[2] Dresser (1994, Footnote 17) on specific occurrences in Oaxaca and Yucatán.

[3] Dresser (1994, 5).

[4] Dresser (1994, 11). In the light of the strategy of including populist forces Salinas's surprising decision to appoint Carlos Tello - a key player during the populist 1982 bank nationalization - as Pronasol's first General Coordinator was a very clever and far-sighted one.

[5] Dresser (1991, 19).

could be more efficiently addressed than before.[1] Since the communities can directly get involved in the more transparent decision making process the difficulties for local bosses *(caciques)* to illegally enrich themselves personally by secretly "privatizing" public resources increased. The communities do have an incentive to follow closely the whereabouts of Pronasol-money, since any unproductive use would be to the detriment of their own vital interest of improving the local social infrastructure. The president's pronounced personal preoccupation renders corrupt practices even less attractive, although the control from (and the local bosses accountability to) the apex of the power pyramid works only on a random basis, since the probability of Salinas visiting any particular project is pretty slim.[2]

While corruption is probably somewhat on the wane it would be naive to doubt that local power brokers would not be able to adapt to the tougher rules and not find more subtle ways to cheat the public. The temptation for municipal administrations responsible for the financial disbursements to excessively postpone them and to pocket the interest revenue is probably one of the somewhat more gentlemanlike frauds to be thought of. Pronasol's *Controlaría General* detected irregularities of several millions of new pesos in the state of Guerrero alone which were attributable to not following the program's regulations of project execution, faking bills and boosting payrolls with imaginary phantom workers.[3] The danger of unlawful alienation of funds is higher the weaker the civil society on the local level is. Only an experienced and selfconscious community actually takes the decisions itself and effective control is possible, whereas for marginalized regions with a heavier dose of paternalism remaining the propagated social control is formal only rather than substantial. The process of developing a politically more involved society is a slow one and without it no effective control of local bosses is imaginable. While Pronasol still enjoys an impressive overall popularity, a poll in November 1992 found that corruption has since recently elapsed as one of the aspects associated with the program. While this perception is not yet very

---

[1] Peniche (1992, 23) and Peña Valencia (1992, 81).

[2] But once it happens it can be extremely embarrassing: "In [...] Nayarit last year, Salinas stopped in a town to meet with local Solidarity committees. After some amicable discussion, one resident stood up and demanded when exactly was the money going to arrive for these fine projects. Salinas turned to the ashen-faced governor and replied: "It was sent four months ago." The next day, the governor purged his Cabinet." Scott (1991, p.4). In March 1992 the director of the *Instituto Nacional Indigenista* in Chiapas was imprisoned together with two subordinates after having been accused and convicted for fraud (Cano 1994, 41).

[3] *Excélsior* (Oct.20, 1991), reprinted in *El Cotidiano* (julio-agosto 1992, 47).

widespread (only 5.3% of the surveyed mentioned it) it has been the *only* negative feature referred to. [1]

Pronasol's main goal with respect to the desired reform of corporatism lies in the innovative co-optation and thereby appeasement of grassroots organizations in the form of Solidarity Committees. [2] For the PRI, an additional advantage of Pronasol is the potential to divide interregional movements, since an element of competition between various localities over the scarce resources is invoked. This complicates the formation of powerful autonomous groups that could challenge the political dominance of the PRI in the way the *neocardenista* oppositional movement succeeded in 1988. This sectoralization and division of demands does actually *undermine solidarity* that could otherwise lead to a cross-sectoral and inter-regional front as happened in the late 1980s: "Labor leaders, urban groups, peasants, and Indians converged in their support for Cárdenas, temporarily forgetting their sectoral struggles. Pronasol, in contrast, underscores particularistic affiliations and goals through the specificity of its programs and regional targeting strategies." [3] The new corporatism is even more centered around president and party than the old one was, since they now don't have to deal with three peak organizations whose individual defection would make a big difference for the whole system, instead they now face over 100,000 dispersed tiny Solidarity Committees that have absolutely no power to influence the rules of the game unless they would form a national council that could articulate their collective interest.

Just like generally impeding corruption, the higher transparency of Pronasol procedures as well as the substitution of wide-ranging discretionary power for binding rules (at least for actors at the *local* level) jeopardize the feuds and interests of the *caciques* on the microlevel. [4] Efforts to maintain their local control become more troublesome. Putting the *caciques* and the informal repression-mechanisms on the defensive and thereby enhancing accountability is certainly a positive side effect. While they are not powerful enough to criticize or confront the presidential initiative

---

[1] Banamex (1993a, 78 and 80).

[2] Moguel (1992, 44). "Salinas señaló lo que serían las futuras bases del vínculo entre el Estado y las Organizaciones campesinas: requerimos, afirmó, »impulsar, una extraordinaria tarea de depuración y recreación institucional [...]« y que »en este fortalecimiento [...] es indispensable que los liderazgos de las nuevas organizaciones estén dispuestos a uno que promueva negociación y concertación y no confrontación.«" Peña Valencia (1992, 79).

[3] Dresser (1991, 21).

[4] Echeverría (1992, 40) and Bailey (1994, 20).

directly they try to save as much of their power as they can by instrumentalizing Solidarity Committees for his clientele and obstructing projects in communities questioning his power and privileges. Once again the degree of their success depends on the speed with which popular leadership and political self-esteem of the communities in question develop.

- ◆ **The Party System.** Party politics belongs in most places to the preferred topics of public and media discussion. Surveying the (print-)media coverage of the past couple of years this became more and more true for Mexico as well. It was hence to be expected, that a sometimes fierce discussion on Pronasol's possible consequences for the transforming party system elapsed.

While it is not unlikely that Pronasol helped the PRI in weakening the left opposition movement around Cuhauthémoc Cárdenas by "stealing the enemy's thunder" (Dresser) it must not be ignored that the PRD gave sufficient reasons for disappointment to its sympathizers itself by falling back into a programmatic vacuum and the failure to overcome the ongoing organizational and partisan "balkanization" on the left of the political spectre. It is therefore not clear how much Pronasol contributed to the poor prospects of Cárdenas to move into the presidential palace *Los Pinos* in 1994 and how much of the blame the "one man party" has to take itself.

Pronasol created a very powerful conflict within the PRI itself, however. Many local party bosses suspect (probably rightly so) that it will reduce their power and hamper personal career prospects. Salinas's initiative has accentuated the smoldering conflict between the *tecnicos* and the conservative *politicos* within the party. The latter suspect that the traditional paths of upward mobility based on seniority, loyalty and patronage are now barred since the proportion of PRI candidates for all kinds of positions that are recruited from Pronasol personnel or Committee leaders has increased considerably. [1] The conventional party career and engagement in one of the corporatist sectors does no longer guarantee the *politicos* to move forward, introducing a considerable amount of bitterness and intraparty resistance, especially since privatization efforts do simultaneously shut down opportunities in the parastatals also. "Pronasol leaders emphasize that positive outcomes were assured only by marginalizing traditional PRI leaders, and that »it's easier to count on the opposition than on the PRI. Party leaders are afraid that the institutional PRI may be coming to an end.«" [2]

---

[1] *El Financiero* (Oct.10, 1991), reprinted in *El Cotidiano* (julio-agosto 1992, 47).
[2] Dresser (1994, 15).

Never before did the fraction of the academic *tecnicos* hold so much power than during the Salinas *sexenio*. Since it is unperceivable that the next PRI-government will rely less on Pronasol in order to gain popularity than the outgoing Salinas one, the disequilibrium between program and party will grow. And with it the resistance of the conservative old-style party ranks will mount. So far they keep their heads down since they have the dubious feeling that - for the time being - Pronasol is a necessary evil in order to regain the party's hegemony and being able to return to business as usual later on. But the moment the *politicos* feel that the PRI has recovered completely from the crisis' aftermaths their position will become more vocal and introduce a self-destructive demarcation line within the party. Pronasol therefore placed a precarious time bomb into the PRI and the long term consequences, which might even include a schism can not yet be forecast.

This leads us directly to the last potential consequence for the Mexican party system that has been debated - the possibility of the offspring of a new "Solidarity Party". This new party would recruit its members from progressive forces within the PRI. The latter proposed during the party's assembly in September 1991 to change the name to "Party of Solidarity", a proposal that has been defeated by angry PRI militants.[1] This reveals once more the mentioned conflict between the rival factions inside the party. The very rift is also observable in the (largely failed) attempt to introduce a higher degree of intraparty democracy by decentralizing candidate selection to the grassroots.[2] The failure and reversal of this development may have frustrated the progressive forces further and increased the centrifugal forces threatening to tear the PRI apart. While the Solidarity Committees appear to be perfect and already existing basis organizations for the new party (compatible with the progressives' idea of organizing the PRI on regional rather than on sectoral grounds) it would be shortsighted to assume that the communities would easily agree to being instrumentalized in such a partisan fashion, even if popular and integrating personalities like Carlos Rojas or Salinas himself were to head the new party. For the time being the not yet firm recovery of the party and the personal popularity and charisma of the president forces the contending groups to stay united. Salinas has not commented the rumours about the new "Solidarity Party", whose leader he is allegedly to become according to some speculation. Whether a united PRI will muddle its way through right into the next millennium is far from certain but right now only a small minority (15%) believes that

---
[1] Dresser (1994, 15) and Peña Valencia (1992, 90).
[2] Bailey (1994, 22).

the modernizing Salinas government intends to transform Pronasol into an autonomous political party. [1]

5. Conclusions

The toll in terms of poverty created by the painful austerity measures that started under de la Madrid and the resulting decline of the system's stability forced the incoming Salinas government in 1988 to react effectively to both threats simultaneously. An initiative that made the economic modernization process more acceptable had to be invented. In his first speech as president, Salinas presented the National Solidarity Program and while the pre-recession level of poverty indicators have in many instances not yet been reached once more, the most recent numbers available indicate that the worst may be over and that poverty is now declining. While this in itself is no water-tight proof of Pronasols effectiveness in reducing poverty and a number of conceptional shortcomings have been identified it is not very likely that a trickle down effect during the recent years of modest per capita growth alone could have achieved the reversal of the trend.

While combating poverty Pronasol has also been highly popular with both the poor and the non-poor alike. This fact, together with the quickly increasing budgetary importance, gave birth to the reproach that the PRI misuses public resources to promote party candidates standing for governor or to even to prop up the PRI's vote at federal elections. Empirical as well as anecdotal evidence suggest that there is certainly some truth in this. Diverting the funds from poor communities towards those that are better off but where strategic elections are round the corner is indeed to be condemned. By curtailing the discretionary power of the central government and introducing an objective key of the statewise distribution of Pronasol investments this partisan abuse could be prevented and thereby the aggregate efficiency of the program in terms of poverty eradication improved. On the other hand, the use of government funds for popular programs that lead to social improvements and higher popularity of the executive is perfectly legitimate.

Reproaching the PRI government that it uses the taxpayer's money for popular programs in order to maximize presidential reelection prospects is a rather helpless

---

[1] *Este País* (July 1992, 27).

gesture. In fact, a governments responsiveness to popular demands is one of the fundamental concepts of a liberal democracy where parties compete for majorities pretty much the same way private companies compete for market-shares in the marketplace. If not even the PRI is able to resist the will of the electorate, this shows - if anything - that Mexico moves towards a more democratic system. While it is still true that no level playing field for all parties exists it can not be maintained that the PRI exploited Pronasol openly by presenting it as a party program. True, president Salinas is heavily identified with the program, but for constitutional reasons he can not be reelected in 1994. The choice of Colosio as the PRI's candidate (instead of finance minister Pedro Aspe, for example) and - although to a lesser extent - the decision for Zedillo after the murder of Colosio could be interpreted as a promise that the popular Salinas-style of governing is to continue in the coming *sexenio*. If the electorate wants it and does therefore not vote for Cardenas and the PRD, so may it be. As long as the elections are fair this time (they may not be so, but this has nothing to do with Pronasol), there is absolutely nothing wrong with the PRI winning if it offers the people what they want. If they don't fulfill (implicit) promises they are going to feel it in the midterm elections and in gubernatorial races all over the country. This is a normal and even welcome feature of all western democracies. If the existence of political manipulation were indeed as obvious as maintained the electoral effect should be minimal, because any voter in his right mind would realize that the PRI tries to bribe him and reduce benefits again after the election. While Mexicans, like all other voters on earth, may not have perfectly rational expectations, they are certainly sceptical and no fools that would take every PRI-promise literally. Critics claiming at the remotest sight of a Pronasol project that pork is around the corner, should think twice. They may be partly right but should nonetheless not forget what the possible alternatives could look like, especially in an environment of reduced aggregate government spending.

The involvement of more and more Mexicans into policy making through the Solidarity Committees will - at least in the longer run - lead to a more open and decentralized political system, even if the results concerning mobilization and especially decentralization are not yet very convincing. The establishment of a civil society is not achieved overnight. Even if the PRI might not be particularly interested in this development it will have a hard time trying to shut the Pandora's Box opened by Salinas and his social project. By creating a separate Ministry and choosing its Secretary as the presidential candidate, Pronasol has been successfully locked in and is therefore bound to survive Salinas's presidency. The process of mobilization is therefore going to continue and prove hazardous for the ruling elite that will have to be more accountable in the future. While the system - and the PRI - have been stabilized for the while being, Pronasol has still other potentials to backfire in store. Once the projects are taken for granted and something as a matter of course the communities will no longer gratefully support the system when a project is realized but could turn towards punishing it whenever the "right" for the project has been rejected and the application has been turned down. When simultaneously the frequently exaggerated individual hopes that are associated with the projects can not be fulfilled, social discontent will actually mount as a result of Pronasol and could get out of control. It is therefore adequate to close with a remark by Denise Dresser who concludes: "Hope is the stuff votes are made of. But unfulfilled hopes are the stuff revolts are made of - and if Pronasol offers more than it can deliver, Salinas's successors may yet discover that the streets of Mexico City can resemble those of Caracas, or Lima, or São Paulo."[1] - Or those of Ocosingo and San Cristóbal in Chiapas!

---

[1] Dresser (1994, 23).

References

Acevedo Pesquera, Luis. 1993. "Concentra 20% de la Población más de la Mitad de la Riqueza." *El Financiero* (May 24):30.

Albarrán de Alba, Gerardo. 1994. "La asignación de recursos de Pronasol, orientada por criterios políticos." *Proceso* (March 14):38-40.

Arroyo Alejandre, Jesús et al. 1988. "Opiniones preelectorales de la población económica y politicamente activa de la Zona Metropolitana de Guadalajara." *Carta Económica Regional* 1(3):1-10.

Aspe, Pedro. 1994. "Balance de la Transformación Económica 1989-94." *El Mercado de Valores* 8:10-22.

Bailey, John. 1994. "Centralism and Political Change in Mexico: The Case of National Solidarity." Forthcoming. In Wayne Cornelius, Ann Craig, and Jonathan Fox, eds. *Transforming State-Society Relations in Mexico - The National Solidarity Strategy*. (mimeo.)

Banamex. 1993: "Socio-Political Pulse." *Review of the Economic Situation of Mexico* LXIX (807-808):69-80.

─────. 1993b. "Poverty in Mexico." *Review of the Economic Situation of Mexico* LXIX (809):143-151.

Basáñez, Miguel. 1991. "Encuesta Electoral 1991." *Este País* (August):3-6.

Cano, Arturo. 1994. "Chiapas y la suerte de Solidaridad." *Mañana* (February):38-41.

Carrasco, Rosalba, and Francisco Hernández. 1993. "¿Cuantos pobres hay en México?" *La Jornada* (November 1):37.

Centeno, Miguel Angel. 1991. "Mexico in the 1990s: Government and Opposition Speak Out." *Center for U.S.-Mexican Studies*. University of California. San Diego.

Chávez, Marco. 1993. "Gap Still Wide Between Rich, Poor." *El Financiero*. International Edition (November 22):4.

Colosio, Luis Donaldo. 1992. "El desarrollo social como elemento de la democracia." *Examen* (December):5-6.

Consejo Consultivo del Programa Nacional de Solidaridad. 1994. *El Programa Nacional de Solidaridad. Una Visión de la Modernización de México.* Fondo de Cultura Económica. México D.F.

Contreras, Oscar, and Vivienne Bennett. 1994. "National Solidarity in the Northern Borderlands: Social Participation and Community Leadership." Forthcoming in Wayne Cornelius, Ann Craig, and Jonathan Fox, eds. *Transforming State-Society Relations in Mexico - The National Solidarity Strategy*. Center for U.S.-Mexican Studies. University of California. San Diego. (mimeo.)

Cornelius, Wayne, and Ann Craig. 1991. "The Mexican Political System in Transition." *Monograph Series* No.35. Center for U.S.-Mexican Studies. UCSD.

Cruz Rivero, Carlos et al. 1991. "The Impact of Economic Crisis and Adjustment on Health Care in Mexico." *Innocenti Occasional Paper* No.13. UNICEF. Florence.

del Castillo, Gustavo. 1992. *Mexico and the United States: The Politics of Free Trade and the Loss of Mexican Options.* (mimeo.)

Dresser, Denise. 1994. "Bringing the Poor Back In: National Solidarity as a Strategy of Regime Legitimation." Forthcoming in Wayne Cornelius, Ann Craig, and Jonathan Fox, eds. *Transforming State-Society Relations in Mexico - The National Solidarity Strategy.* Center for U.S.-Mexican Studies. University of California. San Diego. (mimeo.)

———. 1991. *Neopopulist Solutions to Neoliberal Problems - Mexico's National Solidarity Program.* Current Issues Brief No.3. Center for U.S.-Mexican Studies. University of California. San Diego.

Echeverría, Rodolfo. 1992. "El Programa Nacional de Solidaridad: resultados y perspectivas." *El Cotidiano* 49:37-41.

Gardy, Alison. 1992. "Time to Fine-Tune Mexico's Solidarity Program." *The Wall Street Journal* (December 18):A11.

Gaceta de Solidaridad. 1994. "Balance de Solidaridad, en los hechos" (February 15):3.

Gershberg, Alec Ian. 1994. "Distributing Resources in the Education Sector: Solidaridad's Escuela Digna Program." Forthcoming in Wayne Cornelius, Ann Craig, and Jonathan Fox, eds. *Transforming State-Society Relations in Mexico - The National Solidarity Strategy.* Center for U.S.-Mexican Studies. University of California. San Diego. (mimeo.)

González Gomez, Marco Antonio. 1992. "Indicadores del bienestar social. Una comparación entre los censos de 1980 y 1990." *El Cotidiano* 49:24-28.

Jiménez Badillo, Margarita. 1992. "Programa Nacional de Solidaridad: una nueva política." *El Cotidiano* 49:8-13.

Kraemer, Moritz. 1991. *Neuere Ansätze zur Lösung der internationalen Schuldenkrise.* Frankfurt/Bern/New York. Peter Lang Publishers.

———. 1992. "Lateinamerikas Weg aus der Schuldenfalle - Das Beispiel Mexiko." In Thomas H. Diehl, ed. *500 Jahre Conquista - und kein Ende?* Marburg. 107-141.

Lustig, Nora. 1993. "Poverty in Mexico: An Empirical Analysis." The Helen Kellogg Institute for International Studies. University of Notre Dame. IN. *Working Paper* 188.

———. 1994. "Solidarity as a Strategy of Poverty Alleviation." Forthcoming in Wayne Cornelius, Ann Craig, and Jonathan Fox, eds. *Transforming State-Society Relations in Mexico - The National Solidarity Strategy.* Center for U.S.-Mexican Studies. University of California. San Diego. (mimeo.)

Méndez et al. 1992. "Solidaridad se institucionaliza." *El Cotidiano* 49:60-66.

Mexico Service. 1991. "Poverty in Mexico." (April 24):11-14.

Moffett, Matt. 1993. "A Mexican Program to Spur Development Shows Much Progress." *The Wall Street Journal* (January 8).

Moguel, Julio. 1992. "Cinco críticas solidarias a un programa de gobierno." *El Cotidiano* 49:41-48.

Molinar Horcasitas, Juan, and Jeff Weldon. 1994. "Electoral Determinants and Consequences of National Solidarity." Forthcoming in Wayne Cornelius, Ann Craig, and Jonathan Fox, eds. *Transforming State-Society Relations in Mexico - The National Solidarity Strategy*. Center for U.S.-Mexican Studies. University of California. San Diego.

Olguín, Claudia. 1993. "Creciente Interés por Ligar Empresas de Solidaridad con *Trusts* Nacionales." *El Financiero* (September 6):12.

Parcero López, José. 1992. *México, la revolución silenciosa*. México D.F.

Peña Valencia, Gustavo. 1992. "Programa Nacional de Solidaridad: Entre el conflicto y la concertacion." *Anales* 2(3-4):77-97. Universidad de Gotemburgo (Suecia).

Peniche, Antonio. 1992. "El Pronasol: algunas notas y reflexiones generales." *El Cotidiano* 49:20-23.

Peón, Fernando. 1992. "Solidaridad en el marco de la política social." *El Cotidiano* 49:14-19.

Piñeyro, José Luis. 1992. "El Pronasol: ¿nueva hegemonía política?" *El Cotidiano* 49:58-71.

Presidencia de la Republica. 1992. *Mexican Agenda*. 13th. ed. México D.F.

PRONASOL. 1993. *La solidaridad en el desarrollo nacional. La nueva relación entre Sociedad y Gobierno*. SEDESOL. Marzo 1993.

Rojas Gutierrez, Carlos. 1992. "El Programa Nacional de Solidaridad: hechos e ideas en torno a un esfuerzo." *Comercio Exterior* 42(5):440-448.

Rojas, Alejandra. 1992. "El Gasto Social." *Economía Informa* 202 (February):23-27.

Salinas de Gortari, Carlos. 1982. *Political Participation, Public Investment, and Support for the System: A Comparative Study of Rural Communities in Mexico*. Research Report Series. No.35. Center for U.S.-Mexican Studies. University of California. San Diego.

———. 1993. "Fifth State of the Nation Address." Reprinted in *Foreign Broadcast Information Service* (LAT-93-210). (November 2):11-36.

Scott, David Clark. 1991. "Mexican President Wins Plaudits With Aid to Poor." *The Christian Science Monitor* (February 28):4.

———. 1992. "Mexico..." *The Christian Science Monitor* (September 16).

Smith, Peter. 1992. *The Political Impact of Free Trade on Mexico*. UCSD. (mimeo.

Spencer, Starr. 1993. "Solidarity: Social Program or Political Paradigm?" *Mexico Insight* (September 12):6-7.

Tiburcio, Enrique. 1992. "6 tesis sobre el Programa Nacional de Solidaridad." *El Cotidiano* 49:3-7.

Tiburcio, Enrique, and Aurelio de Alba. 1992. *Ajuste Económico y Política Social en México*. México D.F.

Ward, Peter M. 1994. "Social Welfare Policy and Political Opening in Mexico." Forthcoming in Wayne Cornelius, Ann Craig, and Jonathan Fox, eds. *Transforming State-Society Relations in Mexico - The National Solidarity Strategy*. Center for U.S.-Mexican Studies. University of California. San Diego.

International Poverty Reduction
A Discussion of the Possibilities of Development Cooperation

Hermann Sautter [1]

It is part of the rhetoric of development cooperation to speak of the imperative of "international solidarity". The understanding is that *all* states have the task of contributing towards the conquest of poverty in developing countries. The "Rio Declaration on Environment and Development" puts it as follows: "All States and all people shall cooperate in the essential task of eradicating poverty ... in order to decrease the disparities in standards of living and better meet the needs of the majority of the people of the world". [2] Formulations of this kind can probably also be found in many national development cooperation programmes.

What is meant by "international cooperation" in the reduction of poverty? The concept would seem to express something normative and matter-of-fact, but it conceals fundamental differences in views of the need for action. "International reduction of poverty" can, for example, be understood as the social side of a "global interior policy". This interpretation has gained many proponents in the past few years. Section I sums up their arguments and looks at the weaknesses of this approach. If one doubts the inevitability of a development towards a "global interior policy" and assumes instead the permanent existence of nation states, then "international reduction of poverty" will have to be interpreted differently: in that case, it is more an element of ordered international relations. This order must satisfy certain principles if there is to be a sustained possibility of reducing poverty. Section II deals with this aspect in detail. Within the framework of ordered international relations, development cooperation can also play a role in the reduction of poverty. This article cannot deal with all the questions associated with this topic. The third section concentrates mainly on the question as to which criteria can be used as a basis for donations of development aid if the goal of reducing poverty is to be pursued.

---

[1] The author would like to thank Mr Philip Mann for the translation. Also he would like to thank Mr Achim Blume for performing the calculations in Section III below. This article is also to be published in "Economics" (Tübingen) (forthcoming).

[2] United Nations (1992, 119). Quoted from Principle 5 of the "Rio Declaration on Environment and Development" (Rio de Janeiro) (A/Conf. 155/5/Rev., 1, 13 June 1992) adopted at UNCED.

1. International Reduction of Poverty - Social Component of a "Global Interior Policy"?

The intervention in Somalia, carried out under the auspices of the United Nations, has been interpreted by many people as a sign that the territorial state principle of international law is a thing of the past, and that the international community has an obligation to provide the individual person, regardless of his nationality, with effective protection against coercion and life-threatening need. Nuscheler believes that this intervention marks a turning point, after which "global interior policy is no longer an empty phrase in soap-box oratory". Rather, according to Nuscheler, global interior policy has become reality, albeit only in fragmentary form up to now.[1] At least now, he feels, the way is open for a logical further development of international law in the interest of the universal protection of human rights.

There are two main developments which have led to this understanding of international obligations: first, the erosion of nation-state sovereignty as a result of the increasing interconnection of national companies and, second, the extension of the list of human rights that are worthy of protection. As far as the *first* point is concerned, one can point to the undeniable fact that the *degree of openness* of national economies has clearly *increased* if one considers such factors as export-income ratios and propensity to import, the interpenetration of national financial markets or the internationalization of production. The result is that economic policy in national isolation is scarcely possible any longer. Rather, the *de facto* globalization of markets makes ever more wide-ranging policy coordination imperative. This imperative is also the result of interdependencies that are not passed on via markets and whose global impact is also becoming increasingly obvious. These include global pollution, international migratory flows[2] and the health hazards resulting from the global or regional spread of diseases (AIDS, cholera epidemics). Given the *de facto* globalization of market-based and non-market-based relationships, it is concluded that insistence on nation-state sovereignty no longer takes account of the present-day situation, and that globalization of politics - i.e. the turn to a "global interior policy" - is necessary instead.[3]

---

[1] Nuscheler, Franz (1992, 5).

[2] According to estimates by the International Red Cross, 500 million people are currently on the move in the search for a new, permanent domicile; this is the equivalent of roughly one-tenth of the world's population. However, this figure also includes internally displaced persons. See: Mühlum, Albert (1993, 9).

[3] Senghaas, Dieter (1992, 643).

The *extension of the list of human rights* that has taken place over the past few decades can also be used to substantiate this demand, and this brings us to the *second* point referred to above. The "first generation" human rights consisted in the right of the individual to protection from arbitrary acts by the state. In the 1960s and 1970s, this list of fundamental rights was supplemented by the human rights of the "second" and "third" generation: the right to the free expression of the personality, to "development", [1] to protection against life-threatening need and to "international solidarity". None of these are rights as defined by the "hard catalogue" of rights of political freedom. In many cases, they are more "human rights standards", a special form of international "soft law" which gives rise to the fear that they cannot be integrated into classical international law without this having negative consequences for the latter. [2]

However, the protagonists of a "*global interior policy*" have no regard for these fears. What they demand is no more and no less than a "de-nationalization of international law" and the creation of global social rights which will, in their view, give each individual the right to living conditions fit for human beings. In order to be able to redeem this right, a world state is seen to be necessary. [3] As long as the latter has not been achieved, the territorial state should not, it is felt, stand in the way of people claiming their rights.

It is only logical if the *prohibition of intervention* contained in international law is greatly *relativized* as a result of these considerations. According to a traditional interpretation of international law, intervention is possible if the government of a country is massacring its own people. [4] A "global interior policy", however, extends the list of circumstances legitimating intervention. For example, it would regard intervention as legitimate in cases where national sovereignty was violated by environmental catastrophes caused by one national government ("ecological warfare") or where a chaotic economic policy was driving people from their homes in masses. [5]

The suggestion that an globalized welfare state programme should be honoured by placing certain regions under an *international trusteeship* has also to be seen in this

---

[1] See Bennigsen, Sabine (1989).
[2] Riedel, Eibe H. (1986).
[3] Rolf Knieper's (1991) ideas go in this direction.
[4] Nardin, Terry (1983, 239).
[5] Senghaas, Dieter (1992, 650).

context.[1] It should cover those regions or states that are not in a position to provide their population with the basic essentials. This trusteeship should be exercised by international organizations, in which the countries of the North cannot be overruled by the elites of the "countries of the South". Otherwise - in Menzel's view - there would be a danger that humanitarian action would be thwarted by the resistance of these elites.[2] In this case, therefore, the protection of the individual goes so far as to fundamentally question the constellation of states that has been formed in the course of decolonization since the Second World War.

From this point of view, "international reduction of poverty" is the social component of a "global interior policy". In those cases where one cannot - or rather, "not yet" - speak of a "global interior policy" in the strict sense of the word, there is a call for international agreements between sovereign states. In the end, however, these agreements are seen as the *preliminary stage* on the way to achieving the actual aim itself - the general transfer of national sovereign powers to supranational organizations that are intended to assume a cosmopolitan responsibility for all world citizens.

As early as Kant, one can find the classical *objection* to this suggestion. It was not yet a "global social policy" that he had in mind, yet his objection to a world state as the guarantee of a "global peace policy" can easily be applied to the topic of our discussion.[3] In the "merger of states" Kant sees the danger of a "soulless despotism" arising, which "extirpates the seeds of the good" and finally "degenerates into anarchy". According to Kant, this state is even more difficult to bear than the latent pretext for war that goes hand in hand with the existence of independent states.[4] International peace - or international justice, as one might put it in extension of Kant's argument - cannot be expected from a world power which "weakens all forces" and thus tends to despotism, but from a balance of powers "in liveliest competition with

---

[1] Menzel, Ulrich (1992).

[2] Ibid., 211.

[3] See Kant, Immanuel (1975). English translation from Schwarz (1988).

[4] Kant, Immanuel (1975, 101). The passage reads: "The idea of the law of nations presupposes the segregation of many neighbouring states that are independent of one another, and although such a status is by itself already a status of war ... yet even this status is, according to the idea of reason, better than their merger ... because laws with the enlarged scope of government lose more and more weight, and a soulless despotism, after having extirpated the seeds of the good, inevitably degenerates into anarchy at last".

each other". [1] In short, the world state with a "global interior policy" is more of a horror scenario than a hope.

In more recent debates, Kant's argument is being continued on the level of legal philosophy and political science. Höffe [2] specifies *legal philosophy's* objections to a universal world-state. The main characteristic of a community based on rights is that individuals agree on certain rules for interaction and transfer some of their personal rights to an impartial third party, so that the latter can ensure the reliability of the agreed rules. The constitutional state satisfies this aim. Similarly, it is possible to imagine an international community of common rights. This is formed by *states* which can transfer some of their sovereign powers to international bodies, but with the sole aim of ruling out military conflicts between each other, and in this respect they remain sovereign bodies and their citizens' main guarantee of the rule of law. This aim corresponds to a "world republic" with "minimal-state functions". It is formed by sovereign states which only waive their sovereign powers insofar as this is necessary for self-preservation. Any transfer of powers to international organizations that goes further than this is contrary to the idea of an international community of common rights.

However, the analogy between national and international community of rights ends with the right to self-destruction: while, from the point of view of legal morality, the individual cannot be denied this right, it can be denied to the collective, for in this context "self-destruction" translates as "civil war", which can lead to the annihilation of parts of the population. Those peoples that are threatened by a civil war are therefore entitled to demand help from the outside world.

From the point of view of *political science*, the demand for "world governance" also comes in for criticism. Czempiel nevertheless admits that there is no doubt that the "nation-state world" is a thing of the past. By "nation-state world" he means the existence of discrete states whose interaction takes place mainly on a governmental level. Modern reality, in Czempiel's view is characterized by a mutual infiltration of societies below the governmental level: electronic media know no bounds, multi-national corporations pursue global corporate policies, Western ideas of democracy and human dignity are becoming universal, etc. However, there is no reason why this should be indicative of an irrepressible trend towards a "world state". Rather,

---
[1] Kant, Immanuel (1975, 102).
[2] Höffe, Otfried (1992).

Czempiel feels that there are many possible forms of *institutionalized cooperation* between the traditional "nation-state world" and the "world state". [1] For this reason, he advises scepticism with regard to the idea of "global interior policy". While the idea is appealing, Czempiel believes that it makes use of false parallels, for "the states still exist, they are merely being relativized by interdependence and the transnational cooperation of social agents". [2]

This objection to "world governance" can be formulated even more strongly. Nation-states are far from dissolving themselves. While they have surrendered powers in one way or another they can reclaim these rights again, even though this may possibly involve costs. [3] Although the borders of the nation-states have become more porous, they have not been swept away and "they remain in the background as the ultima ratio for emergencies". [4] The nation-state is indispensable for poor countries, because it is the most logical vehicle to use when putting forward claims on the world of the rich countries, [5] and the bulldozing away of independent statehood must be a nightmare vision for the rich countries, for this would mean the collapse of all barriers against international migration. [6] In addition, it is also difficult to replace the nation-state because it can hardly be imagined how the institutional bases for a functioning *private* economy can be created without it. [7] At all events, the view that the nation-state is being made obsolete by the increasing number of cross-border private-sector links ignores the requirements of efficient private-sector cooperation.

If we sum up these arguments, then it would seem advisable to treat the idea of "global interior policy" with caution. International poverty reduction should be seen more as an *element of ordered international relations,* not as an element of global social policy. In the first instance, this order requires rules which allow an efficient allocation of resources, as sustainable poverty reduction cannot be achieved in any other way. A second necessary element of this order consists of rules that minimize the risk of macro-economic instability. Third, ordered international relations need regulations for development aid that adheres to the principle of subsidiarity. This

---

[1] Czempiel, Ernst-Otto (1992).
[2] Ibid., 103.
[3] Kondylis, Panajotis (1992, 34).
[4] Ibid.
[5] Ibid., 64.
[6] Ibid., 118.
[7] Ibid., 36.

principle stands for the self-responsibility of individuals, private organizations and national governments and for the international duty to improve global conditions to allow individual countries to reduce poverty independently. All these elements of ordered international relations are interrelated, and they must be given due consideration in national frameworks for economic transactions.

In the context of a coherent order of this kind, development cooperation can also play its limited role in reducing poverty. It cannot replace poorly functioning rules of allocation any more than it can replace rules to minimize macro-economic instability. At best, it can support national and international efforts to improve efficiency and stability and encourage national schemes to reduce poverty in developing countries. The second section will sketch this basic outline of an international reduction of poverty, which is to be understood as a feature of ordered international relations.

2. Efficiency of Allocation, Stability and Subsidiarity - Requirements of an International and National Economic Order Serving to Reduce Poverty

2.1. Efficiency of Factor Allocation

It is difficult to imagine a long-term programme to reduce poverty that does without an economically rational use of resources and economic growth. Schemes to reduce poverty in developing countries must therefore be integrated in an economic framework which allows an *efficient allocation of resources* in both a static and dynamic respect. This is not to give the aims of efficiency or growth priority over the objective of reducing poverty. It is merely to say that the one is scarcely possible without the other in the long run. Sustained growth cannot be achieved if a programme to overcome poverty does not aim to improve the human capital of the population, and a permanent conquest of poverty will equally have little chance if the efficiency of allocation is not improved and growth is not stimulated. This applies equally to policies in the national and international sphere.

As far as the *national* sphere is concerned, theoretical arguments or empirical evidence is now hardly needed to show that a *market economy* has advantages over

state control of the economy as far as controlling the process of allocation and growth is concerned. At the same time, however, theoretical and empirical studies - recently, above all, experience with the transformation processes in Eastern European countries - show that the "market economy" is a *state affair* and not a spontaneous process that is in some way completely independent of politically determined parameters. Private interaction on the market presupposes the existence of hard and fast rules, and although some of these can arise as a result of spontaneous agreement between participants in the market, as von Hayek stresses, even in this case these implicitly assume the existence of a legal order, provided by the "external institutions" which are the precondition for the spontaneous emergence of the market's "internal institutions".
[1] State legislation is all the more necessary in those cases where the spontaneous rules formed by market participants are insufficient, be it because the relevant information is asymmetrically disseminated, or be it because "free rider" behaviour can only be ruled out by state control mechanisms. In addition, externalities mean that establishing a legal order for economic transactions is an indispensable precondition for the efficient allocation of resources, and in any event the existence of public goods - without which the production of private goods in a complex economy based on the division of labour is practically impossible - makes state action a condition *sine qua non* for a market economy. It is understandable when, as a reaction against the arbitrary exercise of political and bureaucratic power, the functions of the state in the market economy are played down, but this does not do justice to the real need for state action.

It therefore serves the interest of long-term measures to reduce poverty if industrialized nations make the creation of appropriate economic rules a topic for political dialogue with developing countries. Indeed, the Advisory Board at the Ministry for Economic Cooperation goes one step further and recommends that more attention be paid to the framework conditions in the receiving country when development aid is being allocated. For example, it recommends ascertaining whether commodity markets are ruled by competition, whether imports are regulated by licenses, whether smallholders and small businessmen have access to the formal banking sector, etc. [2]

However, efforts to improve the internal conditions for allocation and growth in developing countries will only be credible if, at the same time, the industrialized nations

---

[1] See Lachman (1962).
[2] Advisory Board at the Federal Ministry for Economic Cooperation (1992).

attempt to provide rules on the *international level* which allow efficient management and sustainable income growth in developing countries. International action to reduce poverty must include a policy on the part of the industrialized nations which does not work against, but rewards the developing countries' own efforts to create productive jobs. In principle, this is possible within the framework of an international order for competition, such as that which has found its expression in the GATT and in the WTO.[1]

However, there is sufficient documentary evidence to show that the industrialized nations are far from respecting the GATT principles when it comes to opening up markets to the benefit of competitive suppliers from developing countries. The agricultural protectionism of the industrialized nations should be mentioned here - which, with the EU's market regulations for bananas, has recently threatened to become a particularly flagrant form of discrimination against poor people in developing countries[2], - the almost insurmountable number of non-tariff trade barriers on the markets for many commercial goods, the signs of bureaucratization of European trade policy with the completion of the Single Market and the concomitant removal of market niches that were still possible under the independent government trade policies of the member states - the list of *protectionist measures* could be continued. Their effect tends to be one of exacerbating poverty in those developing countries that are capable of exporting.

Some *examples* may illustrate this point. The EU's subsidized sugar exports and the USA's import quota policy are mainly responsible for the reduction in income of farm workers in the Dominican Republic and for the unemployment of 50,000 migrant workers from Haiti; in the middle of the 1980s, the import restrictions imposed by the USA and some European governments on garments from Bangladesh led to the collapse of many workshops and thus to an exacerbation of poverty in the country; the trade restrictions laid down in the Multi-Fibre Agreement are keeping the developing countries as a whole from increasing employment in the textiles and garments industry by 20 - 45%.[3] The income losses that have resulted from this far

---

[1] This is also the tenor of Korff's contention that an economy which intends to "serve the common good of the family of man" cannot do without the "market economy" as a "fundamental ordering principle". See Korff, Wilhelm (1992, 4).

[2] See DIW Wochenbericht (1993).

[3] These examples are cited in World Bank (1990, 148).

exceed the resource transfers to the developing countries as a result of financial cooperation.[1]

It has to be concluded that, without a *change in the tenor of trade policy*, the efforts of the industrialized nations to help reduce poverty as part of their development cooperation are completely lacking in credibility. Without a more liberal foreign trade policy on the part of the industrialized nations which is geared to the criterion of efficiency, the conditions for domestic economic reform policies in the developing countries will also be unfavourable. Attempts to improve resource allocation and to increase labour productivity are being obstructed by the industrialized nations' protectionist policies. If the industrialized nations are serious about their duty to reduce poverty in the developing countries [2], then they also have to see to it that priority is given to economic policy course corrections which take the criterion of allocation efficiency and (ecologically qualified) growth stimulation into account.

2.2. Macroeconomic stability

Extreme *fluctuations* in *employment and income in the economy as a whole* hamper any long-term policy to overcome poverty. This is illustrated by the developments in the 1980s. In the wake of the debt crisis, poverty became exacerbated in many developing countries during this period, and this makes increased efforts necessary in order at least to regain the situation before the crisis started.[3]

For this reason, stability has to be aimed for as well as efficiency. Here, I will not go into the bodies needed for this purpose in the developing countries. Some of these are the same as those required with regard to the aims of efficiency and growth: an independent central bank committed to the goal of monetary stability; an efficient banking system to facilitate an intertemporal compensation of individual fluctuations in income; a tax system and a financial administration which can contribute to the stabilization of income fluctuations.

---

[1] The "Human Development Report 1992" speaks of a total loss of income for the developing countries of US$ 75 bn as a result of import restrictions imposed by the industrialized nations. The total amount of government development aid (ODA) flowing into the developing countries in 1990 amounted to US$ 44 bn (UNDP, 1992, 6 and 162).

[2] See United Nations, 1993, 167.

[3] See Schinke, this volume.

The stabilization policy to be pursued by these bodies is already difficult enough for the developing countries. However, they can far less afford to compensate for instabilities caused by the global economy. These may be due to causes that are also beyond the influence of the industrialized nations, but these countries are also quite capable of influencing some of these instabilities politically. One example of this is the international interest shock, caused mainly by the "Reaganomics" of the early 1980s, and the disturbances in international flows of capital that resulted from this. The effects of this policy were not far removed from those of a traditional "beggar-my-neighbour" policy. The increased budget deficit in the USA led to an international "crowding-out" effect which affected the NICs in particular. [1]

The resulting problems with poverty in these countries have already been discussed. Any serious commitment to international poverty reduction on the part of the industrialized nations must therefore also involve the willingness to pursue policies which do their best to avoid shocks to the global economic system. This is not to call for binding cooperation in economic policy between the most important industrialized nations. As regards the declared aim of greater global economic stability, this cooperation may be disadvantageous under certain circumstances. [2] Rather, what is important here is that every one of the important industrialized nations pursues at a *national level* a *monetary and fiscal policy that is geared to stability,* and renounces all forms of "beggar-my-neighbour" policies.

2.3. Reduction of poverty on the basis of subsidiarity

While a policy that is geared to stability and to promoting efficiency and growth on both a national and an international level is a necessary condition for effectively reducing poverty in developing countries, it is by no means sufficient. For many reasons, there is an unequal distribution of human and real capital, which are the main determinants of the individual's income opportunities in a market economy. The *unequal distribution of income* is thus typical of a market economy, which, from the point of view of efficiency and growth, deserves preference over alternative methods

---

[1] I have already discussed the economic-ethical implications of the international debt crisis in: Sautter (1992). This is not to assert that the debt crisis was the sole reason for the exacerbation of poverty in the 1980s, nor that this crisis was solely due to the international interest shock. The situation is more complex. However, it is undeniable that the interest shock was the most important cause of the debt crisis and that poverty in the debtor countries has increased in the wake of this crisis.

[2] Neumann, Manfred J.M. (1991).

of controlling the economy as a whole. This inequality is not only a result, but also in a certain respect the precondition of dynamic markets. However, the distribution should not be too unequal, as otherwise the social consensus which is the basis of the reliability of the rules of interaction in a market economy will be jeopardized. Quite apart from that, the prevention of life-threatening poverty is an ethical imperative [1] that calls for action even without any opportunistic considerations (e.g. "poverty reduction as a means of safeguarding consensus"). The *market institution* must therefore be *supplemented* by institutions specifically designed to *reduce poverty*.

Conflicts can arise here, especially between social policy aims and the goal of allocation control aimed at promoting efficiency and growth. [2] However, these conflicts can be minimized if social policy aims are not pursued via market interventions and if the *principle of subsidiarity* is observed in the fight against poverty. This brings us to the third requirement of international poverty reduction that is to be dealt with in this article. It states that self-help should be given priority over outside aid, and that superordinate social units giving outside aid should be given the task of improving the preconditions for self-help. Taken to its logical conclusion, this means that it is incumbent on each individual to help himself (taking up employment and training opportunities), and that the superordinate unit of the state has to create the framework conditions which permit self-help through private initiative (creation of viable factor and commodity markets, guarantee of free access to the market, provision of the public commodity of primary education). Within the framework of a poverty reduction based on the subsidiarity-principle, it is the task of private "social networks" (families, neighbourhood associations, charity organizations, etc.) to support the individual where he cannot cope with the task of helping himself; the state's task is to create the legal conditions which allow these non-governmental organizations to operate. Whenever private organizations can no longer cope, the state should bring its social policy into action. [3] Finally, if a subsidiarity-based structure to reduce poverty is taken to its logical conclusion, then it is the task of international organizations and bilateral partners to provide financial aid for those countries that are determined to reduce poverty but which do not have the financial means to implement such a policy.

---

[1] Sautter, Hermann (1991).

[2] On the subject of the conflict between the goal of equality and the criterion of efficiency in general, see: Okun, Arthur M. (1975).

[3] Taking Brazil as an example, the structure of a poverty reduction policy based on subsidiarity has been proposed in: Karsch, Thomas, Platino, Carlos and Sautter, Hermann (1992). For the rationale and the elements of international concerted action to reduce poverty, see also: Sautter, Hermann: Problems of an International Social Order, in this volume, 191-211.

Not only the dispute between EU member states and the European Commission about the allocation of power has shown that putting subsidiarity into practice is a tricky process. As regards the tasks of an international policy to reduce poverty, it cannot be expected that the job of defining criteria of what is reasonable and who is responsible will be without its problems. Fundamentally, however, this principle remains unchallenged. It points the way forward for the structuring of national and international programmes. In this context, international programmes to reduce poverty in developing countries are not to be understood as the social dimension of a "global interior policy", but as the assumption of a social duty within the context of ordered international relations.

One might well ask to what extent the industrialized nations' development cooperation corresponds with this aim. How strongly does the reduction of poverty feature in actual donations of official development aid? What criteria can determine aid to individual recipient countries, if the reduction of poverty is to be a priority of development cooperation? The third section is devoted to these questions.

3. The Allocation of Development Aid Within an International Strategy to Reduce Poverty

There cannot be one sole criterion for the distribution of development aid, even if there were only one aim. In addition, many aims play a role in the actual aid policies of donor countries: the influence of voting behaviour in international organizations, safeguarding raw materials and sales markets, taking care of traditional relationships (that may go back to colonial times), securing votes at home (a dominant motive in US foreign aid to Israel) and - something that played an important role in the past - securing and expanding the donor country's sphere of influence. One cannot simply reproach official development cooperation for this. Neither in collectives nor in individuals is purely altruistic behaviour the rule. Action based on self-interest predominates. Rather, the question is whether the long-term interests of the industrialized nations themselves might not be better served by determined efforts to reduce poverty in the developing countries than by a policy that is guided by their own short-term interests only.

Various attempts have been made to *investigate* how far aid distribution policy is *geared to poverty*. For this purpose, Clark has calculated concentration ratios (suits index) of the official development assistance of various donor countries and traced the corresponding Lorenz curves. [1] According to the hypothesis underlying this study, a policy geared solely to the poverty of the recipient countries would be expressed in a "uniform distribution straight line": the cumulated share of ODA of the recipient countries, ordered according to per capita income, ought to develop in strict proportion to the cumulated share of the GNP of all recipient countries. The fact is, however, that the actual distribution curves clearly deviate from this pattern; this is most pronounced in the case of the USA, whose aid distribution structure shows an obvious "middle-income bias". [2] McGillivray uses a different method. [3] He calculates an index from the weighted shares of per capita ODA allocated to a country as a proportion of the sum of per capita aid to all recipient countries (weighting factor is the per capita income of the recipient country). The values on the index range from 0 to 100 (complete neglect of "poverty", as measured by the per capita income of the recipient country, gives a value of 0, exclusive "poverty orientation" in the distribution of aid gives a value of 100). The resulting values fluctuate between 0.63 (USA) and 0.93 (Belgium), thus demonstrating country-specific differences in poverty-orientation, with the aid distribution structure of the USA again showing the lowest orientation to poverty. Finally, Weck-Hannemann and Frey have used regression lines to compare US ODA per capita contributions to recipient countries with the per capita incomes of these countries. The relationship was not statistically significant. [4]

In all these studies, per capita income was used as an indicator of poverty. The meaningfulness of this indicator can be questioned. In many cases, the Human Development Index (HDI) proposed by the UNDP is seen as a more meaningful indicator of the development or poverty of a country. This indicator not only includes the "benefits" of per capita income (which presupposes a declining marginal utility), but also the literacy rate, school education and average life expectancy. [5] If we use regression lines to compare ODA contributions per capita of the recipient country with the poverty indicator (1-HDI), then we get a relationship that is just as statistically

---

[1] Clark, Don P. (1992).
[2] Ibid., 193.
[3] McGillivray, Mark (1989).
[4] Weck-Hannemann, Hannelore, and Bruno S. Frey (1987).
[5] UNDP (1990).

insignificant as was the case with the use of per capita income as a poverty indicator in the study by Weck-Hannemann and Frey. (The regression calculations were performed for the bilateral ODA contributions from the following countries: Federal Republic of Germany, France, Japan, Canada, The Netherlands, Sweden, USA. In none of these cases did the coefficient of determination come to a value above 0.03.)

All these results allow the following conclusion: there is scarcely any relationship between the official development aid granted and the neediness of the recipient countries, regardless of whether this neediness is measured in terms of per capita income or in terms of the HDI index. However, one can ask whether the neediness of a country (however that might be measured) is the most reliable criterion for the granting of official development aid. This question is particularly justified if the "reduction of poverty" is seen as an urgent goal of development cooperation. Should not rather a country's own development efforts be rewarded, i.e. made a criterion for the granting of aid? Section II above referred to the significance of economic policy framework for a strategy to overcome poverty. It might be possible to attempt to quantify the efforts of a country to fulfill these conditions (i.e. its performance), and to derive criteria for the granting of aid from this.

Without wishing to question the justification for this procedure, I would like to ask here what the indicators for a country's own efforts to *reduce poverty* are. On this basis, too, criteria for the granting of aid can be developed. A country's own efforts can be approximately judged from the ratio between the actual and hypothetical value of a social indicator, if the latter describes the degree of poverty reduction a country could itself achieve even *without* specific effort. The more clearly the actual value of a social indicator *exceeds* this hypothetical value, the more one could speak of special efforts to overcome poverty (measured by the height of the selected social indicator). This takes as its point of departure indicators whose *increase* can be interpreted as a success in the fight against poverty (school enrolment rate, for example). The opposite is true of indicators whose *reduction* can be adjudged a success (mortality rate, for example). Here, *falling short* of a hypothetical value can be interpreted as the expression of special efforts to reduce poverty.

On the basis of these considerations, the ratios of the actual and hypothetical values of the following social indicators will be calculated below: 1) school enrolment for girls in secondary schools, 2) proportion of school-age children to have completed primary school, 3) mortality rate for children under five, 4) childbirth mortality. I will explain briefly why these indicators were chosen.

Indicator 1): Women are disadvantaged in the educational system and labour market of many developing countries, and they are over-represented among poor people (population below the poverty line). At the same time, improving the educational standard of women has far-reaching feedback effects on children's educational success, on improvements in health standards and on the effectiveness of family planning. According to Bhalla and Gill, the school enrolment rate for girls in secondary schools can therefore be regarded as a particularly meaningful indicator for a country's social situation. [1] Indicator 2): In the last few years, it has been possible to increase school enrolment rates in the primary school sector in many countries. For many reasons, however, the drop-out rate is very high. This is not least due to the low quality of education. The "completing primary level" indicator is therefore more suited to describing education policy success than the school enrolment rate. Indicator 3): The under-five mortality rate is a meaningful "output" indicator for a country's efforts in health and nutrition policy. As a rule, an extended system of motherhood advice services, health clinics, nutrition programmes, etc. will be reflected in low mortality rates. Indicator 4): It is a similar story with this indicator. It shows the female population's access to the services offered by the health system.

It is to be expected that, all other things being equal, indicators 1 and 2 (3 and 4) will be all the higher (lower), the better a country's structural economic data are: diversification of production, labour productivity standard, amount of capital stock, etc. These economic determinants of social indicators can be expressed in simplified form in the amount of per capita income. It is true that per capita income is a very rough indicator of the level of economic development in a country and of the potential for social policy action in the broadest sense of the word. Here, however, little knowledge can be gained by using more detailed structural data. All the important determinants of economic success are reflected in the amount of per capita income, although it makes sense to allow a time-lag between per capita income and social indicators: past economic successes, reflected in a comparatively high per capita income, have positive effects on the development of social indicators in the following years.

---

[1] Bhalla, Surjit S., and Indermit S. Gill (1991).

The considerations that follow are based on the assumption that there is a positive (negative) relationship between per capita income and indicators 1 and 2 (3 and 4), although it would seem probable that this relationship is non-linear. The higher the level of per capita income, the smaller the additional improvements in indicator values that accompany income increases will probably be. A semi-logarithmic type of functional relationship will therefore probably describe the proposed relationship better than a linear regression equation. Tests that have been carried out confirm this proposition. The regression results used for further calculations are presented in Table 1. The estimated values of the above-named indicators can be interpreted as those successes in the fight against poverty that are to be expected on average on the basis of a country's economic situation.

Table 1
Regression results

	α	β	t value	F value	FG	R^2
ERG	-99.02	20.45	9.44	89.20	60	0.60
PCR	-11.47	11.86	4.56	20.79	60	0.26
CMR	528.64	-64.26	-10.62	112.89	60	0.65
CBM	1,974.30	-241.81	-9.90	98.01	60	0.62

Source: Own calculations with data from UNDP. 1992. *Human Development Report*; World Bank. 1987. *World Development Report*.

Function type: $Y = \alpha + \beta \ln X$

FG = Degrees of freedom

Independent variables (X): per capita income in US dollars (1985)

Dependent variables (Y):

ERG = school enrolment rate for girls in secondary schools (1988)

PCR = proportion of those completing primary school to the total number of primary-school age children (1988)

CMR = mortality rate for children under five per 1,000 live births (1990)

CBM = childbirth mortality per 10,000 live births (1988)

In a *second* stage, ratios can now be calculated between the actual indicator values and these estimated values ("poverty reduction efficiency" or PRE). A PRE value greater than 1 (less than 1) for the indicators 1 and 2 (3 and 4) can be interpreted as a sign that the country in question can show evidence of particular success in combating poverty which goes beyond the standard to be expected from its level of development. It would seem justified to see this as a sign of the determination and efficiency of government policy in the fight against poverty. Table 2 lists those countries with favourable or unfavourable values. Values of >1 in indicators 1 and 2 and of <1 in indicators 3 and 4 are interpreted as favourable, while the opposite holds true for unfavourable values. In the countries listed, all the values are within the defined regions. A mixed picture emerges for 40 other countries whose values are not given here: certain values hint at successful efforts to combat poverty, others at less successful efforts.

It is not surprising that countries like Sri Lanka, China and Malaysia are to be found in the first country group and countries such as Brazil, Guatemala and Venezuela in the second. If one goes along with the above-mentioned consideration, then the countries of the first group ought to be relatively promising partners in a policy to reduce poverty - insofar as they qualify at all for development cooperation (South Korea no longer belongs to this group of countries, and Malaysia too can at best be considered as a partner in individual technical cooperation projects). In those countries belonging to the second group, by contrast, one may justifiably doubt the seriousness of their intention to combat poverty; in addition, fundamental political conditions for a policy of poverty reduction are lacking in the case of Mozambique and Somalia.

Of course, the PRE values given here are not the only possible criteria for the granting of development aid, but one will scarcely be able to ignore indicators of this kind if poverty reduction is to be a priority of development cooperation. In order to examine the extent to which the actual aid distribution structure of individual donor countries is oriented towards the recipient countries' own efforts (as expressed by their PRE values), rank correlation coefficients have been calculated. Here, the per capita aid ranking of the recipient countries has been compared with their PRE ranking. The results are presented in Table 3.

Table 2
Poverty Reduction Efficiency

(PRE value: ratio between actual and estimated values for four social indicators)

	ERG	PCR	CMR	CBM
a) Countries with favourable values				
Sri Lanka	3.39	1.59	0.29	0.33
China	2.08	1.41	0.30	0.22
Jamaica	1.56	1.33	0.27	0.58
Mauritius	1.20	1.37	0.41	0.46
Philippines	1.41	1.09	0.57	0.57
South Korea	1.47	1.24	0.78	0.67
Zimbabwe	1.22	1.14	0.87	0.83
Egypt	2.21	1.47	0.82	0.71
Chile	1.57	0.98	0.46	0.31
Indonesia	1.47	1.26	0.90	0.66
Malaysia	1.05	1.22	0.69	0.88
b) Countries with unfavourable values				
Brazil	0.69	0.26	1.54	1.25
Venezuela	0,95	0.87	2.12	4.06
Somalia	0.43	0.67	1.24	1.47
Mexico	0.93	0.91	1.31	1.18
Bhutan	0.42	0.53	1.01	1.07
Guatemala	0.36	0.49	1.11	1.00
Mozambique	0.84	0.70	1.42	1.07
Pakistan	0.53	0.97	1.14	1.12
Rwanda	0.37	0.83	1.15	1.14

ERG = school enrolment rate for girls in secondary schools (1988)
PCR = proportion of those completing primary school to the total number of primary school age children (1988)
CMR = mortality rate for children under five per 1,000 live births (1990)
CBM = childbirth mortality per 10,000 live births (1988)
(see above for explanations)

Table 3
Rank correlation between ODA [1] distribution structure of various donor countries and PRE values [2] of recipient countries

	ODA/ERG	ODA/PCR	ODA/CMR	ODA/CBM
Netherlands	0.25	0.15	0.44	0.41
Sweden	0.33	0.31	0.26	0.28
Japan	0.21	0.36	0.43	0.28
Germany	0.10	0.23	0.22	0.21
USA	0.21	0.17	0.16	0.23

Source: Own calculations with data from OECD (1990).

[1] ODA: Official Development Assistance, average values 1986-89, per capita in the recipient country in US dollars.
[2] For explanation see above.

Here too, the picture is hardly surprising. There are differences between the aid distribution structure of The Netherlands and Sweden on the one hand and the USA on the other. It is striking that the German distribution structure shows a comparatively low degree of orientation towards the recipient countries' own efforts to combat poverty.

If the reduction of poverty is to be a priority of development cooperation, then a detailed analysis of poverty in the recipient countries is obviously necessary. This should concern itself just as much with macro-economic "performance" indicators as with political and social policy indicators.[1] Indicators of the type presented here can, however, serve as preliminary clues. They provide information about the actual extent of social indicators compared with those that might be expected on the basis of the country's income level. The ratio between these values allows conclusions to be drawn about the efforts a country itself is making to combat poverty.

---
[1] See Sautter, Hermann and Christoph Serries (1993).

4. Summary

"What does the 'international reduction of poverty' mean?" This question stood at the beginning of this article. It can be understood in the sense of a "global social policy", in which supranational organizations assume direct responsibility for reducing poverty in individual countries. A certain sympathy for this view can be detected in several more recent articles from the field of development policy. Nevertheless, a certain amount of scepticism is justified as regards a "global social policy" that is the social component of a "global interior policy". The sovereignty of nation states may be restricted, but as a rule it has not ceased to exist. Nor is it desirable to eliminate the independence of nation states under international law. Neither the developing countries nor the industrialized nations can be interested in this. The international reduction of poverty therefore means the assumption of social obligations in a system of ordered international relations rather than a universalistically perceived global interior policy with a welfare-state character.

The order of international relations must follow certain principles if a long-term policy to reduce poverty is to succeed. These include heeding allocation efficiency, stability and subsidiarity. The industrialized countries can contribute towards reducing poverty in developing countries if they correct their anti-efficiency, protectionist trade policies and if they pursue a monetary and fiscal policy that is geared to stability and that as far as possible avoids triggering global economic shocks. As part of a subsidiarity-based structure to reduce poverty the industrialized countries also have the task of providing aid for those developing countries that cannot cope financially with a determined programme of self-help. This is not intended as a replacement for the recipient countries' own efforts, but as a reward for them.

The question is how the recipient countries' own efforts can be ascertained. This article has proposed a simple method: calculation of the ratios between actual and estimated values of social indicators (PRE = "Poverty Reduction Efficiency"), where the estimated value describes that level of an indicator that is to be expected on the basis of a country's economic potential (as expressed by its per capita income). PRE values greater than one in the case of the school enrolment rate for girls in secondary schools and the proportion of those completing primary school to the total number of primary-school age children, and less than one for child mortality rate and childbirth mortality were interpreted as expressing a country's own efforts to reduce poverty.

This gives us a possible quantitative criterion for the granting of aid which must be supplemented by other quantitative and qualitative criteria.

One can scarcely speak of the donor countries' aid-granting structure being geared to developing countries' own efforts, as measured in the way set out above. Most industrialized countries will therefore have to revise their aid policy if they are serious about their duty to reduce poverty worldwide.

References

Advisory Board at the Federal Ministry for Economic Cooperation. 1992. "Grundsätze der deutschen Entwicklungszusammenarbeit in den 90er Jahren." *Forschungsberichte des BMZ* 102:1-32. Cologne.

Bennigsen, Sabine, 1989. *Das "Recht auf Entwicklung" in der internationalen Diskussion.* Frankfurt/M. etc.

Bhalla, Surjit S., and Indermit S. Gill. 1991. *Social Expenditure Policies and Welfare Achievement in Developing Countries.* World Bank. background paper. August 1991.

Clark, Don P. 1992. "Distributions of Official Development Assistance Among Developing Country Aid Recipients." *The Developing Economies* III-3:189-197.

Czempiel, Ernst-Otto. 1992. *Weltpolitik im Umbruch.* 2nd edition. Munich.

DIW Wochenbericht. 1993. "Bananenfestung Europa." 14(6):175-179.

Höffe, Otfried. 1992. "Eine Weltrepublik als Minimalstaat. Moralische Grundsätze für eine internationale Rechtsgemeinschaft." Typescript (13th Tübinger Gespräch zu Entwicklungsfragen, 23 October 1992).

Homann, Karl, ed. 1992. *Aktuelle Probleme der Wirtschaftsethik.* Berlin. 69-108.

Kant, Immanuel. 1795. *Zum ewigen Frieden. Ein philosophischer Entwurf.* Königsberg. English quotation quoted from Schwarz, Wolfgang. 1988. *Principles of Lawful Politics. An Annotated Translation of Immanuel Kant's Toward Eternal Peace.* Aalen.

Karsch, Thomas, Carlos Platino, and Sautter, Hermann. 1992. *Interdependente Armutsbekämpfung, das Beispiel Brasilien.* Hamburg.

Knieper, Rolf. 1991. *Nationale Souveranität, Versuch über Ende und Anfang einer Weltordnung.* Frankfurt/M.

Kondylis, Panajotis. 1992. *Planetarische Politik nach dem Kalten Krieg.* Berlin.

Korff, Wilhelm. 1992. "Ethische Probleme einer Weltwirtschaftsordnung." *Aus Politik und Zeitgeschichte* 50:3-12.

Lachman, L.M. 1962. "Wirtschaftsordnung und wirtschaftliche Institutionen." *Ordo* XIV: 63-77.

McGillivray, Mark, 1989. "The Allocation of Aid Among Developing Countries: A Multi-Donor Analysis Using a Per-Capita Aid Index. *World Development* 17(4):561-568.

Menzel, Ulrich. 1992. *Das Ende der Dritten Welt und das Scheitern der großen Theorie.* Frankfurt/M.

Mühlum, Albert. 1993. "Armutswanderung, Asyl und Abwehrverhalten. Globale und nationale Dilemmata." *Aus Politik und Zeitgeschichte* 7:3-15.

Nardin, Terry. 1983. *Law, Morality and the Relations of States.* Princeton.

Neumann, Manfred J.M. 1991. "Internationale Wirtschaftspolitik: Koordination, Kooperation oder Wettbewerb." In Jürgen Siebke, ed. *Monetäre Konfliktfelder der Weltwirtschaft.* Berlin. 61-84.

Nuscheler, Franz. 1992. "Plädoyer für einen humanitären Interventionismus." *Entwicklung und Zusammenarbeit* 33(10):4-5.

OECD. 1990. *Geographical Distribution of Financial Flows to Developing Countries* Paris.

Okun, Arthur M.. 1975. *Equality and Efficiency, the Big Trade-Off.* Washington, D.C.

Riedel, Eibe H. 1986. *Theorie der Menschenrechtsstandards.* Berlin.

Sautter, Hermann. 1992. "Das internationale Schuldenproblem aus wirtschaftsethischer Sicht." In Karl Homann, ed. *Aktuelle Probleme der Wirtschaftsethik.* Berlin. 69-108.

―――. 1991. "Armut in Ländern der Dritten Welt als wirtschaftethisches Problem." In Günther Baadte and Anton Rauscher, eds. *Wirtschaft und Ethik.* Graz etc. 117-144.

Sautter, Hermann, and Christoph Serries. 1993. *Inhalt und Methodik von Armutsanalysen. Forschungsberichte des Bundesministeriums für wirtschaftliche Zusammenarbeit und Entwicklung.* No.110. Cologne.

Schinke, Rolf. 1995. "Poverty and Indebtedness in Latin America: The Influence of Changing Prices of Tradables and Nontradables." This volume.

Schwarz, Wolfgang. 1988. *Principles of Lawful Politics. An Annotated Translation of Immanuel Kant's Toward Eternal Peace.* Aalen.

Senghaas, Dieter. 1992. "Weltinnenpolitik - Ansätze für ein Konzept." *Europaarchiv* 47(22):643-652.

UNDP. 1990. "Human Development Report 1990." *Technical Notes.* Washington, D.C.

UNDP. 1992. *Human Development Report 1992.* New York and Oxford.

United Nations. 1992. *Conference on Environment and Development (UNCED).* Rio de Janeiro. 3-14 June 1992, Agenda item 9: The Rio Declaration for Environment and Development (A/Conf. 151/5/Rev. 1) (mimeo.)

Weck-Hannemann, Hannelore, and Bruno S. Frey. 1987. "Was erklärt die Entwicklungshilfe?" *Jahrbuch für Nationalökonomie und Statistik* 203 (2):101-122.

World Bank. 1990. *World Development Report 1990 "Poverty".* Washington DC.

World Bank. 1987. *World Development Report.*

Problems of an International Social Order

Hermann Sautter [1]

1. Introduction

In general it is not difficult to accept the necessity of rules ordering the international trade and currency relations. Individuals in specialized economies need a minimum of secure expectations regarding the actions and reactions of their partners. This security results from regularity, or as one could also say: rule-conformity of interactions. It can be based on customary law, on codexes, informally accepted by the actors or on the written law. In this respect there is basically no difference between economic interactions within a nation and between nations. A difference solely consists in that the rules of interaction within a country can be secured by the monopoly power of the state and the potential of sanctions at its disposal, whilst this is not the case in the international exchange. This by no way means that the economic relations between legally constituted societies are disordered. Hereby voluntarily reached agreements by sovereign partners play a great role. The order of the international trade as well as that of the international monetary and financial relations are founded on the basis of such voluntary agreements. Whether this order is satisfying remains to be seen. It is a fact that certain regularities have been internationally agreed upon, that the corresponding arrangements also foresee the possibility of sanctions in case of violation of rules and that on this basis a positive amount of secure expectation is possible, even if in this regard a lot remains to be improved.

Therefore no doubt for the necessity of an international economic order remains. But what about the necessity of an international social order? Is this expression actually meaningful? How can, by the way, the necessity of such an order be explained, which possibilities are there for realizing it? This is a line of questions whose answers are not easily given. Why these questions are posed shall be illustrated by reference to some facts:

---

[1] The author would like to thank Abenaa Addai for the translation.

- Under the responsibility of western industrialized countries, care packages are dropped from aeroplanes over Curdish refugee camps in Turkey and north Iraq. Neither the Turkish and even less the Iraqi government undertake serious efforts to solve the starvation problem of the Curds. What sense is there in such humanitarian actions if they are not imbedded in a general order of international relations, that facilitate a minimum provision for human beings, irrespective of their national origin?

- The governments of numerous developing countries receive financial aid at "soft conditions" from the western world. The donor countries justify this with the "obligation for international solidarity". The governments of the receiving countries are either not willing or not able - often both -, to undertake serious efforts themselves to alleviate poverty. Is the continuation of the development co-operation with the aim of a world wide reduction of poverty justified under these circumstances? How must the development co-operation be brought into line with other forms of international co-operation to improve the chances of attaining this aim? Must, in other words, the "world order" also contain an international social order and international transfers, that are co-ordinated with an international economic order in such a way that they facilitate a world wide poverty alleviation?

In this context a look at the resolutions of the UN-Conference on Environment and Development (UNCED) is interesting. The "Rio-Declaration", signed by over 150 states, declares the sustainable poverty alleviation as an international task.[1] The "Agenda 21" also passed in Rio contains numerous chapters that oblige the signing states to undertake political activities in the field of trade, finance, technology and development with the aim of jointly enabling a "sustainable development" and thereby overcoming the world-wide poverty.[2] International obligations to alleviate poverty do exist and there are many specific activities directed towards this aim. Often these activities have no meaningful reference to one another, and above all they are not integrated into the remaining forms of international relations. The question of how

---

[1] See "Principle 5" of the "Declaration of Rio de Janeiro"; United Nations Conference on Environment and Development (UNCED), Rio de Janeiro, 3-14 June 1992, Agenda item 9: The Rio Declaration for Environment and Development (A/Conf. 151/5/Rev. 1) (mimeo). The principle reads: "All states and all peoples shall cooperate in the essential task of eradicating poverty as an indispensable requirement for sustainable development, in order to decrease the disparities in standards of living and better meet the needs of the majority of the people of the world".

[2] UNCED (1992): Press Summary of Agenda 21, Rio de Janeiro, 3-14 June 1992.

these relations could be arranged so that the chances of a poverty alleviation augment is therefore not superfluous.

The following considerations on an international social order should be seen in front of this background. It will not be possible to exhaustively deal with the initially mentioned questions here and to design a consistent system of world-wide social policy. The aim is more modest. It is to clear the need for action and the possibilities of action concerning the aim of attaining in each country a minimum of subsistence, adequate to the specific social conditions. The argumentation will ensue in several steps. To begin with the clearing of what can be understood by "national social order" shall be dealt with (2). In a second step the arguments of an international social order (3.1) and finally their feasibility (3.2.) shall be given. Section 4 summarizes the results.

2. The social order as an accepted component of national rules of interaction

The western industrial countries know several forms of regulated public assistance with which all members of the society should be guaranteed a certain minimum standard of life. These regulations define entitlements, they lay down who is liable of fulfilling certain obligations and they try to match entitlements and liabilities with the overall system of economic rules. In the Federal Republic of Germany these regulations are laid down in numerous laws, as for example the Law of Public Assistance (Sozialhilfegesetz), the unemployment insurance or the workmen's compensation insurance. The labour law also contains elements of minimum security, as for example the provision of the German Civil Code, according to which "starvation wages" are immoral (§ 138), and the binding clause of collectively negotiated wages, giving them the significance of "minimum wages". Even the procedural law takes the aim of a minimum subsistence into consideration, for example when setting up certain limits of seizure of household appliances.[1] Securing a minimum level of subsistence is therefore a standing element of the German legal order; the economic system also takes heed of this.

---

[1] A systematic overview of the different forms of individual basic security in the Federal Republic of Germany is given in: Weeber, Joachim (1990).

The reasons why are not difficult to explain. On the one hand it is evident, that in a competitive economy nobody has the guarantee not to fall below a certain minimum income, on the other hand exactly this is seen as intolerable on moral grounds. We can proceed on the assumption that there is an agreement in all western industrial countries that the society has the obligation of guaranteeing for a minimum level of subsistence for all its members. Friedrich A. von Hayek, who is unsuspicious of socio-political generosity, stands for this consent. He sees no reason "why, in a free society, the government shall not grant all persons protection against serious deficiencies by a guaranteed minimum income or a minimum under which no one shall drop". [1] Likewise, the political liberalism does not have any difficulties in accepting the socio-political aim of a guaranteed minimum income: "Ideas exist, that move along slowly, but do not simply fade, as not everybody grasps them instantly. Belonging to these ideas is the thought that a guaranteed minimum income should exist for all citizens of developed, civilized societies". [2] The question arises why this aim should be restricted to already "developed, civilized societies" and whether it does not pose a binding character for developing countries and for a world society, wanting to be civilized. But this question anticipates the reflections of the following sections.

Before coming to them an important principle of a national social order shall be considered, this order being understood as a system of entitlements and obligations which make a minimum subsistence level feasible for every member of society. It is the principle of subsidiarity. It implies that self-help should have priority. Help from outside should not replace but facilitate it. This finds its expression for example in the German social welfare system, in as much as in examining any claim of entitlement the possible own contribution of the applicant and of his family members has to be taken into account. This principle is supposed to minimize conflicts with the objective of efficiency, as this objective is best realized by a high degree of self-responsibility. Self-responsibility is hindered if entitlement claims are laid down without consideration of the individual or family self-help capability.

Summarizing the reflections of this section the following can be said. In western industrial societies a social order is accepted, which ensures every member of the society a minimum subsistence level. This is an integrated part of national rules. Concerning this, moral considerations are substantial, but even without referring to them explicitly,

---

[1] von Hayek, Friederich, A. (1981, 122).
[2] Dahrendorf, Ralf (1987, 157).

economic and legal reflections speak in favour of such an order: It strengthens the reliability of economic rules if social conflicts are reduced by granting a minimum social security to everyone.

3. Arguments for and feasibility of an international social order

3.1. The arguments

3.1.1. The necessity of supplementing the international rules of resource-allocation

The following argument holds on an international as well as on a national level: Within a competitive system, neither income guarantees nor guarantees of a minimum income can exist. It is true that many income differences on an international level are caused by offending against the competition rules. The protectionist trade policy of the rich countries gives an example.[1] In this case it is an ethical demand to care for a consequent application of competition principle. But even a consistent and liberal world trade order could not prevent people within trading countries from becoming or staying poor, either because they are not involved in international trade or exactly *because* they are directly or indirectly involved.

In this respect it is necessary to supplement international rules of resource-allocation through an international social order. As to this necessity there is no difference between the national and the international level. Is there also no difference regarding the ethical reasoning of an international social order?

3.1.2. Ethical Arguments

The answer to this question is not easily given. There are, indeed, many arguments for an international social order. But they are faced by a number of objections. First, the positive arguments shall be dealt with.

---

[1] The World Bank (1990, 121*f*) points out the connection between poverty in developing countries and trade protectionism in industrialized countries.

Within the scope of the religiously founded ethic of Christianity, it does not make sense to restrict welfare to the members of the own society. The original image of Christian charity - the parable of the "good Samaritan" - declares help for distressed members of a foreign society which is hostile to one's own as an action of charity. [1] Christian theologians have extended this individualistic ethical duty to a social-ethical demand. This intends the realization of a "world welfare" which shall give every human being the chance of "becoming subject". It is inconsistent with this "universal common weal", as Nell-Breuning believes, if "some nations live in severe poverty and distress". [2] Nations that are capable of helping are therefore obliged to help the distressed people of other nations.

Other religions also know this dimension of ethical responsibility, even if they are not as distinct as in the Christian tradition. A true Muslim for example is obliged to pay a general welfare tax ("sakat"), with which those shall be supported who are in distress - not only members of the own religion. [3] Some variants of the Confucian cultural tradition stress the universality of ethical obligations, although charity for the own family, the own clan or the own people has priority. [4] The traditional Buddhism perceives "compassion" (the rejection of "greed") as one of the four "divine states of rejection" and the compassionate, devoting assistance for others as a "good deed". [5] It was not until the Reform Buddhism, which evolved from the acquaintance with the western world, that the ethical dimension was extended, beyond the narrow range of the own society.

On the whole, a tendency of universalizing religiously founded demands for supporting the poor is recognizable. Seemingly, with the growing interdependence of the national societies a "world ethos" is evolving, as Küng believes. [6] In any case, the demand for minimum individual safety is supported by nearly all religions of the world, and in increasing manner the world-wide dimension of this task is being recognized.

---

[1] The Bible, gospel according to St. Luke, ch. 10, v. 33-35.

[2] von Nell-Breuning, Oswald (1962, 388f). Also Sutor and Weiler speak of "world welfare" (Sutor, Bernhard, 1991, 302); Weiler, Rudolf (1986, 42). The conception of a "world welfare" is, however, missing in typical presentations of protestant economic ethics, see e.g.: Rich, Arthur (1990, 350f).

[3] Antes, Peter (1984, 68).

[4] See: Seiwert, Hubert (1984).

[5] See Bechert, Heinz (1984). Individual voices from Asian or African countries, from which a complete callosity for other people living in perilous poverty can be concluded, should not be given too much weight. See: Hesse, Helmut (1988, 208).

[6] Küng, Hans (1990).

This is similar in philosophical ethics. In its Anglo-Saxon tradition an utilitarian characteristic can be found. [1] But many ethics philosophers share the opinion that utilitarism alone is insufficient in founding modern ethics, and that moreover deontologic elements are needed. [2] For the formulation of this deontologic dimension Kant's ethic is of fundamental significance, till date. Its basic item, the principle of universalization, expressed by the "categorical imperative", is taken over in one way or another by many of the contemporary ethic philosophers.

Combining utilitarism with the principle of universalization can lead to the statement that it is not obvious why somebody should be legitimated "to require a privileged treatment for his interests just because they are his interests." [3] Seen this way, the use of the own income for the satisfaction of comparatively unimportant necessities is difficult to justify, if by doing so, those are deprived of help who hardly have the basic vital necessities. In this context Patzig doubts the "moral justification" of wealthy industrial societies' idly watching a part of the world's population permanently being threatened by starvation. According to Patzig, the problem is "how far the industrial societies are morally justified to disregard that a large part of the world population outside these societies is far from attaining a minimum level, whose existence within these societies is generally accepted as a condition of any further fulfillment of preferences. One can expect that this collective passiveness or even recklessness will in foreseeable future seem just as awkward to the then living inhabitants of the planet, as we are astonished by the indifference with which even morally sensitive Greeks and Romans took the situation of the slaves, and the bourgeoisie in Europe, at the beginning of the industrial revolution, the situation of the industrial workers as an inevitable fate, which, of course, always only meets others". [4] So, also from a utilitarian approach, combined with the principle of universalization, there is much to be said for an ethical obligation of richer societies of helping individuals of poorer societies.

Against this, it cannot be objected that moral obligations solely refer to "face to face"-relations. It is indeed true that obligations to the nearest (family member, neighbour) are of a special quality. Not correct though is that one can speak of moral obligations of the individual only with respect to his existence as a "private person" but not with

---

[1] See, for example, Frankena, William K. (1986); Mackie, John Leslie (1981).
[2] See, for example, Mackie, John Leslie (1981, footnote 2, ch. 7).
[3] Patzig, Günther (1978, 24).
[4] Ibid., 22f.

respect to his membership of a certain organization in whose decisions he can participate. As a member of an organization the individual also has moral obligations, for example, the obligation of making contributions to enable this organization to donate social services to the destitute. [1]

It is questionable whether the obligation of helping by means of organizations decreases in direct proportion with the geographic distance between potential donators and recipients does, and thereby the anonymity of the relation between each other grows. [2] It is not understandable, however, why for example the obligations towards a citizen of a neighbour country should be greater than that towards a citizen of a different continent. Once the narrow field of the immediate personal relations is exceeded then the differences in the grade of anonymity towards geographically closer or further away living people becomes irrelevant.

Therefore, the above mentioned objection is not capable of weakening the ethical reasoning for an international social order. It would be a wrong understanding of the principle "charity begins at home", if one would declare help for *absolutely* poor foreigners only then admissible if the *relative* poverty of the nearer persons has been alleviated.

3.1.3. The economic self-interest of rich societies in an international social order

Moreover, rich societies have an economic self-interest in an international social order. Natural resources, that are also of interest to the development of prosperity in rich countries, are to be found in the poor countries. Tropical rainforests are an example. They form a pollutant-sink, they stabilize the world climate and they offer a gene reservoir whose safeguarding is of high value to future generations. The poverty in tropical countries however leads the people to the exploitation of these natural resources. [3] Therefore it lies in the self-interest of rich societies to contribute to an alleviation of poverty in such countries and thereby reduce the pressure of exploiting the natural resources.

---

[1] Moral obligations that can be fulfilled on an international level by appropriate institutions are discussed by Shue, Henry (1988).

[2] For a critism of this argument of "concentric circles" see: Enderle, Georges (1985, 182).

[3] For the complex relations between poverty, the destruction of the rainforest and global climate changes, see: Deutscher Bundestag, Referat Öffentlichkeitsarbeit, ed. (1990).

Another argument can be added. The insufficient supply of clean drinking water, the lack of adequate sanitary facilities and the insufficient health services cause diseases in developing countries whose dissemination to other countries can hardly be hindered.[1] Also for this reason the rich countries are well advised to advocate a policy of minimum subsistence in poor countries which includes the satisfaction of material basic needs. Finally, the problem of international migration due to poverty should be mentioned in this context. This poses problems to the rich societies which could be solved more efficiently by poverty alleviation in the countries of origin of the migrants than this is possible in the industrialized countries.

We therefore come to the conclusion that the international trade and monetary order needs to be supplemented by carefully targeted poverty alleviation strategies in developing countries. Ethical considerations add to this reasoning as well as the assertion of economic self-interest of the rich countries. It is plausible to search for a sensible order of such measures, i.e. an international social order, that guarantees a minimum subsistence of the people in all societies with respect to their specific social living standards. The following section deals with the feasibility of such an order.

3.2. The feasibility of an international social order

The basic question here is: How can particular measures of securing an individual, country- specific, minimum of subsistence be brought into a meaningful relationship to each other, so that they can show their full efficiency and do not fizzle out ineffectively? The following propositions shall be developed:

First: Particular measures of securing a minimum subsistence must be integrated into an international and national order of allocation, that is promoting economic efficiency.

Second: An international social order must include the clarification of entitlements and liabilities that are arranged according to the principle of subsidiarity.

Third: An international social order must provide for the avoidance of "the rationality-trap". The claimant must not be encouraged to an attitude that, in the long run, makes the fulfillment of liabilities impossible.

---

[1] See: World Bank (1992).

3.2.1. Efficiency-oriented economic rules of interaction as a necessary condition for the feasibility of an international social order

A sustainable alleviation of poverty is only possible on the basis of efficient economic activities. Temporary success can possibly be achieved by political measures of distribution, that neglect the criterion of efficiency. Lasting achievements however can not be attained this way. Within the scope of the international social order, the actors possessing entitlements and liabilities must be included in a system of rules, that enables efficient economic activity. [1] Experience has shown that this is most likely the case in a market-based economic system, whose functioning is guaranteed through the public allocation of "public goods".

Most countries of the world have owned up to important principles of an efficiency-oriented economic order by the accession to the GATT/WTO and the International Monetary Fund (IMF), even if, through this, they have not formally undertaken the obligation of establishing a certain type of market economy. The international economic relations are, in any case, founded on the market-principle. The question is how reliable this system of rules is and how large its possibilities are to urge each participating country to act according to the rules.

The findings, regarding the reliability of the trade-rules, are not very encouraging. Obviously the precautions contained in the old GATT for securing its own functioning were not sufficient to avoid aggravating violations of its rules. This is principally connected with the lacking of discipline in the trade policy, as defined by the GATT, of the most important international trading partners. Without national discipline in respecting competition rules, a reliable international trade system will hardly be possible. It hence follows: A consistent international *social* order is feasible in the same degree as the most important trading countries take their own obligation serious to support an efficiency promoting international trade order.

Something similar applies with respect to the international monetary order, that is constituted by the IMF. Certainly this agreement contains some possibilities for sanctions for the individual member states. But these possibilities are subject to a characteristical asymmetry: They are much more effective in regard to the deficit countries that are dependent on stand-by-credits, than in regard to the surplus countries; and countries with key currencies are anyhow not subject to the same

---

[1] This argument is also stressed by Hesse, Helmut (1988, 208).

compulsion of rule conformity as the rest of the members of the fund. This constitutes one of the basic weaknesses of the international monetary order.

In recent years a growing openness of the IMF for social objectives could be observed. Thus the annual report 1990 of the IMF reads: "The Fund's increasing focus on poverty issues has influenced its approach to policy analysis and recommendations. A number of arrangements have contained measures to lessen or compensate for the adverse impact of certain economic developments and policies on specific groups among the poor."[1] In connection with the structural adjustment program in Mozambique, for example, food stamps were distributed to those removed from the public service; the structural adjustment program in Bolivia was supplemented through the construction of a fund that finances employment promoting public work and grants newly founded small enterprises opening capital.[2] As favourable as socio-political activities in connection with structural adjustment programs seem, the danger cannot be ruled out, that they lead to the mollification of efficiency promoting adjustment measures, if the IMF were to be bound to socio-political aims. A better way of solving social problems is to establish an independent system of social security.

The political dialogue that is carried out on the different levels of the bilateral and multilateral development co-operation also serves the consolidation of efficiency promoting rules of interaction. This dialogue is supposed to increase the readiness of the recipient countries for economic and social reforms and thereby improve the preconditions for a sustained poverty alleviation in these countries. It is obvious that the credibility of this dialogue rises in the amount that the industrial countries are willing to fulfill their obligations with view to an efficiency oriented international trade and monetary system.

Summarizing these reflections, the following can be stated. A number of institutional regulations exist promoting efficient economic activities on an international and national level. Societies that are respecting these institutions offer relatively favourable conditions for effective socio-political measures. The conditions for success of a social order improve in as much as the deficiencies in these efficiency oriented rules are overcome. Herewith the social order does not become unnecessary because, even the most perfect market oriented rules of allocation do not guarantee for a

---

[1] International Monetary Fund (1990, 42).
[2] Ibid.

minimum level of subsistence. Therefore supplementary measures for securing this level of subsistence are necessary. [1]

3.2.2. A system of subsidiary entitlements and liabilities

It must be the individual, who is entitled to a monetary minimum income or a specific provision in kind that guarantees a minimum subsistence level. His claims are, in the first instance, directed towards private groups such as the family, the neighbourhood or other non-governmental welfare organizations. To the extent that these organizations are overstrained, public organizations must become active, thereby taking into account the capability of the individual or the family of making own provisions. Besides other things, it lies in the responsibility of legal politics and of the education system to make the individual realize being subject of rights including the right of help in distress that cannot be overcome by one's own initiative. It also lies in the responsibility of the legal system to name those public organizations that are obliged to subsidiary assistance. It is the duty of the public financial policy to provide these organizations with the necessary means. [2]

Looking at the administration, developing countries are generally not overstrained in constructing a national social order of this kind. Of course the extent of differentiation of a social order cannot be the same everywhere and of course, the extent increases with a rising level of productivity. But even at a low level, a country should be capable to give out food stamps to the needy, organize basic medical care for low-income families, provide settlements of poor families with clean drinking water, enable children - especially girls - of poor families to visit primary schools etc. The experience of Sri Lanka and some Indian states prove that the administrative capacities of a society, whose economic level of productivity is comparatively low, are not exceeded by activities of this kind. [3] If they really are, these capacities can be enlarged by specific measures of development co-operation.

The construction of a national social order does not stand for a symbol of "luxury". On the contrary: by improving the "quality" of the "human capital", it stimulates the

---

[1] The World Bank also sees the key of overcoming poverty in developing countries in the complementarity of improved rules of allocation and a consequent social policy; see: World Bank (1990).

[2] The author has described the outlines of such a subsidiary system of entitlements and liabilities in: Sautter, Hermann (1991a); same author (1991b).

[3] See: Drèze, Jean; Sen, Amartya (1989).

economic development. Well nourished and educated people are more capable of contributing to the production process and to react to market impulses. The experience of numerous developing countries suggest that a "human-capital approach", as the one outlined, is more likely to lead to sustained development than a "physical-capital approach" that has to pay the accelerated construction of a real capital stock with social passiveness. [1]

Maybe the *financial* capacity of a society is exceeded to guarantee each member a minimum subsistence, within the limits of a subsidiary structure of entitlements and obligations. This is likely to be the case in the less developed countries, where the aggregated poverty gap accounts for a considerable part of the GDP. In the case of Bangladesh, for example, a share of 15% is calculated; adding the transfer costs that accrue from the establishment and the maintenance of public assistance one obtains a total that surely exceeds the financial possibilities of the country. [2]

Within the scope of an international social order the wealthier societies must, in this case, take over transfer obligations that enable the beneficiary societies to fulfill the claim of its members to a minimum subsistence. These transfers can be made in various forms, for example, in form of food aid or monetary aid. [3] Transfers of this kind must be included in the national system of entitlements and obligations in the recipient country; in other words, the international social order must have its counterpart in a national social order [4] whereby on the national as well as on the international level the social order has to be supplemented by rules of efficient division of labour. In this way specific measures of poverty-oriented development co-operation are put into a meaningful context and can develop their intended effectiveness.

The question remains of how an order of this kind can avoid falling into the "rationality trap". Related to this is the question which international necessities for action exist, in those cases, where the national contributions are not made, be it those of establishing an efficiency oriented economic order, or those of establishing a social order.

---

[1] See: World Bank (1991).

[2] The aggregated "poverty gap" is defined as the difference between the actual income and the "poverty line", for all those that lie below a socially specific minimum level ("poverty line"). In the case of the newly industrialized countries, the poverty gap hardly equals to a financial volume exceeding the capacities of the countries. For Brazil, for example, this gap equals to 1.1 % of the GDP (World Bank (1990, 50 f).

[3] For an appropriate proposal see: Reutlinger, Shlomo (1988).

[4] That this connection is not made is seen as one of the deficiencies of the treaty of Lomé, see: Enderle, Georges (1988, 68).

3.2.3. Avoiding the "rationality trap"

A social order is impossible if it seduces the beneficiaries to an attitude that impedes the fulfillment of entitlements or even makes them impossible. What is rational for the individual, namely to react to given impulses in a certain way, becomes irrational for the whole system and herewith its existence is jeopardized. This problem is given on an individual as well as on a social level.

The individual claimant can be in a position in which he is being offered services without having the incentive for self-help. The incentive can, contrarily, lie in exploiting the service system as much as possible. Generous transfers, not connected to the proof of the own capability and whose amount lets own efforts seem unprofitable, are an example.

A "rationality trap" of this kind can be avoided if the claim to public assistance is bound to reasonable own contributions. The "food for work" programs, often practised in development co-operation, are an example of this. Payment of wages in cash or in kind are made in exchange for work requirements.[1] Besides, the danger of abuse can be lowered by verifying the entitlement and by screening public assistance programs. The administrative authorities of a developing country should not be strained with this verification, as research by Drèze and Sen shows.[2] School feeding or "fair price-shops" operated in settlements of the poor are examples for abuse reducing "targeting" of socio-political programs.

In this context the question arises whether the obligation of fulfilling services remains, even if the potential beneficiary does not make own contributions. Respecting individuality in this case requires retention. It is also ethically problematic talking of an obligation of helping in those cases where the recipient rejects all own initiative. At any rate, this is not the typical problem of developing countries. If an apathetic recipient attitude is to be found, then this is generally the result of chronic malnutrition. Here poverty is much less the *result* of lacking activity than its *cause*. The psycho-social studies conducted by Rabanal in the "pueblos jovenes" of Lima, show the extent of the psychological damage resulting from years of malnutrition.[3] The lacking of own initiative can therefore generally not be interpreted as denial of any achievement which

---

[1] See also: Cassen, Robert (1990, section 5.7.).
[2] See Drèze and Sen (1989).
[3] Rabanal, C.R. (1990).

should be answered by retention of public assistance, but rather as a request for targeted effort of overcoming distress. Thereby the psycho-social context in which these services are carried out is quite important. Assistance can contribute to the strengthening of dignity of the beneficiary; but it can also effect the opposite.

Of substantially greater importance is the problem of a "rationality trap" on a social level. Three problematic topics shall be mentioned in this context: the large population growth, the case of non-sustainable forms of settlements and cultivation and the case of political inability and unwillingness to establish the basic provisions for a national social order.

Seen from a Malthusian point of view, transfers are a typical example of social irrationalism, if they are for the benefit of a country that is characterized by large population growth. The compulsion of slowing the population growth resulting from distress is thereby relaxed, the assistance increases the number of beneficiaries. In reality of course things are different. It is exactly distress which causes the high birth rate and through this (cet. par.) high population growth rates, be it because women in this situation see their only fulfillment in life in bringing up children, be it because for them "opportunity costs" of child education is very low as a result of lacking opportunity of education and money-earning, be it because poor families are dependent upon the assistance of children. Specific measures of improving the living standard - especially the improvement of the situation of women - can, on the contrary, reduce the birth rates. [1] Examples are an improved primary school education, facilitating the access to land property - especially for women -, improved access to the formal credit system, improvement of the hygienic conditions, enlargement of employment facilities and special adult education programs. With adequate "targeting" minimum subsistence services must not lead to a "rationality trap" of population policy. The opposite is right: an efficient social order lowers the population pressure in a humane way.

The second problem mentioned consists in the fact that certain forms of settlements and cultivation can possibly not be maintained. In this case transfers can retard necessary structural adjustments; the assistance increases the need for assistance. An example is the settlement on and the cultivation of marginal soil. If the income-deficits of persons cultivating such soil is compensated by national or international transfers, then the settlement and cultivation can be maintained and possibly even

---

[1] See: World Bank (1992, 25).

extended. In such cases assistance must be connected to measures of altering the existing methods of settling and cultivating. Carefully planned actions of resettlement can be one of such measures. [1] It is the task of the political dialogue to care for the integration of international transfers into structural adjustments that, at least in the long run, increase the self-help capacity.

The third problem mentioned consists in the fact that the government of a country is unable or unwilling, or both together, to establish the basic requirements for a national social order. In this case it should be attempted to increase the pressure and the incentive of implementing inner reforms in such a country. It can for example be thought of increasing trade advantages in order to induce the country under consideration to establish assistance facilities. That this argument is not far from reality is confirmed by the fact that during the constitution process of the North American Free Trade Association, binding the date of conceding trade advantages to Mexico to the implementation of certain political reforms in this country was considered. [2] On a different occasion the congress of the USA made the granting of tariff advantages to the former Soviet Union dependent on more liberal emigration regulations for the Soviet Jews. The use of trade policy as an instrument of increasing the pressure and the incentive of implementing certain measures of reforms is by no way new. The implemented, respectively the discussed measures make it clear that even in the international relations at least rudimentary an "interdependence of orders" exists: The trade and monetary order cannot be developed independently of the elements of a social order.

In the extreme case diplomatic pressure and trade policy give no incentives: the legal and political situation of a country is so desolate that a policy of guaranteeing a minimum subsistence cannot be expected. The question is, in this case, whether the world community should give up securing a minimum subsistence of the people in such a country. Respecting the sovereignty of a country would then have priority over the securing of the individual right of living.

It can be doubted whether this is an appropriate understanding of the principle of sovereignty. Even up till now the law of nations allows interventions in a country that violates the freedom of its people; massacres amongst the own people, for example,

---

[1] Wissenschaftlicher Beirat beim Bundesminister für wirtschaftliche Zusammenarbeit (1992, 43).
[2] Compare del Castillo (1992).

justify foreign interventions.[1] The situation of the Curds in Iraq is closely related to this case, the situation in Somalia as well. In such cases it does by no way seem absurd to demand for foreign intervention with the aim of contributing to the pacification of the country and thereby establishing the basic preconditions for a minimum level of provision with vital goods for the people. In this case an international social order would be connected with a general order of the political relations between legally constituted societies; specific measures of fighting hunger would be included in the general relations of the states, and could then be more efficient than without this connection.[2]

4. Conclusion

We come to the following result. The conditions for establishing an efficient international social order are rudimentarily accomplished: An international order - though in need of reforms - to enable resource-allocation exists. Further there are tendencies that aim at clarifying subsidiary claims and liabilities. This can be concluded from the various forms of political dialogues and international obligations of alleviating poverty, whereby the own initiatives have priority. Finally it is not impossible to avoid the problem of the "rationality trap". We are still far away from an international social order in the same formal sense as, for example, an international trade and monetary order. But the outlines of such an order are within sight, and tendencies that will take further shape, can be observed.

Several other questions still need to be settled: How shall, for example, the country-specific individual minimum demand be determined, and who shall determine it? According to which criterion should the obligations of the wealthier nations be settled? How can the contributions of governmental and non-governmental organizations on national and international level be co-ordinated in order to guarantee a minimum subsistence? How can international agreements increase the pressure and incentive of establishing a national social order? The clarifying of these questions will need

---

[1] Nardin, Terry (1983, 239). Nardin strongly emphasizes, by the way, the formal character of an "international morality", that he sees as incorporated in rule-conformity of the nations. Talking of a "universal morality" is, according to him, a regress behind the achievements of the modern law of nations.

[2] The events of the Gulf War have carried the discussion of a "new world order" ahead. Increased interference implies something fundamentally different than the replacing of the international order by a universal state and the devolution of the law of nations by an universal law, see: Sautter, H.: International Poverty Reduction, this volume.

great efforts on an economic, political and legal level. In the presence of poverty in large parts of the world such efforts have high priority.

References

Antes, Peter. 1984. "Islamische Ethik" In Antes, Peter a.o. *Ethik in nichtchristlichen Kulturen*. Stuttgart. 48-81.

Bechert, Heinz. 1984. "Die Ethik der Buddhisten." In Antes, Peter a.o. *Ethik in nichtchristlichen Kulturen*. Stuttgart. 114-135.

Cassen, Robert. 1990. *Entwicklungszusammenarbeit*. Bern/Stuttgart.

Dahrendorf, Ralf. 1987. "Ein garantiertes Mindesteinkommen." In Dahrendorf, Ralf. *Fragmente eines neuen Liberalismus*. Stuttgart. 157-160.

del Castillo, V., Gustavo. 1992. *Mexico and the United States: The Politics of Free Trade and the Loss of Mexican Options* (draft, March 1992).

Deutscher Bundestag, Referat Öffentlichkeitsarbeit, ed. 1990. *Schutz der tropischen Wälder - eine internationale Schwerpunktaufgabe*. Bericht der Enquête-Kommission des 11. Deutschen Bundestages "Vorsorge zum Schutz der Erdatmosphäre". Bonn.

Drèze, Jean, and Amartya Sen. 1989. *Hunger and Public Action*. Oxford.

Enderle, Georges. 1988. "Das Lomé-III-Abkommen: Eine Strategie zur Überwindung der Armut in Entwicklungsländern?" In Hesse, Helmut, ed. *Wirtschaftswissenschaft und Ethik*. Berlin. 47-70.

———. 1985. "Sicherung des Existenzminimums für alle Menschen - eine Herausforderung für Ethik und Wirtschaftwissenschaft." In Enderle, Georges, ed. *Ethik und Wirtschaftswissenschaft*. Berlin. 163-180.

Frankena, William K. 1986. *Analytische Ethik. Eine Einführung*. München (4th ed.)

von Hayek, Friederich, A. 1981. *Recht, Gesetzgebung und Freiheit. Vol. 2: Die Illusion sozialer Gerechtigkeit*. Landsberg a. Lech.

Hesse, Helmut. 1988. "Internationale Wirtschaftsbeziehungen als Gegenstand der Wirtschaftsethik." In Hesse, Helmut, ed. *Wirtschaftswissenschaft und Ethik*. Berlin. 195-214.

International Monetary Fund. 1990. *Annual report 1990*. Washington D.C.

Küng, Hans. 1990. *Projekt Weltethos*. München/Zürich.

Mackie, John Leslie. 1981. *Ethik*. Stuttgart. Original version: Mackie, John Leslie. 1977. *Ethics*. Harmondsworth.

Nardin, Terry. 1983. *Law, Morality, and the Relation of States*. Princeton N.J.

von Nell-Breuning, Oswald. 1962. "Die ethische Begründung der Entwicklungshilfe." *Jahrbuch des Instituts für Christliche Sozialwissenschaften*:388ff.

Patzig, Günther. 1978. *Der Unterschied zwischen subjektiven und objektiven Interessen und seine Bedeutung für die Ethik*. Göttingen.

Rabanal, C.R. 1990. *Überleben im Slum*. Frankfurt/M.

Reutlinger, Shlomo. 1988. "Efficient alleviation of poverty and hunger. A new international assistance facility." *Food Policy* (February):56-66.

Rich, Arthur. 1990. *Wirtschaftsethik. Vol. 2*. Gütersloh.

Sautter, Hermann. 1991a. "Armut in den Ländern der Dritten Welt als wirtschaftsethisches Problem." In G. Baadte, and A. Rauscher, eds. *Wirtschaft und Ethik*. Graz. 117-144.

Sautter, Hermann. 1991b. "Armut in Entwicklungsländern - ein wirtschaftsethisches Problem." *Wisu (Das Wirtschaftsstudium)* 21(5):421-427.

Seiwert, Hubert. 1984. "Ethik in der chinesischen Kulturtradition." In Antes, Peter a.o. *Ethik in nichtchristlichen Kulturen*. Stuttgart etc. 136-167.

Shue, Henry. 1988. Mediating Duties. *Ethics* 98(4):687-704.

Sutor, Bernhard. 1991. *Politische Ethik*. Paderborn etc.

The Bible. Gospel according to St. Luke, ch. 10, v. 33-35.

United Nations. 1992. *Conference on Environment and Development (UNCED)*. Rio de Janeiro. 3-14 June 1992, Agenda item 9: The Rio Declaration for Environment and Development (A/Conf. 151/5/Rev. 1) (mimeo).

Weeber, Joachim. 1990. *Monetäre Mindestsicherung in der Bundesrepublik Deutschland: Bestandsanalysen, Konzeptionen und Folgewirkungen*. Frankfurt/M. etc.

Weiler, Rudolf. 1986. *Internationale Ethik. Vol. 1*. Berlin.

Wissenschaftlicher Beirat beim Bundesminister für wirtschaftliche Zusammenarbeit. 1992. *Grundsätze und Schwerpunkte der deutschen Entwicklungszusammenarbeit in den neunziger Jahren*. München. 43.

World Bank. 1990. *World Development Report: Poverty*. Washington D.C.

World Bank. 1991. *World Development Report: Development as a Challenge*. Washington D.C. Ch. 3: "Investments into Man".

World Bank. 1992. *World Development Report: Development and the Environment*. Washington D.C.

The authors

Moritz Kraemer
Research Fellow, Volkswirtschaftliches Seminar, Georg-August-Universität Göttingen.

Dr. Eduardo Lizano
Professor, Academia de Centroamérica, San José, Costa Rica.

Dr. Hermann Sautter
Director of the Ibero-America Institute for Economic Research and Professor, Department of Economics, Georg-August-Universität Göttingen.

Dr. Rolf Schinke
Academic Director of the Ibero-America Institute for Economic Research, Georg-August-Universität Göttingen.